MULTILINGUAL WRITING IN ENTANGLEMENT

Multilingual Writing in Entanglement

Becoming With Others Through Chronotopic Figuring and Unpredictable Encounters

XIQIAO WANG

UTAH STATE UNIVERSITY PRESS
Logan

© 2025 by University Press of Colorado

Published by Utah State University Press
An imprint of University Press of Colorado
1580 North Logan Street, Suite 660
PMB 39883
Denver, Colorado 80203-1942

All rights reserved

 The University Press of Colorado is a proud member of
Association of University Presses.

The University Press of Colorado is a cooperative publishing enterprise supported, in part, by Adams State University, Colorado School of Mines, Colorado State University, Fort Lewis College, Metropolitan State University of Denver, University of Alaska Fairbanks, University of Colorado, University of Denver, University of Northern Colorado, University of Wyoming, Utah State University, and Western Colorado University.

ISBN: 978-1-64642-760-4 (hardcover)
ISBN: 978-1-64642-761-1 (paperback)
ISBN: 978-1-64642-762-8 (ebook)
https://doi.org/10.7330/9781646427628

Library of Congress Cataloging-in-Publication Data

Names: Wang, Xiqiao, 1977 December 2– author.
Title: Multilingual writing in entanglement : becoming with others through chronotopic figuring and unpredictable encounters / Xiqiao Wang.
Description: Logan : Utah State University Press, [2025] | Includes bibliographical references and index.
Identifiers: LCCN 2025016644 (print) | LCCN 2025016645 (ebook) | ISBN 9781646427604 (hardcover) | ISBN 9781646427611 (paperback) | ISBN 9781646427628 (ebook)
Subjects: LCSH: Academic writing—Study and teaching (Higher)—Case studies. | Multilingual persons—Education—Case studies. | Multilingual education—Case studies. | College freshmen—Case studies. | English language—Study and teaching (Higher)—Chinese speakers—Case studies. | English language—Rhetoric—Study and teaching (Higher)—Case studies.
Classification: LCC P301.5.A27 W37 2025 (print) | LCC P301.5.A27 (ebook) | DDC 808.06/6378—dc23/eng/20250610
LC record available at https://lccn.loc.gov/2025016644
LC ebook record available at https://lccn.loc.gov/2025016645

Cover illustration by Thiago/Adobe Stock

Contents

List of Illustrations   ix

Foreword: Re-Worlding Multilingual Writing & Writing Studies With Entanglement
   Paul Prior   xi

Preface   xxi

Acknowledgments   xxvii

Introduction   3
   Transnational Migration and Multilingual Writing   3
   An Entanglement Perspective for Multilingual Writing Research   8
   Methodology for the Project   14
      Institutional Context   15
      Participants   19
      Researcher Positioning   22
      Data Collection   23
      Data Analysis   26
   Limitations   27
   Overview of the Book   29

1. Theorizing Multilingual Writing in Entanglement   32
   Thinking With Mushrooms   32
   Multi-Species Relationships   34
   Becoming With Others   39
   Dwelling on Unpredictable Encounters   43
   Chronotopic Figuring   47
   An Entanglement Framework   55

2. Becoming With the River   57
   Spatializing Nature in Multilingual Landscape   57
   Meeting Morgan   62
   Encountering the River   63
   Writing the River into Meaning   69
   Becoming With the River   76

3. Turning Toward Thickets of Relationships   80
   Translation as Rhetorical Practice   80
   Translating the River Into an Intimate Friend   84
   Translating the River Across Coordinated Life Worlds   91
   Entanglements Could Fail   98
   Translating Through Thickets of Relationships   106

4. Dwelling on Unpredictable Encounters   111
   Looking for Unpredictable Encounters   111
   Meeting Leo   114
   Finding the Calligraphy Story   116
      Unexpected Detours   121
      Surprising (Re)discovery   125
      Unintended Consequences   131
   What Do Unpredictable Encounters Show Us?   138

5. Following Chronotopic Figuring   141
   Rhetorical Silence   142
   Performing Strategic Silence   145
   Masking Second-Generation Privilege   149
   Exercising Censorship to Navigate Perilous Class Identity   155
   Chronotopic Figuring   161

6. Working With Multilingual Writers in Entanglement   166
   Reconsidering Pedagogical Practices in First-Year Writing   168
      Supporting Precarious Relationships   168
         Snapshot   168
         Recommendations   172
      Listening to the Polyphony of the Academia   173
         Snapshot   173
         Recommendations   177
      Encounters With New Cultures and Disciplines   178
         Snapshot   178
         Recommendations   181

Destabilizing Deficit Perspectives   181
   Snapshot   181
   Recommendations   186
Asset-Based Pedagogy in Bridge Writing   187
   Translation Narrative   188
      Procedure   188
      Affordance   189
   I Am From Poetry   192
      Procedure   193
      Affordance   193
Enacting Asset-Based Pedagogy   197

Conclusion   201
   Writers In-Becoming With Others   204
   Thickets of Relationships   205
   The Surprising Ways of Encounters   206
   Chronotopic Figuring   207
   Asset-Based Multilingual Writing Pedagogy   209

Epilogue   213

Appendix   216
References   219
Index   231
About the Author   245

Illustrations

Figures

2.1. Morgan's WeChat Moments Remix of "At My Front Door"   65
2.2. Opening Scene in Morgan's Memoir Draft   71
3.1. Peer Review Annotations (Jessie and Ryan)   93
3.2. Morgan's Draft With Instructor Comments   101
3.3. Memoir Final Draft   105
4.1. Leo's WeChat Moments of July Meeting With Calligraphy Teacher   118
4.2. Leo's September WeChat Post   127
4.3. Leo's September WeChat Moments Post and Peer Comments   133
5.1. Multimodal Title Page for Leo's Memoir Assignment   148

Boxes

3.1. Excerpts of Morgan's Annotation of Peer Review Feedback   103
4.1. Comments on Leo's July WeChat Post   122

Table

6.1. Contrasting Perspectives on the Purpose of Teacher Conference   183

FOREWORD

Re-Worlding Multilingual Writing & Writing Studies With Entanglement

PAUL PRIOR

It is an honor to be writing this preface for a scholar I have learned much from and a book I greatly admire. In *Multilingual Writing in Entanglement: Becoming With Others Through Chronotopic Figuring and Unpredictable Encounters*, Xiqiao Wang articulates an innovative vision for writing theory, research, and pedagogy, particularly for working with multilingual writing and writers. The book weaves together an incisive argument for a theoretical-methodological shift to *entanglement*, richly detailed case studies of the entangled activities of two multilingual writers (Morgan and Leo) around undergraduate university study in the US, and pedagogical stories, reflections, and recommendations emerging at the intersection of the case studies, curricular redesign, and entanglement.

What is an entanglement framework and what is at stake in proposing and taking it up? Wang weaves together work on fungi and their mycorrhizal formations (Sheldrake, 2020; Tsing, 2015); Barad's (2007) intra-active agential realism that details how quantum mechanics matters for understanding of, and inquiry into, the ongoing production of our worlds; and Haraway's (2016) post-humanist call for *sympoiesis* (making and becoming with), which Haraway describes as "a word proper to complex, dynamic, responsive, situated, historical systems . . . a word for worlding-with, in company" (p. 58).

https://doi.org/10.7330/9781646427628.c000a

A key value of approaching entanglement from these post-humanist perspectives of fungi, intra-active mattering, sympoiesis, and worlding is that, unlike the metaphoric rhizomatics of Deleuze and Guattari (1987), these accounts of complex biotic, abiotic, and symbiotic entanglements offer seriously grounded models for flat ontologies.

Wang's attention to fungi and living worlds likewise respecifies metaphoric allusions to literate/semiotic ecologies. Her focus on unpredictable encounters, surprise, indeterminacy, and emergence rescues notions of ecology from machinic tropes that center fixed materialities and coherent systematicity. In biology, selection of model organisms for research is recognized as key to findings. Our ways of conceptualizing writing, learning, and society have been grounded in one model, the human, and in our cultural investments/beliefs about ourselves. Shifting the model toward fungi-in-ecologies (where humans may or may not be present and active) is thus radical in its implications for theoretical and sociopolitical vision. Feminist-materialist and decolonial and Indigenous scholarship has developed those implications, particularly in challenging human exceptionalist ideologies and their many invidious categorical boundaries and practices (e.g., Bang, 2017; Haraway, 2016; Nxumalo et al., 2022; Tsing, 2015).

Shifts in worldview of such magnitude are challenging. Voloshinov (1986) observed in 1929 that accounts of language (and signs) routinely seek a fixed source, whether in synchronic impersonal systems of language or the generatively expressive souls of people; he argued both poles are wrong, that language and sign phenomena in general are "purely historical phenomen[a]" (p. 82). The ruts of thinking and acting with everyday semiotic tropes and terms (Prior & Olinger, 2019) are so worn that the ontological shift to a historical-dialogic perspective remains not only controversial almost a century later but also difficult to consistently maintain even for theorists, researchers, and teachers who accept it. Voloshinov's call for emergent historicity grounded in Marxist perspectives got a boost in the same era from physics's revolutionary theoretical and experimental recasting of the world around quantum mechanics. As Barad (2007) argues, quantum mechanics is an account of the universe we all inhabit, not of odd anomalies of small bits of matter, an account with radical ethico-onto-epistemological implications for projects of knowing, doing, and becoming (cf. Prior et al., forthcoming). To resist slippage to conventional worldviews, Barad de-centers language and metaphors grounded in common sense and reified in Cartesian-Newtonian ideologies. Instead of static worlds where given and autonomous objects simply interact, Barad argues for *intra-active* agential accounts focused on constantly emergent *becoming, entanglement,* and fused *spacetimemattering.*

Over the last 30 years, and thus harder still to grasp, biology is having its quantum moment as symbiosis fractures tables of neatly ordered species (types) and member organisms (tokens), finding instead symbiosis, where organisms are holobionts (multispecies consortia) and species are metagenomically meshed with their environments (Gilbert, 2017; Margulis et al., 2011; McFall-Ngai, 2024). At the same time, the detailed molecular phenomena of life have turned out to be dynamic, nothing like the notion of clockwork machinery. The simple idea of genetic-code-driven lifeforms has been increasingly challenged by precise accounts of complex, dynamic, open life processes. Announcing the need for a new biology, Woese (2004) argued: "The time has come to replace the purely reductionist 'eyes-down' molecular perspective with a new and genuinely holistic, eyes-up, view of the living world, one whose primary focus is on evolution, emergence, and biology's innate complexity" (p. 175).

Wang's account of multilingual writing as entanglement draws together this new picture of worlding not just theoretically (tracing multiple conversations that support it) but also empirically (detailing historical-ethnographic analyses that illuminate it) and pedagogically (offering guidance on its implications for supporting multilingual writers in their chronotopic trajectories of becoming). She observes that entanglement encourages her "to engage with transformative encounters, curated and emergent partnerships, indeterminate outcomes, conceptual trespassing, and negotiation and innovation as core features of multilingual writing" and then ticks off some key stakes for writing studies in shifting to entanglement:

> This view problematizes the myth of the singular author by pointing to the role of reciprocal partnerships in open assemblages. It invites us to observe writing and the writer as co-emergent in open articulation of the world along with natural, cultural, and literacy others. It focuses on negotiation across linguistic, cultural, and rhetorical differences as the norm and invites the researcher's efforts to follow the weaving and figuring of meaning through the mediation of semiotic repertoires and spatial-temporal configurations. It encourages an intentional departure from the modernist preoccupation with coherence, pattern, and clarity and instead provides a lens towards the slippery, ephemeral, and messy aspects of the world in becoming through the intra-active open articulation of multiple players and dwellers. It embraces surprises and improvisations as the norm of

coordinated, collaborative survival. It places the writer in the world, knotted within and emerging through historical trajectories and contingencies. (This volume, p. 55)

Methodologically, entanglement attunes research to *chronotopic figuring*, to semiotic fibers of the unexpected, the subtle, fleeting and routine events and patterns that fall outside the dominant ideological spotlight. Wang notes critical "moments of literacy work materialize through language innovation, which often evades our attention not only because they unfold through fleeting decisions that fold into seemingly routine part of language practices and thereby becomes invisible, but also because they are rarely captured, surfaced, and theorized" (this volume, p. 197).

This book is centrally about what happens when such obscured moments, connections, and practices are captured, surfaced, and theorized. Wang provides fine-grained analysis of "the messy, indeterminate, negotiated, and mobile writing processes" of two Chinese international students, Morgan and Leo, tracing their multilingual writing and living "across FYW classrooms, social media, and other significant locales of their natural, cultural, and literacy landscapes" (this volume, p. 7). Wang depicts Morgan and Leo as not only students in classes or writers but as whole persons entangled and intra-acting with others (human, technological, and natural) as they forge fascinating literate practices and lives.

Extending her earlier research on the transnational life worlds and semiotic practices of Chinese international students (Fraiberg et al., 2017) and close accounts of Morgan's translation practices around an honors writing assignment (Wang, 2020), Wang pulls together 2 years of focal research on their common university campus followed by 5 years of follow-up study as Morgan and Leo completed degrees, did graduate work at other institutions, and took up professional positions in the US and China:

> A deep dive into the literacy practices of Leo and Morgan has surfaced aspects of their multilingual writing processes that often elide research attention: ephemeral encounters that energize and inspire writing, reciprocal relationships that sustain the productive distribution of writing labor, accidents and surprises that steer contours of writing in unpredictable ways, and the chronotopic figuring and thickening of writing and identity practices across multiple historical trajectories. Analysis guided by such theoretical ideas has alerted me to the need to move our gaze beyond the singular moment of writing in one spacetime and for one

purpose and to trace the emergence of writing across multiple moments of being, living, and making meaning across lines of differences. (This volume, p. 166)

Wang's account of her research methods initially seems familiar: interviews, observations, and collection of texts (drafts, responded-to drafts, final papers, online exchanges, course materials). Her ability to engage fluently in embodied and online translingual spaces of Chinese and English much like Lam (2009) and her repeated, iterative engagement with the writers across time and contexts much like Roozen (2020) add rich depth to her analyses.

However, the specific relationships Wang forged with Leo and Morgan around "observations" are especially striking for research on writing:

Sometimes we met in my office immediately after their writing class to debrief about classroom activities, brainstorm for ideas for their assignments, process setbacks, and strategize for new challenges. Sometimes we met in one of the campus cafeterias where we ate, chatted, wrote, and studied together, with discussion about writing foregrounded or backgrounded depending on our priorities for the day. Sometimes we connected late into the evening through WeChat as they shared screenshots of their essay drafts, feelings of frustration or achievement, and questions about a writing task at hand. I sometimes followed them to corners on campus where they liked to spend time reading, socializing, or idling (e.g., the bank of a campus river, a sunny corner in an instructional building, a bench under a beautiful birch tree in a secluded corner) to get a sense of the rhythm of their daily routines and ephemeral encounters that prompted self-sponsored writing. Other times I walked with them on their daily routes from dorms to instructional buildings, as their cell phones rang with incoming messages and their replies in voice memos. On a few occasions, I participated in or witnessed informal WeChat discussions or WeChat Moments posts followed by comments, which involved literacy brokers from the students' social networks. (This volume, pp. 25–26)

It also becomes clear she was an active participant (e.g., engaging with Morgan and Leo about professors' comments or the fine-grained connotations of different translation options). The power not only of go-along mobile methods (Nordquist, 2021) but of such relationships is key to these cases and the book. As Hengst (2010) observed, "Relationships track a uniquely dialogic interaction order, a shadow network of times and places knotted together by the co-presence of certain people, a historical with-ness that allows for common ground" as "temporally, spatially, and culturally dispersed itineraries of personal relationships form a complexly networked trajectory through space-time that challenges the assumption that chronotopes come neatly organized in coherent and bounded scenes" (p. 117). A key methodological implication of the *with-ness* documented in this book might be simply stated: to study multilingual writers in entanglement, become entangled with them.

Across Chapters 2 and 3, Wang's analysis of, and engagement with, Morgan's writing illustrates her entanglement framework in detail—moving beyond broad-stroke characterizations to trace polyphonic assemblages in action. For example, as she traces Morgan's 11 drafts of a FYC essay and multiple and multilingual responses to it (the most consequential being self-sponsored intra-actions with others she knew well), Wang displays how Morgan and her essay become-with the local river she writes about and regularly encounters in varied moods, with varying atmospheres, and amid varying social activities:

> Becoming with each other is the name of the game. The river, Morgan, and multimodal texts, which moved the river towards meaning across visceral experiences, images, and writing in Chinese and English, are ontologically heterogeneous partners that become who and what they are in relational material-semiotic worlding. (This volume, p. 76)

Wang is able to trace in detail how certain words ("ebullient," "roar") came to be in the final text while others, like "murmur," disappeared and what was as stake in these seemingly mundane lexical choices. Tracing this "extensive knotted textual history" amid "thickets of relationships" that distributed translingual processes of translation (cf. Gonzales, 2018), negotiated cultural differences, and managed affect, Wang vividly portrays the importance of entanglement for understanding Morgan's texts, Morgan's becoming-with, and the institutional and informal currents that shaped the flows of Morgan's multilingual writing.

After a similar tracing of Leo's calligraphy memoir in Chapter 4, Wang offers in Chapter 5 a deep dive into Leo's silences, social restraints, and semiotic reticence as he navigated tricky social positionings around second-generation government youth in modern China; worked to align with, protect, and support his professional parents; and built toward an aspirational future marked by accomplishment and wealth but not flashy display. The chapter illuminates what is at stake in taking an entanglement perspective that neither reifies nor erases the person but rather traces semiotic-material-chronotopic string figuring as intra-active phenomena. Wang keeps writing and literate practice in view but here generatively highlights what is *not* spoken, written, worn, or done, what is erased or channeled into private spaces.

In the final chapter, Wang discusses how asset-based pedagogies and multimodal activity (Shipka, 2011) played out in Morgan's and Leo's work, focusing particularly on a team's innovative pedagogical retheorization and redesign of a bridge course. Although centered in that course, wandering-with the students also allowed Wang to observe how Morgan and Leo intra-acted with the campus writing center, with other instructors and students, with networks of friends and fellow students locally and globally, an entangled pedagogical ecology. Some early audiences of her approach expressed concern that entanglement perspectives could disrupt many investments typical of writing instruction and schooling (single authorship, writers' voice, plagiarism, stable and neatly ordered tasks and assessments). Taking up those concerns, Wang shifts to reflecting on her own experiences as a biliterate scholar/multilingual writer, nicely highlighting the rich resources, connections, and conversations that she has sought and that are routinely institutionally structured to support faculty writers. That reflection highlights the irony that universities often constrain and question kinds of resources and collaborations among undergraduates that they invest in and support for faculty. Wang argues that entanglement perspectives underscore the value of pedagogical moves that "seek to build connections across academic units; enable the mobility of emerging drafts across languages, modes, writers, and readers; support relationships students forge with each other, teachers, and mentors; encourage continuous efforts to recognize, name, and retool strategies; and help students recognize the value of attunement and improvisation" (this volume, p. 199).

Recalling Lemke's (2000) widely cited account of dynamic temporal scales, which suggested "all human activity takes place on one or more characteristic timescales" (p. 273), Wang observes that entanglement resists images of separate scalar planes and that "chronotopic figuring instead paints a picture of eco-social arrangements that involve the dynamic knotting and figuring of multiple spacetime relationships across scales" (p. 55). *Multilingual Writing in Entanglement: Becoming With Others Through Chronotopic Figuring and Unpredictable Encounters* offers a masterclass in painting such pictures of dynamic knotting and figuring, of how semiotic activity is encountered and enacted and with what consequences as writers, readers, activities, technologies, societies, and ecologies actively entangle, and are entangled, in worlding that educators can at best work to follow, understand, attune with, and become-with.

References

Bang, M. (2017). Toward an ethic of decolonial trans-ontologies in sociocultural theories of learning and development. In I. Esmonde & A. Booker (Eds.), *Power and privilege in the learning sciences: Critical and sociocultural theories of learning* (pp. 115–138). Routledge.

Barad, K. (2007). *Meeting the universe halfway: Quantum physics and the entanglement of matter and meaning.* Duke University Press.

Deleuze, G., & Guattari, F. (1987). *A thousand plateaus: Capitalism and schizophrenia.* (B. Massumi, Trans.). University of Minnesota Press.

Fraiberg, S., Wang, X., & You, X. (2017). *Inventing the world grant university: Chinese international students' mobilities, literacies, and identities.* Utah State University Press.

Gilbert, S. (2017). Holobiont by birth: Multilineage individuals as the concretion of cooperative processes. In A. Tsing, H. Swanson, E. Gan & N. Bubandt (Eds.), *Arts of living on a damaged planet* (pp. M73–90). University of Minnesota Press.

Gonzales, L. (2018). *Sites of translation: What multilinguals can teach us about digital writing and rhetoric.* University of Michigan Press.

Haraway, D. (2016). *Staying with the trouble: Making kin in the Chthulucene.* Duke University Press.

Hengst, J. (2010). Semiotic remediation, conversational narratives and aphasia. In P. Prior & J. Hengst (Eds.), *Exploring semiotic remediation as discourse practice* (pp. 107–138). Palgrave Macmillan.

Lam, W. S. E. (2009). Multiliteracies on instant messaging in negotiating local, translocal, and transnational affiliations: A case of an adolescent immigrant. *Reading Research Quarterly, 44*(4), 377–397.

Lemke, J. (2000). Across the scales of time: Artifacts, activities and meanings in ecosocial systems. *Mind, Culture, and Activity, 7*(4), 273–290.

Margulis, L., Asikainen, C., & Krumbein, W. (Eds.). (2011). *Chimeras and consciousness: Evolution of the sensory self.* MIT Press.

McFall-Ngai, M. (2024). Symbiosis takes a front and center role in biology. *PLoS Biol, 22*(4). e3002571.

Nordquist, B. (2021). Following labors of recontextualization: Toward a pedagogy of translingual mapping. In J. Kiernan, A. Frost & S. Malley (Eds.), *Translingual pedagogical perspectives: Engaging domestic and international students in the composition classroom* (pp. 191–211). Utah State University Press.

Nxumalo, F., Nayak, P., & Tuck, E. (2022). Education and ecological precarity: Pedagogical, curricular, and conceptual provocations. *Curriculum Inquiry, 52*(2), 97–107.

Prior, P. Hengst, J., & Olinger, A. (forthcoming). *Situated, historical, embodied semiosis (SHES): A unified framework for semiotic activity.* DeGruyter/Brill.

Prior, P. & Olinger, A. (2019). Academic literacies as laminated assemblage and embodied semiotic becoming. In D. Bloome, M. Lucia Castanheira, C. Leung & J. Rowsell (Eds.), *Re-theorizing literacy practices: Complex social and cultural contexts* (pp. 126–139). Routledge.

Roozen, K. (2020). Coming to act with tables: Tracing the laminated trajectories of an engineer-in-the-making. *Learning, Culture and Social Interaction, 24*(March). Article 100284.

Sheldrake, M. (2020). *Entangled life*. Random House.

Shipka, J. (2011). *Toward a composition made whole*. University of Pittsburg Press.

Tsing, A. L. (2015). *The Mushroom at the end of the world: On the possibility of life in capitalist ruins*. Princeton University Press.

Voloshinov, V. (1986). *Marxism and the philosophy of language*. Harvard University Press.

Wang, X. (2020). Becoming multilingual writers through translation. *Research in the Teaching of English, 54*(3), 206–230.

Woese, C. R. (2004). A new biology for a new century. *Microbiology and Molecular Biology Reviews, 68*(2), 173–186.

Preface

I started a modest gardening project during the global Covid-19 pandemic. Seeding began in early February 2020 in the corner of my sunroom, whose south-facing windows allowed for 6 hours of sunlight and cool temperatures throughout the day, two critical conditions for producing stubby, healthy seedlings rather than leggy and fragile ones. When the dangers of random snow flurries started to dissipate in early April, I moved platters of inch-tall seedlings back and forth, sunbathing them during the day in the backyard and retrieving them in the afternoon. The caprice of spring temperature variations strengthened the root systems of my seedlings, preparing them for healthy, hardy lives despite all the adventures nature had to offer. Only after Memorial Day weekend did I contemplate planting the most robust seedlings into the garden. Anxiety over devastating frosts was slow to fade.

I relied on information printed on the seed packets to anticipate blooming cycles for different types of flowers. In my mind, my garden would produce flushes of vibrant colors throughout summer. Hardy dianthus would be the first to produce bundles of purple, white, and pink flowers in early spring but would phase out when summer heat approached. The perennial Shasta daisies and black-eyed Susans were late bloomers but would continue to produce splashes of bright yellow and white well into early September. The annuals,

Cape daisies and zinnias, would start to bloom in early spring and continue to do so into late fall. Dahlias, late arriving, would last throughout fall. My vision for the garden started in my head; plotting of the land concretized through careful measurements and doodle maps on paper; my plans and ambitions changed with arguments with other members of the family, who imagined different uses for the land. We negotiated an agreement that ensured equitable division of labor. The most challenging task for me, the gardener, would be the regular pruning in the heat of summer to prevent the plants from tangling into voracious gnarls.

In reality, my tender plants were very much at the mercy of animal neighbors with enormous appetites, including a family of deer, a rabbit couple, and a lone groundhog, who operated with variant foraging schedules to deprive me of the joy of summer blossoms. Surprisingly, it was a Korean chili plant that my husband insisted on planting next to my daisies that saved the day. It produced flamboyant chili peppers that burned our tongues and fingers upon touch and repelled the animals who frequented my garden, thereby preserving a few bouquets of daisies and zinnias for me to boast about to my neighbors.

As winter approached, I prepared the garden by uprooting and composting annuals, trimming and sheltering perennials, and retrieving, drying, and storing dahlia tubers for replanting the next spring. As my hands soiled from digging, cutting, and planting, my mind wandered into the world of writing, which was populated by unfinished sentences and paragraphs, quotes and annotations from literature review, new and old books whose extended edges were jagged by colorful sticky notes, and ethnographic data at various stages of processing and analyzing. My productivity as a writer fluctuated with my mood as an amateur gardener, which fluctuated in accordance with the feasting schedules of critters that shared the flowers and fruits of my imagination and labor. Therefore, the quality and quantity of writing to emerge, like my flowers, were often at the mercy of my groundhog neighbor. The cyclical rhythm of my professional life intersected with the temporal rhythms of seasonal changes; the life cycles of our animal neighbors; and the daily routines of cooking, cleaning, parenting, and other household chores. My writing was entangled with my garden in many ways.

In the months and years to follow, my gardening and writing projects continued to entangle. Gardening allowed me to ponder, recuperate from, and play with ideas for the all-consuming enterprise of book writing. It provided useful distractions from episodes of intensive reading, annotating, data analysis, and drafting, punctuating my days that were otherwise dominated by teaching, meetings, and mentoring carried out remotely through the mediation of my laptop. The physical acts of digging, weeding, pruning, dead-ending, and thinning moved my body in ways sedentary writing did not; tactile engagement with soil, thorns, petals, and earthworms also moved me imaginarily as my mind wandered into the multiplicity of intellectual terrains I traverse, including the world of matsutake mushrooms and the worldly journey they took as a valuable commodity (Tsing, 2015) and the numerous ethnographic slices of transnational lives detailed by scholars I read. While I was gardening, elusive ideas surfaced, connected, and sparked, often compelling a rushed trip inside to record them before they disappeared again.

At the same time, research writing figured into my daily contemplations about the prosperity and plight of my flowers, my futile efforts to grow mushrooms in the garage, and my children's thrill as they strategized to outsmart and outrun the groundhog. My reading about the underground world of fungi helped me shift the human perspective with which to consider the joy, excitement, and puzzlement I experienced in growing and sharing my garden. From reading and writing, I gained new appreciation of the multiple temporal rhythms of the worlds of animals and plants, which entered harmonious and discordant relationships (groundhog spotting at dusk became a reliable predictor of garden "massacres" my children were excited to report the next morning). These daily contemplations in turn shaped how I developed metaphors for describing and theorizing the intricate and contingent ways in which multilingual living and writing take shape through coordinated partnerships across life worlds. My gardening and writing invited efforts to disentangle the multiple spatial contours and temporal trajectories of multilingual writers that we have often failed to notice because they are drowned out by the singular, instructor-facilitated temporal rhythm of the monolingual writing classroom.

Many pleasant and unpleasant surprises arose from the intended yet uncontrollable becoming-with of the amateur gardener, frolicking children, hungry critters, sturdy daisies, fragile roses, voracious weeds, fragrant herbs, and devilishly spicy Korean peppers. My garden served as a constant reminder that unpredictable encounters make life happen, that such encounters defy fences, taxonomies, theoretical binaries, and ontological categories, and the fact that our interpretation of the effects of such encounters vary with the perspectives of humans, animals, or plants. Despite the many theoretical binaries that continue to separate and hierarchically order distinct ways of being, perceiving, relating, and making meaning in the world, my garden reminds me that my being, as multilingual writer, ethnographer, writing researcher, parent, and aspirational gardener, is entangled with the auspicious and suspicious others. The multiple life worlds I weave and am woven into can enable my intellectual movement with fluidity; they can also stall my thinking and change my being.

It was in my garden, and by extension in the world of mushrooms, that I found resonances in theoretical ideas that informed my ongoing ethnographic inquiry into the contours of multilingual writing. This book is my effort to notice, surface, and theorize the physical, emotional, and intellectual labors of multilingual writing in entanglements. Such labor—messy, mobile, distributed, and indeterminate—often remains invisible to writing researchers because immense efforts are taken to teach, regulate, and routinize the material and discursive practices that are believed to make writing happen; when they do become subjects of scholarly and pedagogical inquiry, they often surface as grammatical errors, linguistic oddities, and writing slippages to be eradicated as writing teachers work industriously to help edit messy texts toward closer approximation to academic conventions undergirded by monolingual and monocultural norms. In this book, I enter the backstage scenes of multilingual writing, with all its mess, indeterminacy, surprise, and mobility, as meaningful sites for discovering and making meaning, negotiating across linguistic, cultural, and rhetorical differences, and living multilingual lives. I do so by offering a book-length study of the writing and identity practices of two Chinese international students, Morgan and Leo, as they continued to forge their paths as multilingual writers through the various assignments entailed in first-year writing (FYW) classes, including a bridge writing class I taught and also honor-designated first-year composition (FYC) classes they took at a public university in a midwestern state of the United States. I provide detailed analysis of how their writing assignments took shape through the passing of ideas, stories, phrases, and strategies from one writer/reader, language/mode, and spacetime to another. I followed these writers as they mobilized their writing across reading and writing tasks assigned in FYW classes, creative and interactive literacy activities on social media, self-sponsored and instructor-facilitated writing and reviewing sessions, and social and leisure events that appeared to have nothing to do with writing on the first look. Following such passing, I argue, provides important insights into how writing unfolded through these multilingual writers' imaginary and embodied entanglements with messy and contingent assemblages of natural, cultural, and literacy others.

However, descriptive accounts that celebrate multilingual writers' achievements are not my sole purpose. I am interested in developing theoretical and methodological tools for engaging with messy, ephemeral, and capricious entanglements through which multilingual living and writing unfold. If, as Karen Barad argues, "specificity of entanglement is everything" because it changes with each intra-action among agential forces human and nonhuman, discursive and material, natural and cultural (2007, p. 74), we are compelled to ask how seemingly insignificant particularities of writing entanglements, such as an ephemeral encounter with natural beauty or a seemingly idiosyncratic decision to delete a social media post, inform our understanding of writing and writing pedagogy for multilingual, translingual, and monolingual writers alike. To do so, I resort to intra-action, which is a term Barad (2007) coined to signal that all biological beings and discursive and material mattering are constantly becoming with others in moments of sensing, acting with, and responding to each other, to theorize how multilingual writers become with others in entanglements of complex, dynamic, responsive, situated, and historical systems.

Throughout this book, I argue that attention to seemingly insignificant particulars, methodologically inconvenient anomalies, frivolous idiosyncrasies, and unpredictable encounters provides ways to unravel the indeterminate and determinate ways in which visceral reactions, bodily sensations, affective exchanges, and inspirations tangle with durable literacy practices, collective imaginaries, historical meanings, and prescriptive norms to shape multilingual writing. My efforts to follow, capture, theorize, and represent the ephemeral, messy, and surprising features of multilingual writing co-emerged with my intellectual and physical labors of wandering and dwelling in my garden and in the world of fungi. Mushrooms showed me the need and ways to account for the vast and invisible underground expanse, fragile and sustained partnerships, unpredictable, life-making encounters, and temporal polyphony of life worlds forging coordination. Throughout this book, I rely on mushrooms as my guide into the messy, precarious, and surprising ways of multilingual writers becoming with others through collaboration, negotiation, and improvisation.

Acknowledgments

The writing of this book is as messy, indeterminate, and dispersed as the entangled multilingual writing processes I follow and theorize. I have been fortunate to encounter and connect with incredible people throughout my research. Their questions shape my inquiries; their voices inevitably surface in my writing. I am grateful first and foremost to Morgan and Leo, whose generosity, humor, and trust gave me the opportunity to explore the complexity of multilingual writing in ways that had not previously been possible. As I mentally drafted this acknowledgement on my daily walk through the beautiful Schenley Park in Pittsburgh, I reminisced about similar walks I took with them on the beautiful campus of Michigan State University. It was during these walks, when we talked about our own triumphs, challenges, fears, and joys as multilingual writers, that the bits and pieces that eventually assembled into the book began to emerge.

I am grateful to my University of Pittsburgh colleagues, Annette Vee, Gayle Rogers, Benjamin Miller, and Alexander Hidalgo, who have provided much needed insight, wisdom, and advocacy throughout my writing and publishing process. The book especially benefited from the sharp eyes and creative insights of colleagues who read and listened as I developed drafts, delivered presentations, and strategized for revisions. I appreciate the amazing graduate students I have been fortunate to work with at Pitt, whose curiosities and criticality pushed me to further articulate my theoretical metaphors through the lens of mushrooms. My special shout-out goes to Caro Pirri, who arrived at Pitt in the same year as I did and held my hand as we navigated the many unpredictable turns during the publishing process.

My colleagues at Michigan State University—Steve Fraiberg, Peter DeCosta, Joyce Meier, and Julia Kiernan—have modeled how well-designed research could simultaneously advance theory, develop pedagogy, and enact change. I thank them for setting good examples for how to engage with others as compassionate human beings, dedicated teachers, and inquisitive researchers. I also wish to express my appreciation to the opportunity to participate in the research led by Ellen Cushman, which renewed my interests in research and brought me onto a decade-long journey to understand and support multilingual writers.

The research I present in this book developed through many conversations with groups of scholars across disciplinary fields. A 2016 symposium that Peter DeCosta organized at Michigan State University brought into convergence the voices of Suresh Canagarajah, Esther Milu, Jyotsna Singh, and Steven Fraiberg, who provided invaluable feedback on the initial efforts to write the case study about Leo into meaning. Their insights, which alerted me to the importance of relationships and networks, vibrate through my writing in Chapters 2 and 3.

I am thankful to Rebecca Lorimer Leonard and colleagues at the 2018 Elbow Symposium for the Study and Teaching of Writing at University of Massachusetts Amherst, which honed my understanding of transnational, multilingual literacies as an area of inquiry that required continuous interdisciplinary traversal and methodological attunement.

The 2020 Dartmouth Summer Seminar gave me a space to develop methodological rigor necessary to make sense of messy ethnographic data. I am indebted to the scholars who gave insightful feedback on my work during the seminar: Christiane Donahue, Charles Bazerman, Dylan Dryer, Chris Anson, Mya Poe, Bradley Dilger, and Jason Swarts. My colleagues who joined me in an informal study group after the conclusion of the seminar—Kevin Roozen, Calley Marrota, Dan Ehrenfeld, and Ana Cortez—helped me develop the research narrative that appears in Chapter 4. Their questions were especially helpful for my thinking about classed identity practices in transnational contexts.

I appreciate my colleagues Sidury Christiansen, Peng Yin, and Tairan Qiu, who offered great conversations in a chronotope study group led by

Eva Lam, where we engaged in collective reading in an emerging body of interdisciplinary scholarship that pushed me to consider the theoretical and methodological affordances of spacetime as embodied and representational resources. Their incredible agility to traverse disciplinary barriers motivated me to develop the concept of chronotopic figuring.

I continue to benefit from the generosity of scholars in the field. Conference conversations with Kate Vieira, Nancy Bou Ayash, Xiqioye You, Hannah Rule, and Cydney Alexis have been essential in enriching and complicating my thinking about the embodied, material, and negotiated aspects of multilingual writing.

I am immensely indebted to the mentorship of Paul Prior, whose generosity manifested in his guidance that steered my precarious effort to engage with mushrooms, plantations, and quantum physics; Paul has read multiple drafts throughout my invention, drafting, and revision process and thanks to his wisdom, I was able to survive what often felt like a never-ending journey. I am incredibly grateful to Paul for agreeing to write the foreword for this book, which drew on a long dispersal of conversations we had at conferences, through email exchanges, on the margins of evolving drafts, during study group intra-actions among colleagues genuinely intrigued by and invested in the ideas we each bring, which best illustrate my own becoming with others through multilingual writing in entanglements. I will always remember Paul's advice to "follow the agent," which helped to frame the research questions I pursue and the methods that I adopt.

The three reviewers for Utah State University Press read my manuscript with care and insight. I thank them for their generous, thoughtful response to my work. Thanks to their engagement, my revised manuscript presents a much more focused analysis of entangled multilingual writing, where much innovation and negotiation take place.

I thank my graduate advisor, Kevin Leander at Vanderbilt University, for what he has taught me. My curiosities and perspectives are deeply rooted in readings and conversations that took place in and around the beautiful Rotunda in Wyatt Center. Words are inadequate to convey how much I have learned from all those who have taught and guided me at Vanderbilt.

Finally, my gratitude goes to my partner, Tianfu, and my two daughters, Brooke and Raina, whose love and sacrifice made the fruition of this project a possibility. I am especially thankful to Brooke, who brought my rambling explanation of fungi, entanglement, and multilingual writing into an artistic design, which informed my ideas for the book cover. I wish to express my profound admiration for Raina, whose adventurous spirit and warm encouragement have pushed me to embark on impossible hikes, try strange dishes, and develop curious projects. As I write this acknowledgement, the spawn bags we inoculated with shiitake and oyster mushroom spores are showing first signs of mycelial growth.

    I dedicate this book to my parents. I continue to draw strength from their unwavering support and enduring love. They gave me the name Xiqiao (bridge to the west), which embodies a dream and aspiration shared by generations of intellectuals in my family. This book, I hope, is one way to respond to cross-generational efforts to build bridges, with which people and knowledge are mobilized despite geographic, cultural, and linguistic barriers.

MULTILINGUAL WRITING IN ENTANGLEMENT

Introduction

Transnational Migration and Multilingual Writing

My inquiry into multilingual writing in entanglements builds on research that unravels the complex relationship between transnational individuals' semiotic repertoires, literacy practices, and intersecting global and local forces that shape the exigencies and contours of migration. Broadly, such scholarship has argued that situated literacy activities of transnational individuals cannot be understood in isolation from other forms of cultural, geographic, and imaginary forms of border crossing, which provide such individuals with experiential and linguistic resources and allow them to develop transnational funds of knowledge (Lam & Christiansen, 2022; Karimzad & Catedral, 2021; Guerra, 1998; Medina, 2010; Sanchez, 2007; Skerrett, 2012). As transnational migrants negotiate myriad academic, social, and career challenges, they draw on shifting semiotic repertoires and literacy and identity resources developed in spaces that span multiple geographical territories (Lam & Warriner, 2012; Lorimer Leonard, 2017; Sarroub, 2002; Vieira, 2016). Specifically, transnational migratory processes allow migrants to acquire a "bi-focal" lens with which to view their experiences, develop strategies to disrupt meta-narratives, stigmatizing labels, and nefarious politics through which dominant social discourse portrays migrants, and forge multiple affiliations across transnational networks (Lam & Christiansen, 2022; Suárez-Orozco & Suárez-Orozco, 2001). Transnational migrants mobilize and attune dynamic semiotic repertoires, which encompass wide-ranging print-based, visual, gestural, affective, and imaginary resources to perform, destabilize, and redefine literacies required to meet the new demands of changing social and cultural circumstances (Christiansen, 2017; Yi, 2010; Wang, 2019b). In such accounts, transnational students' multilingual, multimodal, and multisensory repertoires co-evolve with experiential and linguistic resources enabled by and propelling multiple forms of physical, virtual, and imaginary border crossing (Lorimer Leonard, 2015; Rubinstein-Avila, 2007; Vieira, 2019).

In composition studies specifically, scholars have used mobility as a framework to theorize the strategic ways in which multilinguals move textual meaning and attune writing-related dispositions, practices, and knowledge across languages and modalities (Fraiberg, 2010; Gonzales, 2018; Wang, 2019a). Such a view reflects conceptual turns toward languages as practice-based, adaptive, and mutually constitutive linguistic, cultural, and ideological structures. Viewing multilingual writing as sites for embodied, affective, and negotiated rhetorical practice, translingual perspectives recognize language differences as linguistic innovations, highlight language users' agency in working through language ambiguities for strategic gains (Creese & Blackledge, 2010; Horner et al., 2011; Lu & Horner, 2013; Li, 2018) and theorize multilingual writing as coordinated and innovative performance of semiotic repertoires in reaction and resistance to historically inscribed norms (Alvarez, 2018; Li, 2018; Lillis & Curry, 2010).

More specifically, composition scholars have argued that translation, broadly construed, is a core process of all writing, which is always implicated within the traffic of ideas, concepts, symbols, and discourses (Ayash, 2019; Gonzales, 2018; Horner & Tetreault, 2016; Pennycook, 2008). As multilinguals' literacy practices carry intense legal, social, and professional consequences and fulfill important social functions, they are creative interpretations that materialize through the ongoing negotiation of language, rhetorical, and cultural systems and traditions. Composition scholars have argued that multilingual writing is a creative process through which meanings are continuously discovered, interpreted, formulated, and mobilized across languages and rhetorical situations (Lu, 2006; Schor, 1986). Indeed, multilingual writing, like any act of writing, is an inevitable outcome of reworking historically developed practices and meanings because each uptake of a word, phrase, or language emerges from ongoing attempts to populate historical meanings with new intentions and modifications. Such a revised view of translation as rhetorical practice enables multilingual and monolingual writers to view language as dynamic, fluid, and negotiable (Ayash, 2019). Yet the intense physical, emotional, and intellectual labors entailed in such language work have often remained unseen to multilingual writers who use and benefit from them as well as writing instructors who work with multilingual writers (Wang, 2020).

As multilingual students' literacy lives are complexly intertwined in migratory processes and shifting semiotic repertoires, it becomes necessary to expand our analytical gaze toward the expansive literacy landscape of transnational students, especially their writing extracurricular activities, where multilingual writing vibrates with great energy, often in dynamic connection to forms of academic writing experienced and expected in writing classrooms. An emerging body of research has paid closer attention to the fluid fashion in which writing, reading, and digital literacies continue to connect, cross-fertilize, and engage in contestation across spaces. In writing studies, scholars have explored the intricate connection between self-sponsored literacy practices that take place beyond the writing classroom (Fraiberg, 2017; Gere, 1994; Rounsaville, 2014; Roozen, 2012; Yancey, 2004; Yi & Hirvela, 2010), which expands our understanding of writers' discursive repertoire in connection to the literate landscape they traverse. Digital spaces emerge as an important sphere of the literacy landscape of transnational students, who routinely traverse multiple digital platforms and networks to not only access but also participate in transnational dispersal of news, cultural events, and political advocacy. Transnational students weave together writing technologies and digital tools to engage in globally distributed forms of youth culture, to author and perform identities, and to develop simultaneous affiliations with local and translocal communities of diaspora (Black, 2005; Lam, 2009; Takayoshi, 2015; Wang, 2024). Furthermore, these scholars have examined self-sponsored, digital literacies such as fanfiction, personal, and collaborative writing within and across digitally mediated interest and study groups (Fraiberg & Cui, 2016; Wang, 2017; Zhang-Wu, 2021) to facilitate literacy learning in formal spaces. As these authors and others observe, self-sponsored writing activities create opportunities to practice writing for authentic purposes, in multiple genres, and in service of school writing (Roozen & Erickson, 2017). In these self-sponsored writing spaces, transnational students develop agentive identities and positive relationships with literacy through collaborative play, constructive peer feedback, and interest-driven writing activities. In documenting the forms and functions of various digital literacies, such research has provided richly nuanced accounts of the multifaceted literacy experiences of transnational students.

Together, writing researchers have grappled with the complex entanglement of semiotic, affective, socioeconomic, geopolitical, and cultural circumstances through which multilingual writing emerges, while calling attention to the strategic and negotiated ways in which transnational students traverse literacy spaces that are deeply implicated with cultural, linguistic, political, and ideological differences. At the core of such work is also attention to a holistic view of multilingual students' semiotic and rhetorical repertoires, which are honed through wide-ranging communicative tasks that are fundamentally mobile, dynamic, and networked across complex assemblages of texts, technologies, brokers, spatiality, and trajectories. While richly textured accounts of transnational students' literacies have extended our understanding of what Jody Shipka calls the "potentials of alternative, hybrid, mixed, and experimental forms of discourse" (Shipka, 2016, p. 3), they are limited in several ways. First, in operating with dichotomous views of social spaces that divide the literate landscape that writers inhabit (e.g., church, social media, classroom), such studies often overlook the simultaneously fluid, frictive, and fixed ways in which literacy practices pass from one person, space, language, and mode to another or the dynamic ways they continue to connect, extend, and give rise to new exigencies for writing (Lorimer Leonard, 2017). In fixing an analytical gaze on specific locales of students' literacy performance, we have yet to unravel the complex ways in which reading, writing, and digital literacies are meshed, reconfigured, and entangled across spaces to fulfill the literacy expectations entailed in multilingual living. Second, such research has often conceived transnational students' literacy practices developed across language, cultural, and rhetorical differences as discrete dimensions of their literacy lives, while overlooking how writing expertise developed in one language and rhetorical tradition might connect with writing-related knowledge and practices acquired in another. As such, current research has yet to arrive at a productive reconciliation of celebratory accounts of multilingual writing as transformative, agentive, and empowering and the plight of such students working to fulfill the literacy expectations of university classrooms. Lastly, as Pamela Takayoshi (2018) has rightly noted, in focusing on the sociality of writing, current research has not adequately examined the messiness of the writing processes of individuals working through, with, and against ideologically inscribed norms, identity scripts, and power structures. In celebrating multilingual writing as the achievements of agentive and strategic language users, we have yet to fully notice or adequately theorize the messy, indeterminate, and surprising aspects of writing. That is, we have only begun to notice how surprising discoveries, ephemeral encounters, unintended consequences, and unsettling accidents upend ideas and drafts, redirect writing contours, and compel writers to explore new possibilities and forge new relationships through and with writing.

This book is an effort to notice the messy, indeterminate, and surprising aspects of multilingual writing, which I argue to be the exigencies and outcomes of multilingual writers working through differences, in collaboration with others, and toward open articulation of meanings. To do so, I provide fine-grained analysis of the messy, indeterminate, negotiated, and mobile writing processes of two Chinese international student writers. This book-length study of two students' multilingual writing and living builds on careful tracing of their literacies across FYW classrooms, social media, and other significant locales of their natural, cultural, and literacy landscapes, allowing me to enter the backstage scenes of their writing, to follow hidden themes and emerging connections across multiple literacy spheres and spacetimes, and to document the intense intellectual, emotional, and physical labors of writing across differences. This deep dive alerted me to the many unexpected yet productive juxtapositions between ephemeral encounters and their long-lasting effects, delightful and alarming surprises, and unintended detours despite exhaustive plans. I now recognize these juxtapositions, which I initially noticed as methodologically inconvenient accidents, oddities, and anomalies during the research process, as windows into the writers' constant effort to work through the mess of writing labor. They drive and move writing through entanglements, when living and nonliving things (e.g., readers, reviewers, friends, trees, rivers, animals) that otherwise populate the natural and cultural worlds of writers are woven into dynamic and mobile assemblages to provide powerful exigencies for discovering, making, and articulating meaning. To think with mess and surprises, I begin by exploring the improvised, spontaneous aspects of writing labor, which emerges from visceral reactions to ephemeral, fleeting, and chanceful configurations of worlds-in-articulation. Doing so invites me to pay close attention to multilingual writers' organic and haphazard acts of shuttling across languages, genres, and modes as an essential part of navigating capricious, messy, and complex multilingual living. To understand why and how certain ephemeral encounters achieve lasting emotional, affective, and imaginative impact or gain mobility across languages, modes, and spacetimes, I follow the semiotic threads of memories, sensations, knowledge, and practices accumulated across moments of multilingual writing and living and observe how such threads forge and fork in simultaneously predictable and what Haraway (2016) calls "tentacular" ways to make writing happen.

An Entanglement Perspective for Multilingual Writing Research

My effort to grapple with mess, surprises, and indeterminacy as the outcome of multilingual writers encountering, connecting with, and relating to natural, cultural, and literacy others draws on a long tradition of composition scholarship informed by ecological metaphors developed partially in critique of earlier cognitive models of writing, which often depict the solitary writer immersed in their ideas, isolated from the forces of the social world, and performing codified and unified writing processes. For writing scholars interested in imagining and enacting research in a time when writing flourishes in forms and functions across spaces, metaphors informed by ecological studies usefully guide conceptual and methodological efforts to examine writing as a "complex, diffuse, and messy" phenomenon (Law, 2004, p. 2). That is, an ecological perspective begins with the recognition that how we perceive, comprehend, discover, and articulate meaning simultaneously reacts to and evolves with our environment (Coe, 1975), attends to the complex relationships writers form with readers, texts, and broader social systems of meaning making (Cooper, 1986), and examines writing as distributed, collaborative efforts of networks of writers, readers, texts, and tools acting and interacting in parallel with each other through interrelated, complex, socially constituted systems (Syverson, 1999).

Positioning eco-composition as a site to explore "complex interrelationships between the human activity of writing and all of the conditions of the struggle for existence," Sidney Dobrin argues that how we operate within and against the systems in which we find ourselves "is both a matter of discursive maneuvering and a matter of physical and material positioning, and consequence" (2001, pp. 12–13). Some take an ecological conceptualization of writing to examine the materiality of spaces where writers are situated, noting how the material bodies, structures, and actions are complexly interconnected to enforce normed and raced discursive conventions and to discursively, performatively, and materially shape how writers dwell, labor, and get evaluated in such spaces (Inoue, 2015). Others extend ecology to examine the expansive and diverse assemblages of cultural, social, technological, disciplinary, and material networks that circulate and interact to shape how and why we write (Mays, 2017). A compelling example of such sociorhetorical ecologies can be found in Anis Bawarshi's discussion of rhetorical genres as powerful ecosystems within which the individual and the social are mutually reproduced (2001). As he illustrates, the genre of the "Patient Medical History Form" plays an important role in mediating the interaction between patient and doctor, enabling socially recognizable identities, inviting typified activities, and invoking ideological constructs of Western notions of medicine that inform how doctors recognize symptoms and devise treatment plans. In efforts to name and theorize writing ecologies, these authors have unraveled the importance of messy relationships in driving the co-evolution of writers, the symbolic and material structures of their environments, and normalized expectations for identities, practices, interactions, and relations. As Weisser and Dobrin suggest (2001), an ecological perspective focuses on the multiplicity of relationships between words, thoughts, writers, readers, material and imaginary spaces, and temporal trajectories, which enable the co-constitutive existence of writing and natural and cultural worlds writers encounter, traverse, and inhabit (p. 2).

Ecological attention to relationships offers a lens to consider writing and rhetoric as intimately related to place, environment, nature, and location. For multilingual writing research, attention to relationships allows us to observe seemingly idiosyncratic writerly choices, such as the translation of a word from Chinese into English or the writer's strategic deployment of a rhetorical strategy resonating across rhetorical traditions as mutually constituted with an expansive universe of material, natural, and cultural systems operating at various scales. Multilingual writing-in-entanglement is fluid, emergent, and transformative because it is a complex system involving "great numbers of parts undergoing a kaleidoscopic array of simultaneous interactions" (Syverson, 1999, p. 3). Ecology therefore provides a lens to get at the fluidity and complexities of writing as a phenomenon rather than the individual writer as a distanced, strategic designer. Ecological entanglement not only allows us to observe the strategic and purposeful ways in which writers formulate relationships, weave semiotic repertoires, and simultaneously enact and shape material and symbolic environments, but also encourages us to notice the spontaneous ways in which relationships, repertoires, and environs coalesce in unexpected ways, invite improvisations, and redirect contours because writers respond and adapt in reaction to unpredictable, random, and ephemeral forces that ripple through fluid interconnections.

Throughout this book, I build on and extend ecological metaphors by exploring propositions offered by scholarly efforts to think with and about fungi, which are famously collaborative, capricious, and innovative creatures that make life possible. I draw on theoretical metaphors developed by fungi scholars (Sheldrake, 2020; Tsing, 2015) to propose several ways for considering multilingual writing as the outcome and medium through which multilingual living takes shape. I argue that fungal entanglement provides useful ways to observe and theorize reciprocal relationships, unpredictable encounters, and chronotopic figuring as central features of multilingual writing. Ways in which fungi forge reciprocal relationships with trees, rocks, animals, and humans to make collaborative living happen mirror the becoming of the multilingual writer through sustaining relationships the writer strategically and unwittingly forges with other forms of being. Fungi's ability to entangle across categorical boundaries helps to shift our analytical gaze away from texts, languages, writers, and writing technologies as independent entities with determinate boundaries and properties. Instead, fungi provide a way to theorize multilingual writing as unfolding through coordinated and improvised assemblages of writers, readers, literacy brokers, writing technologies, texts, and material and semiotic environs, which are achieved through the constant attuning of and innovations with expansive repertoires of writing-related knowledge and practices. Unpredictable encounters across lines of differences, which drive transformative relationships between fungi and their unlikely partners, similarly energize new affective and imaginative possibilities for multilingual living and writing. Placing mushrooms and multilingual writing in entanglement offers useful insights into facets of multilingual lives that extant research has yet to fully explore. For one thing, how can we study writing as the outcome of divergent, layered, and conjoined projects that make up multilingual students' life worlds? What does it mean to observe multilingual writing as articulation of world-in-becoming when an open-ended gathering of the writer and natural, cultural, and literacy others (re)configure in response to fickle material and semiotic environments? How do we understand writing as determinate and indeterminate happenings when strategic coordination of relationships and unpredictable encounters play equally important roles in directing its contour? In important ways, the move toward entanglement makes it possible and necessary to notice the unruly, random, serendipitous, indeterminate, and improvised aspects of multilingual writing as meaningful sites of inquiry.

Following multilingual writing in entanglement involves conceptual and methodological moves that intentionally burst categories, trespass boundaries, complicate dichotomies, and upend identities (Tsing, 2015, p. 132). Such transgressive moves begin with conscious efforts to dislodge what Karen Barad (2007) critiques as "remnant anthropocentric and representationalist assumptions" rooted in binary conceptions that pit nature against culture, human against nonhuman, and discursive against material practices. Following life-in-entanglement therefore rests upon serious reconsiderations of where to look for evidence of writing and what to look for. By shifting our analytical gaze away from the false assumption of the agentive human who weaves natural, material, semiotic, and symbolic resources into the social fabric we inhabit and navigate, we then begin to feel "accountable for the role we play in the differential constitutions and differential positioning of the human among other creatures, both living and nonliving" (Barad, 2007, p. 136).

As the open-ended gathering of multiplicity of life forms, relationships, and communicative repertoire is essential for the resilience and productivity of life-in-coordination, multilingual writing vibrates with energy from multiplicities stitched together through dynamic relationships, which carry with them layers of historically developed spatial and temporal meanings. As Fleckenstein et al. (2008) usefully argues, "ecological research enacted rhetorically" (p. 390) aims to achieve "resonance *among* the metaphors that undergird our conceptualization of the phenomenon of study, our methods of study, and our enactment of those methods" (p. 389). That is, theoretical constructs informed by ecological metaphors necessitate retooling of ethnographic methods for capturing and accounting for multilingual writing in entanglement. Below I provide an outline of propositions for researching writing from an entanglement perspective and explain how these propositions inform my conceptualization of the phenomenon, my method of study, and my ongoing efforts to attune the theoretical and methodological tools for following multilingual writing in entanglement. In doing so, I respond to Donna Haraway's invitation to consider the "polytemporal, polyspatial knottings" for examining how natural, cultural, and literacy beings are woven into contingent, dynamic, and complex patternings through multilingual writing (2016, p. 60).

NOTICING BECOMING-WITH. Writers change and are changed in shifting entanglement with the natural, cultural, and literacy others. I look for material and semiotic practices of these others, their inventions and improvisations, meanings they acquire through associations with humans and cultural institutions, and their ability to affect, inspire, soothe, and agitate multilingual writers and writing through inter- and intra-actions in heterogeneous temporalities and spatialities. In doing so, I draw on Barad's agential realism to note the constant co-emergence and becoming of fused *spacetimemattering* rather than observing the interaction of persons and objects against static spacetime configurations (2007). Such a perspective guides my analysis that "amplifies accounts of the creative, improvisational, and fleeting practices through which [beings such as] plants and insects *involve* themselves" in writers' lives (Haraway, 2016, p. 69). Such a view positions researchers not as designers of research apparatuses or observers of naturally occurring phenomena but as part of entanglement and world-in-articulation. It also recognizes that our practices as writers and researchers entail material/discursive practices that differentially enact boundaries, properties, and meanings.

TURNING TOWARD THICKETS OF RELATIONSHIPS. Entanglement provides an analytical footing for mapping the intersecting multiplicities that are fluid, ephemeral, and archaic. Such a move toward multiplicities and relationships allows writing researchers to connect concrete acts of reading, inventing, conversing, sketching, drafting, outlining, inscribing, translating, reviewing, conferencing, revising, proofreading, and editing as co-constituted with a web of literacy brokers, forms of being, semiotic resources, writing technologies, texts, lived spatiality, and temporal rhythms. As ideas, texts, memories, and artifacts are mobilized and continue to form expanding relationships, it becomes important to notice and theorize literacy activities as ways of being in the world and forms of life that are always in the making through relationships. It becomes equally important to observe how semiotic fibers form "complex, multifarious chains of transformations in and across representational states and media" (Prior & Shipka, 2003, p. 181). Multilingual writing becomes part of how multilingual writers make, inhabit, fiddle with, and transform natural, social, and imaginary worlds.

DWELLING ON UNPREDICTABLE ENCOUNTERS. Relating and encountering across differences do not always result in desirable outcomes for players unwittingly drawn into the semiotic and material tapestry of the world. Research efforts with an eye toward the multiplicity of relationships, sites, and perspectives do not benefit from theoretical and methodological tools that aim at precise models, predictable outcomes, and replicable designs. An entanglement perspective follows, anticipates, and prepares for unintended consequences from unexpected connections of unlikely partners. Instead of pursuing the promise of certainty, entanglement encourages us to appreciate the analytical value of messy multiplicities, fluid relationships, porous boundaries, and indeterminate ways. Instead of asking how multilingual writers *draw upon* semiotic resources, cultural tropes, and literacy experiences, entanglement asks how literacy activities emerge through the transformative encounters of life forms, semiotic resources, and spacetimes in unpredictable ways and explores how writers are physically, affectively, and imaginatively *moved by* encounters with human and nonhuman others. As a result, moments erupting with surprises, serendipities, anomalies, and improvisations become meaningful sites of inquiry.

FOLLOWING CHRONOTOPIC FIGURING. I draw on metaphors of chronotopic lamination (Prior & Shipka, 2003) and string figuring (Haraway, 2016) to coin the term "chronotopic figuring," which provides a way to think about how multilingual writing takes shape through ongoing figuring of semiotic, emotional, and material fibers, which simultaneously encode languages, practices, and identities with historically developed spatial and temporal meanings and provide opportunities for layering, blending, and hybridization. Drawing on how fungi hyphae tip forge and fork as living and moving beings (Sheldrake, 2020; Tsing, 2015), I explore how these fibers continue to forge new connections and create new possibilities, and at the same time I explore how they retain stabilized meanings that are figured and reconfigured in tentacular and messy ways (Haraway, 2016). I propose chronotopic figuring as a method for "tracing [and] following a thread in the dark" and for finding "their tangles and patterns . . . in real and particular places and times" when encounters, stories, feelings, memories, and various ways of articulating their meanings are passed on and received, made and remade, picked up and dropped (Haraway, 2016, p. 3). Chronotopic figuring allows me to observe the thickening of meaning across spacetimes and to follow the dynamic patterning that solicits passing and response in indeterminate ways. As a theoretical and methodological tool, this concept provides a lens for considering the transformative heterogeneity of relationships, practices, and identities and for observing how unpredictable encounters across differences give rise to novel solutions, provide old strategies with new purchase, and invite negotiation across differences.

In writing entanglements, movement is the norm and manifests in multiple forms. Writers are physically mobile as they move from a teacher conference to a scheduled writing center consultation and then to lunch with a friend, where writing surfaces as a topic to be discussed, strategized, and negotiated.

Even when writers are not physically on the move, texts might travel far through the mediation of technology—a draft is sent through WeChat file share to friends who are spatially and temporally distanced. The circulation of intertextually linked documents is accompanied by interanimating streams of exchanges taking place across multiple modalities—textual vestige of track-change edits quickly disappear with each mouse click to accept a change; digitally mediated conversations between two transnationally distanced friends juggling time differences allow writers to strategize for revision; asynchronously managed interactions through voice memos are produced during a bustling day of one literacy broker when the other is sound asleep; face-to-face meetings at the writing center encode a different ideology that determines what kinds of help and support are desired and delivered; language irregularities are viscerally experienced and valuated through accented, shaky voices of the international student reading her essay. It is these messy, ephemeral, and indeterminate scenes of writers collaboratively negotiating through language, cultural, and rhetorical differences that I follow, unpack, and analyze in this book. To surface, describe, and theorize these spatially and temporally dispersed backstage scenes of multilingual writing, I pursue the following research questions.

- How does multilingual writing emerge through focal students' ways of experiencing, feeling, knowing, understanding, and relating to natural, cultural, and literacy others in their multilingual lives?
- How does indeterminacy, manifesting in surprises, detours, and unpredictable encounters, energize, drive, and direct multilingual writing?
- How does multilingual writing take shape through spatially and temporally dispersed chains of composing activities across language, cultural, and rhetorical differences?
- How do multilingual writers transform with multilingual writing through the dynamic passing and translating of meaning across persons, languages, modes, activities, and spacetimes?

Methodology for the Project

In 2014 and 2015, I traced five international students as they migrated from reading and writing classes offered at the English Language Center into a bridge writing course and regular/honor FYW courses housed in the Writing Department at a large, public university in a midwestern state of the United

States. My broader aim was to understand how Chinese international students navigated the myriad literacy tasks offered at these academic units, which were responsible for introducing language practices of the academia to multilingual writers. Out of the five students, I was able to develop strong rapports with Morgan and Leo (all names are pseudonyms), which enabled ongoing inquiry into their literacy, social, and professional lives beyond first-year writing.

INSTITUTIONAL CONTEXT

Like many institutions of higher education across the US, the university had witnessed a rapid and drastic increase of international students, from a 5% to 8% annual increase from 2012 to 2017, so that as of 2017 international students constituted 14.5% of the entire undergraduate student body, with significant drops in the number of international students enrolled at the university during and after the Covid-19 pandemic ("Statistical report"). Such demographic changes engendered drastic changes to the cultural and linguistic realities on and off campus—Asian restaurants and grocery stores flourished in the college town; license plates on vehicles were customized to reference linguistic codes and cultural tropes from diverse countries of origin; in and out of classes, students constantly switched between languages, dialects and distinctly accented Englishes as they helped each other grapple with course content; instructors received writing assignments completed in various approximations of standard, edited, written English. Indeed, the linguistic reality of the classroom mirrored what translingual scholars call a new global norm, which is marked by the increasing traffic among peoples and languages shaped by and shaping the global reach and use of new communication technologies and networks (Canagarajah, 2012).

Most international students received an introduction to official language practices of the academy through a sequence of coursework housed across different academic units, including the English Language Center, the university's writing center, and bridge, regular, and honors FYW classes housed in a stand-alone rhetoric and composition program.

ENGLISH LANGUAGE CENTER. The English Language Center and its Writing Lab aim to help international students "improve English language skills before beginning academic course work at the university" by providing "English language instruction against a backdrop of American life and academia" (English Language Center, 2022). International students offered with conditional admission to the university are placed in level-appropriate courses within the Intensive English Program (IEP) based on their Test of English as a Foreign Language (TOEFL) scores and performance on placement tests administered by the center. With a strong focus on improving students' reading, writing, listening, and speaking skills, IEP courses offer explicit instructions on vocabulary and grammatical structures and provide opportunities for students to gain experiences with texts of dynamic structures and purposes and varying degrees of complexity and abstraction. Students are promoted through the program in accordance with a combination of class performance and test results before they "graduate" into FYW courses offered at the Writing Department.

THE BRIDGE WRITING CLASS. The First-Year Writing Program is housed in the Department of Writing, Rhetoric, and Composition, which offers more than 200 sections of bridge, regular, and honors FYW classes to more than 7,000 undergraduate students annually. FYW courses share a curriculum consisting of five major writing assignments (literacy narrative, cultural artifact, disciplinary literacy, remix, final reflection). Positioning "inquiry, discovery, and communication" at the core of the curriculum, the FYW curriculum supports a recursive process of posing questions, pursuing answers, and making knowledge through personal, practical, and cultural inquiries (Department of Writing, Rhetoric, and American Cultures, n.d.).

At the time of my study, the bridge writing class (WRA 1004/0102) served a large population of first- and second-year international students, some having taken coursework through the IEP program, others directly placed in the bridge writing class based on their testing scores for the writing portion of standardized tests (SAT, TOEFL). Most international students take the bridge writing class before taking the required regular or honors sections of FYW classes. During the decade from 2010 to 2020, the bridge writing class annually served 500 to 900 international students, which constitutes as high as 5% to 8% of the undergraduate population ("Statistical report," 2016). The learning goals and curriculum of the bridge writing class traditionally mirrored those of regular FYW classes that followed. Instructors often referred to the "old" bridge writing class as a "pre-peat" because it used the same FYW curriculum, with individual instructors making decisions about discarding one of the standard five projects. It was also a course that instructors without ESL training tended to avoid.

In response to such pedagogical concerns and demographic changes, a group of teacher scholars, including myself, engaged in collaborative pedagogical work that resulted in a reinvented curriculum and new learning goals for the course, which framed students' languages and cultures as "sites of inquiry and resources for student learning" and supported the use of multimodality "as means to identify, understand, and place the 'self,' and to communicate that knowledge to others" and to foster the students' "introduction to, and integration into" the university culture (WRA 1004/0102, n.d.). As I will continue to explore and discuss, specifically in Chapter 6, the bridge writing course operates with asset-based curriculum and pedagogy through assignments and activities that depart from the curriculum of regular FYW courses.

HONORS FIRST-YEAR WRITING COURSE. Undergraduate students enrolled in the university's Honors College can take honors-designated FYW courses to fulfill the college's requirement. During my research, international students were significantly underrepresented in the honors sections of FYW. Only a handful of international students enrolled in the honors-designated writing course each year, with five sections offered annually to serve over 200 students during 2014–2016, which was roughly 2% to 3% of the entire undergraduate population. My informal conversations with international students suggested that most students turned away from honors sections because of their perceived lack of capacity to cope with the intensive reading and writing tasks expected in the course. Honors sections share the curriculum of FYW, with individual instructors making adaptive decisions about extra reading assignments, ranging from additional articles assigned for each class to whole books assigned for the semester.

WRITING CENTER. The university's writing center operates with an "expansive view of literacy, writing, and pedagogy," which "[challenges] the notion of standard English" and "[promotes] diverse understandings of writing and the disciplines in which they are situated" (Vision Statement, n.d.). Aiming to support student writers throughout the writing process, the writing center encourages writing center consultants to move away from roles as proofreaders and instead to focus on working with student writers to identify goals for invention and revision at different stages of the invention, drafting, and revision process.

As evidenced here, multilingual writers' experiences with writing and writing instruction at the university are shaped by an entanglement of teachers, curriculums, pedagogies, and learning goals variously informed by individual, programmatic, and disciplinary frames for theorizing, valuating, and instructing writing, which further entangle in broader interdisciplinary conversations around monolingual, multilingual, and translingual pedagogies to create opportunities and fissures as students work to mobilize writing-related knowledge and practices across courses.

As multilingual writers traverse across these programs, they experience dissonances that introduce opportunities for learning and challenges for navigating competing, sometimes conflicting expectations for writing. For instance, the explicit instruction on grammar and vocabulary and sustained attention to formulaic writing genres at the English Language Center often contrasted with the FYW curriculum's emphasis on helping students to develop the ability to use introspection and reflection to guide their ongoing inquiry into cultural and disciplinary curiosities and to revise writing-related goals and strategies. Similarly, language irregularities manifesting in student writing, variously shaped by linguistic, rhetorical, and cultural differences, are differently perceived, valued, and leveraged by teachers, whose pedagogical practices are shaped by their own employment statuses, professional training, personal experiences, and writerly idiosyncrasies. As I will detail in the following chapters, language irregularities that are blanketed as grammar mistakes by a writing teacher or used as sites of inquiry into rhetorical differences could unravel the complexities of the institutional entanglement of academic units and programs with distinct structures, values, and practices.

Running parallel to the formal learning space was also a digital space that played an important role in international Chinese students' learning. WeChat is a popular smartphone application with 1,200,000,000 active monthly users in China and 70,000,000 users (about twice the population of California) outside of China (Tencent Technology [Shenzhen] Company Ltd., 2020). Of interest for my research is the Moments function of WeChat, comparable to the Wall function for Facebook, which allows users to display personalized content in reverse-chronological order for selected circles of friends. The ebb and flow of the students' WeChat activities mirrored the changing flows of their literacy activities in the writing classroom particularly and their cultural experiences at large, with their posts ranging from documentation of reading and writing activities within and beyond FYW classes, sharing of popular cultural content (e.g., memes, jokes), performance of talents (e.g., video clips of Leo performing magic tricks, street dances, and piano scores), sharing of achievement or frustration in the FYW class, and broader efforts to connect to transnational networks of friends, family, and professional relations. As my analysis will show, self-sponsored literacies on WeChat played an important role in enabling the ongoing entanglement of the writer with and through ephemeral encounters that inspire writing, moments of improvised and orchestrated writing, ongoing efforts to attune and reconfigure semiotic and material repertoires for writing across differences, and personal and professional relationships that enabled the chronotopic figuring of the multilingual writing process.

PARTICIPANTS

Morgan and Leo were Chinese international students attending the public university. Both students took different sections of the bridge writing class I taught during their first year, before enrolling in honor-designated FYW classes, within and beyond which my research took place. At the time of my research, they were sophomores, with Morgan having declared her major in finance and Leo yet to submit his application for admission into the Business College.

Both students attended highly selective traditional high schools in China and were variously prepared for the intensely competitive college entrance exam that was used by Chinese universities to determine admission decisions. Morgan completed the 3-day exam and received a good score that earned her admission to a prestigious university in Beijing, the capital city of China. Not satisfied with this outcome, her family decided to send her abroad for postsecondary education. Leo, on the other hand, was informed of his family's decision to send him abroad right before the exam; he walked out of the math and science portions of the exam, using this dramatic performance to voice his defiance of what he called a "torturous" testing system many of his peers had to suffer through. While Morgan took a gap year to prepare for the TOEFL exam and complete her college application for US universities, Leo arrived at the university on conditional admission, which was determined by his TOEFL score below the university's admission threshold. Leo was required to take classes from the English Language Center for a semester before he "graduated" into the regular university curriculum during his second semester.

Both students claimed they were ill-prepared for their applications to and first experiences with the university because they attended traditional Chinese high schools rather than international high schools, which offered curriculums mirroring that of typical American high schools and provided students with extensive resources for navigating SAT and TOEFL exams. According to Morgan, this gap, coupled with a haphazard application process, led to her application being incomplete without a SAT score and a less-than-ideal TOEFL score. These factors, Morgan argued, damaged her application and failed to land her in an Ivy League university of her dream, which she was determined to pursue for her postgraduate degree. Leo, on the other hand, was satisfied with the outcome of his application and took a go-with-the-flow approach to life at the university.

Morgan used a popular class label of the 屌丝 (*diaosi*, loser) to suggest she was from a less affluent family in China and inherited little social, cultural, and financial capital that could propel her upward social mobility (Szablewicz, 2014). She was energized by ambitious academic and professional goals. When I asked Morgan to select a pseudonym for herself, she spurted out "Morgan" without hesitation. The name, taken from Morgan Stanley, a leading financial investment firm she hoped to join upon graduation, reflected her emerging career aspirations and intense desire for the cosmopolitan identity of a global elite (Wang, 2019b). Ambitious goals weighed heavily on Morgan as she worked tirelessly to maintain a solid GPA and assiduously sought out professional resources that would allow her to find a job in the United States. Her planner was densely populated with due dates, deadlines, and plans.

Leo, however, reluctantly identified himself as a second-generation government official, as his parents held important positions in a state-owned enterprise and a regional hospital. Leo took a more exploratory and relaxed approach to coursework, sampling a wide range of classes from theatrical performance, art history, and political science, dropping classes when course content failed to meet his expectations or became so challenging as to jeopardize his GPA. Keenly aware of his family's influence and professional connections, Leo was not deeply invested in discovering professional development opportunities at the university; instead, he worked hard to maintain a high GPA and took pride in the fact that he was a high-achieving student in his general education classes and core courses in his major. Throughout my research process, Leo was quite open about his intention to return to China after completing his postgraduate studies, where he could pursue a successful career in business with the support of his family.

Leo and Morgan had different experiences with the university's honors program. Morgan was not admitted to the Honors College because of a clerical error that placed her in a bridge writing class during her first semester, which prevented her from fulfilling course requirements based on which invitation letters from the college were awarded. To address this "administrative error," Morgan made numerous visits to the registrar's office and used her "broken English" to negotiate her way into the program. Her experience in the honors FYW class was emotionally tumultuous as well, as she struggled with a reading- and writing-intensive curriculum themed around topics in American history. Specifically, Morgan struggled to fulfill the expectation for critical reading, which was assessed through regularly administered reading quizzes (Wang, 2019a). She also struggled with the course's focus on argumentative writing, which invited students to critically engage with entrenched American assumptions and values. Morgan's efforts to seek clarification from her writing instructor turned increasingly confrontational, as her instructor seemed to perceive her efforts as "bargaining for a better grade." The stress she experienced in the FYW classroom specifically and at the university broadly led to Morgan resorting to her peer networks for writing-related support. Despite her extensive efforts, Morgan received a 3.5 out of 4.0 from the honors FYW course, which she lamented for having negatively affected her otherwise perfect GPA of 3.95.

Leo received an invitation to join the Honors College at the end of his first year. When he was informed that honors students were required to take a "special section" of FYW, he exhausted his peer resources to identify instructors who were known as harsh or friendly to language irregularities manifesting in international students' writing. It was through pure scheduling coincidence that an instructor highly recommended by his peers was to teach an honors section of FYW. Leo decided to enroll after careful weighing of the risks (the negative impact of a challenging course on his 3.95 GPA) and rewards (a chance to prove himself as a sophisticated writer). Recognizing that his peer network would not be of much use in this writing class, in which he was one of only two international students, Leo worked actively to develop a cordial relationship with his instructor, who came to appreciate his thoughtful and creative approach to course assignments. In the classroom, Leo impressed his teacher and classmates with a series of skits and presentations he delivered successfully with effective props, well-crafted speeches, and entertaining interactive activities. Leo received the highest possible grade in the class. To a certain extent, the trajectories of students like Morgan and Leo mirrored the experiences of "traditional high" students that Zhang-Wu explored through her case studies (2021).

It is worth mentioning that both Leo and Morgan mobilized rich literacy expertise developed in their home language to help them navigate the honors writing classes. Both students were avid readers and once entertained the possibility of pursuing creative writing professionally, an aspiration partially fueled by the commercial success of a new generation of young Chinese writers such as Han Han and Guo Jingming. Both students were accomplished writers whose narrative essays were read and analyzed as exemplary texts in classes; both students received awards in regional and national writing contests. Rich literacy experiences in their home language allowed them to develop a repertoire of rhetorical strategies, creative writing techniques, and meta-vocabulary for naming attributes of good writing. The confidence and ease with which they maneuvered writing and their popular cultural expertise easily flowed into their digital literacy practices, as they used social media to sample a variety of cultural texts from niche communities of youth culture (e.g., Japanese anime, memes, Korean variety TV shows, and Hollywood movies) to perform their literacy and class identities. The mobility of writing-related knowledge and strategies, from Chinese and English, from printed to multimodal, turned out to be an adventurous and precarious enterprise. Although both students were well-versed in the literary devices commonly discussed and practiced in FYW (e.g., personification, hyperbole, metaphor/simile), their efforts to translate such rhetorical knowledge into successful English writing were fraught with challenges at semantic, rhetorical, and cultural levels (Kiernan et al., 2016; Smith et al., 2017; Wang, 2020). To navigate such high-stake writing, both students leveraged their established and emerging relationships and resources to help them succeed. WeChat often became a space to process tumultuous emotions, seek support from peers and family members, and share knowledge and expertise. It is such creative and perilous work of weaving streams of literacy experiences, semiotic repertoires, and relationships into shifting entanglements that made their cases compelling for my research.

RESEARCHER POSITIONING

I taught Leo and Morgan in different sections of the bridge writing class prior to their enrollment in two different honors FYW classes. I invited their participation in my research because of the strong rapport I was able to build with the students and their willingness to share aspects of their writing with me. My own background provided useful insights into these multilingual writers' literacies. As an international student who came to the United States from China in my early 20s and a writing instructor at the time, I had experienced similar struggles in adding English to my linguistic repertoire. My proficiency in Mandarin and English; lived experiences of cultural, linguistic, and disciplinary transition; and familiarity with the FYW curriculum helped me develop a degree of rapport that was essential for exploring the students' literacy practices. However, rich points of investigation also emerged from marked differences in our educational experiences and class identities. These differences were especially visible through my limited knowledge of digital technologies, literacy pedagogies, and educational trajectories that powerfully shaped the students' semiotic and rhetorical repertoires. Similarly, my upbringing in socialist China, prior to national policy shifts that propelled dramatic economic transformation, allowed me to recognize class-specific privilege and societal-wide wealth disparity arising as the result of increasing social stratification and shifting class structures in China. My curiosities as a cultural outsider created a space where cultural differences and class nuances became a site of inquiry, students' literacy and identity practices as objects of analysis, and their linguistic and cultural expertise as resources for learning.

I was entangled in the students' writing in many ways: as a former teacher to provide clarification and guidance, as a writing researcher to learn about their writing-related triumphs and struggles, as a friend to discuss and vent about the many challenges life had to present, and as a mentor to provide advice on academic success and career development. Following the students' multilingual writing in entanglement mobilized me physically, affectively, and imaginarily. As a writing researcher, I followed the movements of bodies, ideas, texts, and conversations by partaking in acts of inventing, drafting, reviewing, and revising that were dispersed across acts of eating, walking, and idling. I was willing but nonetheless surprised by how I could be affectively moved by the thrills and surprises of being in the moment to observe multilingual writing becoming through encounters, inspirations, setbacks, conversations, and revisions. Throughout the research process, I became increasingly aware that my way of being and relating to their writing entanglements necessarily and inevitably transformed everyone's experiences. I partook in the students' imaginary traversals across literacy spheres and trajectories as I made efforts to string figure disparate streams of activities, semiotic and rhetorical repertoires, discussions of writing-related knowledge, practices, and dispositions, and imaginaries of academic, social, and professional lives, identities, and aspirations.

DATA COLLECTION

An entanglement perspective for writing research compelled my own active involvement in and contribution to a research ecology that spanned natural and cultural worlds. To entangle in my research was to be immersed in a multilevel, multifaceted environment, which fused the knower, the known, and the material surrounding the acts of knowing (Haraway, 2016). Doing so meant that I actively participated in the production of ethnographic understanding by tracing the messy linkages and attending to ephemeral and elusive feelings, affects, and bodily sensations arising from unintended partnerships and unpredictable encounters. In my ethnographic inquiry, I ventured into the backstage, mobile, and less visible aspects of writing. In this direction, my ethnographic methods of data collection (see Appendix) built on and extended previous efforts in sketching the contours of literate activity by working to capture literacy activities in situ. In situ observation data, captured through participant observation field notes and audio recordings, were coupled with multilingual writers' own efforts to document and annotate their literacy lives (e.g., WeChat Moments posts and screenshots), retrospective interviews, and student artifacts associated with literacy tasks expected in FYW classes.

The primary source of data was collected during the academic semester when students took the honors FYW classes (fall semester of 2014 for Morgan and spring semester of 2015 for Leo), with intensive data collection unfolding during their writing processes for the first writing assignment, the Learning Memoir assignment (hereafter referred to as Memoir), because this assignment provided rich opportunities for multilingual writers to surface, describe, and analyze personal and cultural experiences as resources for learning. Memoir, the first assignment in the course, "invite[d] students to consider their experiences with learning in and out of school to encourage them to reflect on the relationship between their learning histories and present lives" ("About the FYW curriculum"). It embodied an important learning objective of FYW—positioning students' own knowledge and experiences as important resources for generating new understandings of rhetoric, literacy, and culture. During the four weeks dedicated to the assignment, Morgan's instructor used class time to engage students in guided reading of autobiographical narratives by American authors (e.g., Maya Angelou, Amy Tan), identify and explore meaningful literacy experiences through inventive activities, and further develop creative writing techniques and reflective insights through peer review and instructor conference. Similarly, Leo's instructor used autobiographical narratives in a course reader specifically designed for the FYW curriculum (DeJoy et al., 2011), along with readings from the Writing Spaces series (Lowe & Zemliansky, 2011) to help students identify, name, and practice creative writing techniques. The culminating artifact was a narrative essay of approximately five pages. This assignment therefore provides exigencies for students to locate familiar personal and cultural experiences as sites of reflective inquiry and meaning making. Leo and Morgan both commented on the fact that their daily encounter with a new culture invited ongoing scrutiny of familiar, established assumptions, norms, and practices, which provided rich resources for writing. Alongside intensive data collection around students' writing processes in situ, I used semistructured interviews and field observations to broadly explore students' literacy history, writing-related knowledge, practices, and theories, and their experiences of transitioning into the university life academically, socially, and professionally.

For each student, I conducted three semistructured interviews in a mix of Chinese and English, each lasting 60–90 minutes. These interviews broadly explored students' literacy experiences, identities, and educational histories. To capture their school- and self-sponsored reading, writing, and digital literacies, I conducted weekly observations of the students engaging in literacy work in locales of their choice, each lasting 45 to 90 minutes. I observed the students performing a wide range of literacy tasks at different stages of their writing process, including reading assignment descriptions; brainstorming and doodling; outlining; reading; preparing a reading response; drafting, translating, reading, and responding to peer review; rehearsing for a class presentation; or processing experiences in relation to the writing class. I gathered multiple drafts that contained edits and comments from teacher conferences, in-class peer reviews, writing center consultations, and self-sponsored peer reviews, along with inventive artifacts (outlines, annotated reading materials, and notes) and WeChat posts they created during my research. Following this period of intensive data collection, I also followed their literacy and professional trajectories through informal conversations (approximately twice a year) throughout the course of their college career and beyond.

I used interviews and observations to explore and identify multilingual writing in entanglement. To achieve this goal, I followed Morgan and Leo into the various locales where literacy work happened. Sometimes we met in my office immediately after their writing class to debrief about classroom activities, brainstorm ideas for their assignments, process setbacks, and strategize for new challenges. Sometimes we met in one of the campus cafeterias where we ate, chatted, wrote, and studied together, with discussion about writing foregrounded or backgrounded depending on our priorities for the day. Sometimes we connected late into the evening through WeChat as they shared screenshots of their essay drafts, feelings of frustration or achievement, and questions about a writing task at hand. I sometimes followed them to corners on campus where they liked to spend time reading, socializing, or idling (e.g., the bank of a campus river, a sunny corner in an instructional building, a bench under a beautiful birch tree in a secluded corner) to get a sense of the rhythm of their daily routines and ephemeral encounters that prompted self-sponsored writing. Other times I walked with them on their daily routes from dorms to instructional buildings, as their cell phones rang with incoming messages and their replies in voice memos. On a few occasions, I participated in or witnessed informal WeChat discussions or WeChat Moments posts followed by comments, which involved literacy brokers from the students' social networks. By providing minimal structure to such conversations and encouraging the students to direct their own literacy activities during these meetings, I was able to observe in situ acts of multilingual writing emerging through the complex coordination of multiple life worlds of resonant, discordant temporal rhythms and spatial arcs, negotiation of meaning across languages, modes, and minds, and multidirectional flow of information through channels sustained by writing technologies and digital tools. Attending to entanglement necessarily directed my gaze toward the complex ways in which writers, things, environs, and ideas are woven into heterogeneity through carefully cultivated relationships and unpredictable encounters.

DATA ANALYSIS

Triangulated reading of multiple streams of data allowed me to map multiplicities of relationships, follow multilingual writing processes on the move, and attend to unpredictable encounters that gave rise to impromptu acts of writing. Moreover, following multilingual writers across multiple episodes of composition and multiple entanglements of multilingual living surfaced writing-related theories and practices that were rendered irrelevant unless read against the backdrop of literate lives that spanned linguistic, cultural, geographical, social, and rhetorical boundaries. In the same vein, I attended to accidents, surprises, anomalies, silences, and slips as equally useful as well-articulated intentions, designs, and strategies in revealing the dynamic ways in which multilingual writing took shape.

Data analysis was recursively organized throughout the research process to explore how the making and movements of meanings, identities, and practices take shape through emergent, shifting entanglements of writers and other forms of being and living, languages and modes, technologies, and tools. In light of the theoretical focus on entanglement as a unit of analysis, my first pass at data analysis focused on identifying assemblages of living human (peers, friends, consultants, instructor) and nonhuman (rivers, trees), material (texts, digital tools, writing technologies), semiotic (languages, modes, jokes), visceral (memories, feelings), and conceptual (identity labels and narratives, writing-related theories and practices, genres) agents that gave shape to tentatively stabilized literacy events (e.g., a casual walk that invited an idea for writing, crafting a bilingual outline for an essay, posting a multimodal message on WeChat, conversation with a friend or teacher).

My second move focused on exploring how a literacy event emerged through the multilingual writer's entanglement with the natural, cultural, and literacy others, such as observing how writers were moved by encounters that generated visceral reactions and feelings and exploring how such encounters mobilized or left traces of memories, imaginaries and representations that reconfigure the natural, cultural, and literacy others. Simultaneously, I observed how a literacy event buzzed with temporal rhythms of multiple life worlds and historical trajectories in coordination, which not only wove into juxtaposition multiple voices, perspectives, and contours of writing, but also reconfigured these life worlds and trajectories by inserting new meanings and enabling new relationships among them. Such an understanding was achieved through triangulated reading of interviews, informal observation field notes, drafts, social media posts, and interactions to identify contours of meanings moving across persons, texts, languages, modes, and spacetimes, with questions asked about which and how human, nonhuman, material, semiotic, and conceptual elements were entangled in open articulation of the world.

Following multilingual writing in entanglement then compelled my attention to how literacy meanings and identities located in an embodied spacetime simultaneously enacted meanings brought from afar, gained mobility or mobile potentials, string figured with meanings and practices emerging in other spacetimes, and achieved determinate and indeterminate contours and effects. Following the entanglement of ideas, identities, and practices through the lens of chronotopic figuring enabled systematic examination of how multiple semiotic fibers, voices, and practices could be woven into meanings that were simultaneously durable and innovative.

Limitations

With its detailed accounts of two focal students' multilingual writing processes, this book aspires to achieve depth and nuance, rather than width and generalizable patterns. Its narrow focus on a small sample of students from one demographic, namely accomplished Chinese international student writers, echoes Zhaozhe Wang's argument that a "dynamic view of difference as emerging and relational" is needed to disrupt the institutional discourse of diversity that operates within the neoliberal economic and political climate to stabilize, reify, flatten, and capitalize on the vast and varied experiences of a growing population of multilingual students (2024, p. 166). That is, the analysis points to the profound differences despite seemingly shared linguistic, cultural, and rhetorical backgrounds of the students—their approaches to, beliefs about, and practices with writing. A deep dive into these writers' idiosyncrasies, affiliations, inspirations, and encounters reveal important insights about language and identity practices they develop across life-spans. As such, the insights developed therein could be applicable to an increasingly heterogeneous population of diverse students, including domestic multilinguals, native speakers of historically underprivileged varieties of English, speakers of world Englishes, and international, multilingual students from other linguistic and rhetorical backgrounds. By detailing multilingual writing processes as unfolding through the emergence of the writer across linguistic, rhetorical, writerly, and cultural differences, these ethnographic case studies further complicate Paul Matsuda's critique of the "myth of linguistic homogeneity in the U.S. college composition," which has been facilitated by the "concomitant policy of linguistic containment that has kept language differences invisible in the required composition courses and in the discourse of composition studies" (2006, p. 641).

Even though these case studies are very focused on the lived experiences of two students, the fine-grained analysis, informed by an entanglement framework, provides conceptual and methodological tools for attending to the messy, indeterminate, and improvised dimensions of writing, which extends our understanding of the dynamic, mobile, and distributed nature of writing for multilingual, monolingual, veteran, and novice writers grappling with writing across rhetorical situations, disciplinary contexts, and professional fields. This deep dive into the backstage scenes and invisible trails of multilingual writing enhances our understanding of multilingual writing, simultaneously strategic, ephemeral, and improvisational, as the exigencies and outcomes of working through linguistic, cultural, and rhetorical differences. Insights, and mobile methods used to generate such insights, contribute to the repertoire of writing research methods for engaging with writing as mediated, distributed, and dispersed phenomena across writers' literacy landscapes and lifespans.

Overview of the Book

Chapter 1 presents entanglement as a theoretical framework and unpacks useful conceptual and methodological tools for multilingual writing research. I develop theoretical metaphors informed by fungi and ecological studies to discuss ways writing researchers might usefully engage with the messy, ephemeral, unpredictable, and chronotopically layered aspects of the writing phenomena. I draw on ecological examples to discuss four entanglement propositions: becoming with others, turning to thickets of relationships, dwelling on unpredictable encounters, and following chronotopic figuring. Each of these propositions guide the analysis in body chapters.

Chapter 2 explores how Morgan's multilingual writing stayed in becoming with a campus river. I begin this chapter with an account of how an unexpected encounter with the Red Cedar River moved the multilingual writer physically, affectively, and imaginatively. The ephemeral encounter was so powerful that it invited Morgan into an intimate partnership with the river, which traveled into her drafting and revision of the Memoir assignment. Inviting nature back into Morgan's literacy landscape, I explore how her multilingual writing was co-constituted and co-emergent with lived spatiality that she traversed daily, life forms wittingly and unwittingly woven into her literacy landscape, and unpredictable encounters with nature, which also continued to gain reflective, affective, and imaginary possibilities with the writer through multilingual writing. A close analysis of the continuous reconfigurations of the river provides compelling evidence of how boundaries and binaries that arbitrarily separate nature/culture, writers/brokers, English/Chinese are constantly redrawn.

Chapter 3 turns to thickets of relationships and explores how relationships stitch patchworks of multilingual writing and living into meaning. Figuring spatially and temporally distanced episodes of translating, reviewing, and revising into a mobile assemblage, I trace the semiotic labor of writing the river into meaning across drafts, languages, and writers/readers, noting specifically how the river continued to gain expressive purchase and transformed by staying emergent through its movements. Following its mobile trajectory, I analyze how each textual, linguistic, and affective passing of the river was fraught with opportunities for innovation as well as needs for negotiation. I discuss how attention to relationships enriches our understanding of translation as rhetorical practices by demonstrating how meanings were subject to open negotiation through collaborative efforts to manage cross-language relations, develop affinities, and retool semiotic repertoires.

In Chapter 4, I dwell on unpredictable encounters in Leo's multilingual writing as sites of meaning making. I begin by tracing the emergence of a calligraphy story, which served as the centerpiece of Leo's Memoir assignment. I describe how the theme of the story was repeatedly taken up in alternation or juxtaposition across real and (re)imagined times and observe how such iterations entered resonant and dissonant harmony as Leo continued to discover and articulate its meaning. In so doing, I pay particular attention to unpredictable encounters, surprising discoveries, unexpected detours, and unintended consequences, which not only generated multiple ways of reading and interpreting the story but also produced intense feelings of thrill and trepidation that redirected Leo's writing indeterminately. Paying attention to indeterminacy allows me to explore how streams of literacy and identity practices came together in sporadic but consequential coordination to shape seemingly idiosyncratic decisions Leo made as a writer. I look for ways in which stories, insights, and practices reverberated with their own histories, rhythms, and melodic lines to enter intended and unexpected coordination.

In Chapter 5, I draw on theories of rhetorical silence to further explore how Leo's strategic silences were negotiated across multiple temporal trajectories to perform and resist dominant narratives and social discourses around his class identity as a second-generation government official. Namely, I examine how Leo made strategic decisions to silence certain life experiences, hush personal and professional aspirations, and erase his own digital footprints. A chronotopic reading of strategic silence compels attention to Leo's multilingual writing as reverberating with narratives, controversies, and practices associated with his class identity, which was modeled and practiced in schooled, family-sponsored, and self-sponsored literacy activities, cultivated through years of familial training and warning, and reflected the ebbs and flows of social political circumstances in China. A chronotopic analysis of Leo's strategic silence shows it to be a strategy for those in positions of privilege to survive intensified public scrutiny and government surveillance against the backdrop of increasing social and economic disparity and intensifying social discontent in China (Jiang, 2013).

Chapter 6 points to gaps between multilingual students' lived realities and pedagogical practices that often perpetuate monolingual and monocultural ideologies and thereby impede student learning. Building on snapshots that reveal mismatches between student experiences and teacher practices and expectations, I offer ideas for how entanglement could inform an asset-based pedagogy by supporting precarious relationships, enabling polyphonic conversation across academic units, contemplating and leveraging unpredictable encounters, and enabling chronotopic figuring. I then present concrete examples of curricular moves through assignments that enact an asset-based pedagogy, each complete with an overview, procedure, and analysis of exemplary student work.

Together, the ethnographic snapshots I provide throughout the book illustrate how conceptual and methodological attention to entanglement, rather than writers, reveals how dynamic, temporaneous, and improvised relationships direct the contours of multilingual living and writing. Placing shifting, contingent relationships at the center of analysis invites attention to the surprising energy and opportunities for innovation that emerge from the working of unintended coordination, unpredictable encounters, and indeterminate meanings. These relationships bring into partnership, conversation, and contestation worlds and lives with their own semiotic, material, and temporal histories. As much as indeterminacy manifests in fungal hyphal tips that fork and fuse in their search for a friendly tree root, multilingual writers/writing stay emergent as the outcome of precarious, surprising, and productive relationships that make up multilingual lives. Following chanceful encounters, improvised connections, and anomalous adventures that hardly fall within the purview of writing researchers' ethnographic gaze, I argue, allows us to notice the mess of working across biological, cultural, linguistic, and spacetime differences as a core feature of multilingual writing on the move. On one hand, unpredictable encounters set into motion dynamic semiotic repertoires and writing-related knowledge, strategies, and practices. Reciprocally, the movements of writers, resources, practices, and texts propel encounters as multilingual writers enter polyphony with the many others in their ongoing efforts to attune their rhetorical and semiotic repertoires to fulfill literacy, social, and professional purposes.

1
Theorizing Multilingual Writing in Entanglement

Thinking With Mushrooms

In the summer of 2018, I was traveling for research in Guizhou, China, where I tasted the best wild mushroom chicken soup ever. My colleagues from Guizhou University and I sat in the courtyard of a farm-to-table restaurant, which was also the family abode of the Chen family. We watched the owner haggling with mushroom pickers over the price of wild mushrooms measured in bags. Teams of veteran mushroom pickers typically consisted of older villagers knowledgeable of the mountainous terrain and children who were surprisingly sophisticated mushroom connoisseurs. They played their part as the grumbling seller, muttering words of complaint that they had been cheated out of fair prices, while they swiftly unloaded bags of mushrooms onto the concrete floor of the Chinese courtyard, shared recipes for cooking with each type of mushroom, and waved goodbye, barely containing their triumphant smile over a successful transaction. We chatted over fragrant Chinese tea, our table a mere meter away from the owner/chef, who leisurely washed the mushrooms in large basins of spring water pumping out of a bamboo pipe connected to the family well. She took the time to educate us about ways to distinguish delicious mushrooms from poisonous ones. We watched in delight as she generously portioned mushrooms into a pot of chicken soup boiling on an open fire. We slurped the hot, delicious soup along with spicy side dishes and strong local beer, asking for refills that she happily delivered. This mushroom feast, only available during a small window of several weeks of the summer season, grew from a long Chinese culinary tradition that regards mushrooms as a "delicacy of the mountain." When I returned from my research trip, I was feeling so emboldened by my newly gained knowledge of mushrooms that I started and failed in several attempts to grow shiitake and oyster mushrooms from spores I purchased on Amazon. After my messy and laborious experimentation in bags of pasteurized straw, buckets of moist wood chips, and patches of soil in a shady corner of my garden, I proceeded with a small literature review to diagnose my failures and to direct future endeavors. My amateur attempt to grow the mountain delicacy drew me into the capricious world of mushrooms.

The more I was drawn into learning about, working with, and relating to mushrooms, the blurrier the boundaries between my cultural and natural worlds became. Was it my own fascination with mushrooms, renewed through the research trip, and my puzzlements over the many failed attempts to grow my own, that motivated my reading of scholarship outside my disciplinary purview? Was it my reading about mushrooms and their remarkable ability to forge collaborative partnerships with companion species such as trees, insects, and humans that sensitized me to forms of collaboration in the multilingual worlds I visited and revisited in ethnographic data? Could that be the reason why I allowed wild strawberries, Chinese chives, mint, and green scallions to coexist with my flowers in an otherwise industriously hand-weeded garden? Could it be that my own material and discursive practices of managing flowers, vegetables, and mushrooms alerted me to inklings of multiple life worlds and boundary-blurring practices in the multilingual lives of others and myself, practices I had previously ignored? How was it that my garden actively remade me, my case studies, and the structure of the book when I was supposed to make and remake the garden?

In this chapter, I follow fungi scholars into the world of mushrooms and explore how thinking with mushrooms shifts my ongoing effort to capture, theorize, and understand multilingual writing. First, I draw on the notion of multi-species relationship to consider the dynamic, messy ways in which multilingual writing takes shape through cultivated and unexpected relationships with natural, cultural, and literate beings and worlds. I then discuss how the notion of "becoming" disrupts boundaries, attributes, and taxonomies that have positioned the writer as the focal point of analysis, thereby allowing us to position the multilingual writer as emergent with shifting entanglements of material and semiotic environs with spatial and temporal particularities. Learning to dwell on unpredictable encounters that energize and result from precarious, cross-species collaboration, I detail how mushrooms show us the ways to explore unintended outcomes and surprising departures as sites of meaning making, innovation, and negotiation across linguistic, cultural, and rhetorical differences. Lastly, I use chronotopic figuring, a concept I adapt from chronotopic lamination (Prior & Shipka, 2003), to explore how polyphonic assemblage (Tsing, 2018), a concept used to examine the convergence of multiple temporal trajectories of life-making projects, provide useful ideas to trace and unravel the complex layering of transnationally mobilized imaginaries, narratives, and tropes that differently position multilingual and transnational lives.

Thinking about and relating to mushrooms move me away from analysis of multilingual writing as the outcome of strategic negotiation across differences (Wang, 2019b, 2020). Instead, thinking with mushrooms redirects my gaze toward writers' ephemeral encounters with, visceral reactions to, and affective relationships with cultural, natural, and literacy others for how such encounters unpredictably inspire, energize, and steer writing. Mushrooms also compel me to dwell on the surprises, messes, and indeterminacies that prevented an easy, linear reading of students' efforts to write their experiences and identities into meaning. As I continue to learn about, cook with, relate to, and think along with mushrooms, they become an important agential force that shapes and reshapes the ethnographic studies I present in this book. In what follows, I discuss the key theoretical propositions that guided my thinking and analysis with mushrooms.

Multi-Species Relationships

> When we smell a truffle's aroma, we receive a one-way transmission from [the] truffle to the world. The process is comparatively nuance-free. To attract an animal, the aroma has to be curious, and delicious—yes. But most of all it has to be penetrating and strong. It doesn't really matter whether their spores are scattered by a wild boar or a flying squirrel, so why be picky? Most hungry animals will chase a delicious smell. Moreover, a truffle doesn't change its aroma in response to your immediate attention. It can excite, but it isn't excitable. Its signal billows out loud and clear, and once begun, it is always on. A ripe truffle broadcasts an unambiguous summons in chemical lingua franca, a pop scent with mass appeal

that could cause Daniele, Paride, two dogs, a mouse, and me to converge at a single point under a bramble bush on a muddy bank in Italy.
—Merlin Sheldrake (2020, p. 35)

This snapshot depicts a November day that Merlin Sheldrake spent truffle hunting in the hills around Bologna, Italy. It points to intricate relationships that bring multiple lives and world-making projects into entanglement to make collaborative survival a possibility. This understanding of life as the outcome of cross-species relationships changes the focus of our effort to comprehend the world. Life, viewed from the perspective of fungi, requires the interplay of many kinds of beings. Anna Tsing used "interspecies entanglements" (2015) to account for ways in which entangled world-making projects overlap, allowing room for more than one way of being and living. Each organism changes everyone's world by making ecological living places, altering earth, air, water, and the world for everyone else. Bacteria make our oxygenic atmosphere, and plants help maintain it. Plants live on land because fungi digest rocks into fertile soils. Contrary to humanist conceptions that position humans as the measure of all things and observer of nature from above or afar (Barad, 2007), the world of fungi invites a post-humanistic view that works from the proposition that humans have always been involved in multispecies world-making.

As shown in this scenario, the world of fungi provides concrete examples for understanding entanglements through the lens of reciprocal partnerships and open assemblages (Tsing, 2015; Sheldrake, 2020). Various types of mycorrhizal fungi exist for most of the year as mycelial networks, which are sustained through a reciprocal relationship they share with trees. Fungi make life possible for trees by unlocking nutrients from rocks and repelling harmful insects and fungal competitors. In turn, fungi's survival is made possible through their relationship with friendly trees, which reciprocate with lipids and sugar. Truffle's underground habitat, which deprives the mushroom of access to air currents or visibility to wild animals, makes the dispersal of spores a difficult achievement. The ingenuous solution is a distinct smell, the outcome of evolutionary entanglement between the fungi and animal tastes. This delicious, vociferous, and penetrating smell of the truffle, distinct within the crisscross of the forest's smellscape, lures bears, dogs, pigs, elk, and humans to excavate the fungi's fruiting body. Fungi entangle with insects and animals, communicating their readiness through chemical signatures intelligible to those best positioned to help it disperse its spores. Truffle dogs' capacity to discover subterranean truffles draws humans into the partnership, as they train dogs for the purpose of consuming and capitalizing on the culinary delicacy.

Multiplicity of agential forces, living and non-living alike, are drawn into open assemblages to drive lives and world-making projects. Livelihoods are made possible through the material practices (e.g., photosynthesis, decomposition), resources (e.g., zinc and calcium that fungi unlock from rocks, lipids and sugars that trees produce), and networks of relationships that bring soil, air, light, trees, subterranean mycorrhizal, and human and animal mushroom hunters into dynamic relationships. It is no longer possible to adopt a humanist gaze to view fungi merely as a valuable commodity to be excavated, traded, cooked, and consumed. Mushrooms are as agential as humans in stitching together the patchwork of worlds inhabited by mushroom pickers and dealers, ethnographers and scientists, restaurateurs, and food connoisseurs. In mushrooms we find a compelling example of what Donna Haraway termed "sympoiesis," which captures how living and nonliving beings are always "making with" and "worlding with" each other in complex, dynamic, responsive, situated, historical systems (2016, p. 58). In this view, all the players, encompassing truffles, dogs, bears, and a host of other friendly or hostile insects and herbivores, enter open-ended assemblages and participate in the ongoing becoming-with-each-other at all sorts of sizes and scales, through diverse kinds of relationalities and with varying degrees of openness to opportunistic assemblages (Haraway, 2016, p. 60).

Michael Hathaway (2022) provides compelling examples of how Indigenous Yi people in Yunnan, China, jostle their daily and seasonal patterns of work and how they reconfigured their century-long relations to other living beings (e.g., corn, goats) in attunement to the rhythms of the mushrooms' world-making. In noting how Yi mushroom hunters study insects' sensory worlds and hunting strategies, seeing insects as "actively learning and coming up with new ways to act in the world in ways that mirrored their own improving abilities to find matsutake" (p. 149), Hathaway offers an ontological and epistemological view of the world, which is informed by Yi cosmologies shaped by shamanism, Buddhism, and Taoism. In important ways, entanglement opens the door for non-Western ontologies, which see the world as full of sentient beings capable of observation, interpretation, learning from other species, and acting with purpose. Such accounts disrupt colonial ontological claims about relationships between people and the natural world, one resting upon the trope of human domination and exploitation of nature. In efforts to reveal the complex, symbiotic relationships that weave mushrooms, plants,

Yi and Tibetan people, and animals into assemblages, these scholars offered ways to develop what Bang (2017) calls "trans-ontology," which "opens the possibilities for plurality of ontologies beyond the West to distinguish it from the notion of ontology steeped in Western intellectual traditions" (p. 117).

Entanglement, made possible through relationships across semiotic, material, and ontological differences, highlights the role played by an expansive repertoire of codes and practices. The world of fungi buzzes with "languages" of many kinds. The actions and behaviors of fungi and plants are informed by what is happening in the sensory worlds they explore through their leaves, roots, and hyphal tips. They co-develop ways to manage the constant flurry of biochemical interactions that sustain their reciprocal livelihoods. The mycelium of fungi mingles with crowds of microbes to sense sources of nutrients, proliferate within them, and send nutrients through a sprawling network of connections among themselves and with trees. They actively sense, interpret, and respond to the chemical emissions of others to gauge if they can branch and fuse into a mycelia network. Trees face the challenge of communicating and connecting with mycelia networks amid "chemical babble in the soil where countless other roots, fungi, and microbe course and engage" (Sheldrake, 2020, p. 37). Millions of root tips explore the soil and learn to discern beneficial fungi to admit into their root systems and to repel harmful ones that could cause disease. Mushrooms signal their maturational readiness through gaseous dispersion of chemical signals that communicate appealing smells evolutionarily aligned with animal preferences. Truffle hunters and their dogs develop their own ways of reading the forest and communicating the location, depth, and type of a find through coded gestures, wagging tails, or one-pawed versus two-pawed digs. As such, the communicative repertoire comprises kinesthetic, semiotic, chemosensory, visual, bio-informational, tactile, and gestural "languages" that are "spoken" across categorical differences. Additionally, commercial transaction around the precious mushroom relies on the lingua franca of a global supply chain, which operates with practices and technical language for sorting, packaging, pricing, and transporting the perishable delicacy, whose economic value diminishes when its signature aroma quickly dwindles once metabolism terminates. Entanglement, a symbiotic configuration of fungal mycelium, trees, and animals are entangled with a social ensemble of languages, codes, and practices, which continue to reconfigure biological and cultural worlds-in-becoming.

With its attention to evolving repertoires of semiotic-material resources and practices that make relationships possible, an entanglement perspective sits comfortably with translingual theorists' call to attend to writers' multilingual, multimodal, and multisensory semiotic repertoire of print-based, visual, gestural, affective, and imaginary resources (Canagarajah 2011; Creese & Blackledge, 2010; Gentil, 2011; Horner et al., 2011; Hornberger & Link, 2012). From an entanglement perspective, writing is not just a cultural achievement but it also emerges through intimate relationships that are enabled, sustained, and arising from communication with other forms of beings across multiple lines of ontological and semiotic differences. Such a view has the potential to expand current research's focus on transnational individuals' sociolinguistic landscape as spanning geographical, cultural, and linguistic borders and operating with power-invested structures for valuating multilingual writers' effort to write for geographic migration, economic prosperity, emotional intimacy, and educational and professional mobility (Dong & Blommaert, 2016). That is, entanglement invites our attention to writers as embodied and emplaced in their semiotic and material environs, interacting with biological and cultural being, and moved by affective energies of many kinds.

This understanding of the vast underground system as being interconnected, transactional, adaptive, and messy informs my thinking about the aspects of multilingual writers and multilingual writing that often remain invisible. My colleagues and I (Fraiberg, Wang, & You, 2017) have provided detailed accounts of multilingual, international students' literacy practices as deeply entangled in underground literacy and social networks, which fuse, forge, and extend with the development of new relationships and transactions around literacy and material resources, shifting social positionings. These webs of connections resemble the tentative, irregular, exploratory, and indeterminate underground mycelial networks, which take shape when fungal hyphae, or streams of fine tubular cell structures, continuously branch, fuse, and tangle into a network. In such accounts, the performance of literacy work is often entangled in improvised partnerships, some merely transactional and fleeting in nature while others continue to fuse and grow in productive, reciprocating, and mutually sustaining ways.

This view of contingent and transformative entanglement as sustained through reciprocal partnerships in open assemblages and mediated by expansive semiotic repertoires encourages an intentional departure from the modernist preoccupation with coherence, pattern, and clarity and instead provides a lens toward the slippery, ephemeral, and indistinct aspects of the world in becoming through the intra-active open articulation of multiple players and dwellers. To follow multilingual writing in entanglement, one must wander with writers, observe how their narratives and practices connect through reciprocal relationships, and be prepared to follow contours of writing that are simultaneously strategic and exploratory, goal-driven and indeterminate, predictable and irregular.

Becoming With Others

> One of the best-studied cases is that of the fungus Ophiocordyceps unilateralis, which organizes its life around carpenter ants. Once infected by the fungus, ants are stripped of their instinctive fear of heights, leave the relative safety of their nests, and climb up the nearest plant—a syndrome known as "summit disease." In due course the fungus forces the ant to clamp its jaws around the plant in a "death grip." Mycelium grows from the ant's feet and stitches them to the plant's surface. The fungus then digests the ant's body and sprouts a stalk out of its head, from which spores shower down on ants passing below. If the spores miss their targets, they produce secondary sticky spores that extend outward on threads that act like trip wires.
> —Merlin Sheldrake (2020, p. 96)

Entanglement redirects the gaze of the ethnographic researcher by challenging the conception of plants, animals, and humans as self-contained individuals. Bodily boundaries that seemingly separate the zombie fungi from the carpenter ants or the plants they disperse spores from do not hold fast. Zombie fungi move into the body of carpenter ants, compelling the ant to move into a zone with just the right temperature and humidity to allow the fungus to fruit and disperse its spores from a strategic height. They do so by becoming a prosthetic organ of the ants' bodies, which grows to as much as 40% of the biomass of an infected ant. Hyphae wind through the ants' body cavities from heads to legs, enmeshing their muscle fibers and coordinating their activity via an interconnected mycelial network. Through the working of a chemical it produces, the fungi help the ants "forget" their instinctive fear of heights and create a condition with ample time for the fungi to digest the ant's body. Whereas the outside surface of the body may seem evident, bodily boundaries that end with outside surfaces, such as skin or bark, stop making sense in the example of zombie fungi and carpenter ants.

It is through entanglements that boundaries are configured and reconfigured, bodies are made and disintegrated, and (im)possibilities of life materialized. In scenarios such as these, what was perceived as intrinsic boundaries that separate what is inside and outside becomes "intrinsically indeterminate" (Barad, 2007, p. 160). Attending to entanglements therefore suggests that we conceptually "span boundaries and transgress categories" (Sheldrake, 2020, p. 18). The study of life in entanglement invites a conceptual shift away from a view of plants, fungi, and animals as self-contained individuals with intrinsic boundaries and inherent properties; rather, the analytical gaze is directed toward relationships complete with competition, cooperation, and contingency as well as the improvisational ways in which boundaries are (re)drawn, properties are (re)articulated, and meanings are (re)made. It is relationships, not the individuals, that stitch the natural and cultural worlds together and make collaborative survival possible.

This attention to indeterminate boundaries and properties allows us to reconsider binaries that seemingly separate the knower and the known, representation and phenomenon, culture and nature as negotiated rather than assumed. Entanglement is propelled by intra-actions of multiple forms of living and being, whose boundaries and properties are redrawn and reconfigured in the process of articulating the world-in-becoming (Barad, 2007, p. 139). In contrast to interaction, which rests on the supposition of components with determinate boundaries and properties relating to each other without being transformed, Barad uses the term "intra-action" to emphasize the specificity of material entanglements in their agential becoming, where entities are transformed. This line of thinking challenges the fundamental assumption that the world is composed of individual objects with determinate properties independent of their agential becoming or the assumption that such individually bounded entities could be measured and represented by the knower that is intrinsically separated from the phenomenon to be known. In what they call a performative approach, the material and semiotic practices of knowing, representing, making, and being with the world depend on the intra-action of elements in shifting entanglements. As Barad describes, a physicist's effort to "see" atoms with the aid of a microscope is not simply a matter of gazing into it as a spectator but an achievement that requires a complex set of practices, such as tinkering with the instrumentation with intuition and ingenuity, honing of tactile techniques in tune with the specificities of the tool, and learning to discriminate between unwanted noise and desired signal along with all kinds of ways of manipulating the atom. That is, "the practices of knowing are specific material engagements that participate in (re)configuring the world" (Barad, 2007, p. 91). The knower, the known, and the apparatuses of material and semiotic practices for knowing all change through their contingent entanglement.

Entanglement thus offers a way to revise writing research's tendency to locate the autonomous writer at the center of meaning making and encourages us to look beyond the strategic ways in which writers mobilize networks of semiotic repertoires, affiliations, relationships, tools, and practices to write multilingual lives and transnational life worlds into meaning. The humanistic lens views the writer as the distanced knower of the cultural and natural worlds, strategic designers of meanings, disseminators of such meaning in mobile networks, and agitators of power-invested discourses that hierarchically valuate languages, credentials, and identities. The writer searches inwardly and outwardly for ideas for writing. In their efforts to discover, invent, and materialize meaning, they weave together patchworks of semiotic resources, affiliations, tools, and bodies of knowledge to succeed (Lam & Christiansen, 2022; Suárez-Orozco & Suárez-Orozco, 2001; Wang, 2019b). While multilingual writing research has fully recognized the messiness entailed in these efforts, such messiness is often interpreted against the backdrop of cognitively, socially, and pedagogically orchestrated and stabilized processes to achieve comprehension, coherence, and clarity. In so doing, such research has embraced an anthropocentric celebration of humans as "an individual apart from all the rest," the "unit of all measure," and "finitude made flesh" (Barad, 2007, p. 134), thereby bestowing on writers the privilege of distance, from which to observe, reflect on, and represent the world, which is perceived as either a passive and uncontested slate awaiting scientific observation and cultural inscription or resources subjected to capitalistic transformation and exploitation (Tsing, 2005, 2015). The preoccupation with the determinate process of knowing, analyzing, and representing the world from an objective stance has contributed to the modernistic project of controlling and manipulating nature. As John Law suggests, however, much of the social and natural realities we grapple with are "vague, diffuse or unspecific, slippery, emotional, ephemeral, elusive or indistinct, changes like a kaleidoscope, or doesn't really have much of a pattern at all" (2004, p. 3).

Entanglement, viewed from the lens of mushrooms, ants, and plants, disrupts human exceptionalism, which attributes to mushroom pickers, industrialists, photographers, students, and writers the ability to drive and make social phenomena such as truffle hunting, beekeeping, scientific research, and writing. As an anthropocentric view tends to celebrate human exceptionalism, manifested in our ability to transform, harness, and exploit the natural world, it reduces nonhuman mechanisms of surviving, collaborating, and producing into inanimate objects merely reacting with mechanical predictability. Fungi, on the other hand, show us how their lives are vibrant and vital in articulating meaning and building lives/worlds. Fungi show us that worlds are made through improvised performances of an ensemble of players spanning categorical boundaries listening to, interacting with, and responding to one another in real time. From an entanglement perspective, theoretical boundaries that enable imagination of species as self-organizing and self-making entities fail to hold. Instead, entanglement offers a way of seeing life as the dynamic worlding-with ecological assemblages of companion organisms interpenetrating, looping around and through, eating, digesting, and partially assimilating each other (Haraway, 2016).

From this perspective, multilingual writing is enabled through writers in open articulation of the world along with companion species and natural, cultural, and literacy others through the mediation of semiotic and material practices broadly defined. A writer sitting on a riverbank, feeding squirrels, and enjoying a leisurely afternoon might spur a social media post that features photos of the feasting squirrel, the clear, blue sky, and fellow students idling on green lawns bathed in golden sunlight. The message, semiotically rendered through languages and emojis, might further elucidate the significance of the restful moment at the end of a busy day. From an entanglement perspective, the writer and the squirrel engage in playful intra-action through various material practices, such as the squirrel learning to stop human pedestrians, demanding and retrieving food, and even posing for a photo; the pedestrian, in their decision to slow down, take a break, and feed and laugh with the squirrel, is also indeterminately transformed. The fleeting interaction might transform the squirrel (e.g., its diet, foraging habits, and physique) and the human (e.g., I had a student who habitually packed a bag of peanuts and changed his daily commute just for the squirrels) equally. As much as the writer moves (with) these components, the writer is moved and (re)made in the same dynamic. Writing is not a mere act to signify or articulate static meaning but is enmeshed with material practices of interacting and feeling with the other and finding available semiotic means to render the experience meaningful and memorable. Observing the writer acting, interacting, and intra-acting with others allows us to notice how boundaries, properties, and meanings are iteratively and dynamically enacted. Looking beyond writing as the consequence of the writer's effort to write *about* the world, an entanglement perspective posits that writers are themselves part of open-ended practices that materialize and configure *with* the world.

Furthermore, an entanglement perspective challenges the very humanist supposition that binarizes human and nonhuman, culture and nature. Entanglement invites nature back into the literacy landscape of multilingual writers and directs the writing researcher's gaze toward the multiplicity of relationships writers forge with cultural, natural, and literate beings of all shapes and sizes. As the world of mushrooms shows us, nature is much more than a static entity, location, reference, or source for human activities. Rather, nature, as all matter, is "dynamic [material] articulation/configuration of the world," through which determinations of boundaries, properties, and meanings are differentially enacted (Barad, 2007, p. 151). Entanglement therefore recognizes "the permeability of social and biological worlds as well as the inextricable positioning of the researchers within those worlds" (Fleckenstein et al., 2008, p. 394). In this view, nature is not the backdrop for cultural activities but an agential force that drives writing and emerges through writing. As I turn my gaze toward nature, new curiosities sprout. Inspirations flare through encounters with nature; writers resort to nature for solace and healing; writers' contemplations about their relationships with nature revise their own capitalistic gaze of it. Writers physically, affectively, and imaginatively move through and become with nature.

Dwelling on Unpredictable Encounters

> One can confront hyphae with microscopic labyrinths and watch how they nose their way around. If obstructed, they branch. After diverting themselves around an obstacle, the hyphal tips recover the original direction of their growth. They soon find the shortest path to the exit, just as my friend's puzzle-solving slime molds were able to find the quickest way out of the IKEA maze. If one follows the growing tips as they explore, it does something peculiar to one's mind. One tip becomes two, becomes four, becomes eight—yet all remain connected in one mycelial network. Is this organism singular or plural, I find myself wondering, before I am forced to admit that it is somehow, improbably, both.
> —Merlin Sheldrake (2020, p. 45)

Fungal hyphae are especially skilled in navigating labyrinths of messy connections, exploratory paths, and tentative solutions. When faced with a forked path, fungal hyphae do not choose one but branch and explore both routes. When obstructed with an obstacle, they branch, nose their way around, and recover the original direction of their path once the obstacle is passed. They fuse and fork into sprawling, interlaced webs strung through the soil, below the surface of the ocean, animal bodies dead or alive, floorboards and old books, improvising their ways through the mess and mass of forms of living and being across ontological differences. As Merlin Sheldrake relays, wood-rotting fungus growing within a block of wood spread radically outward in all directions until it encounters a new block of wood, which would change the behavior of the entire network. The exploratory mycelium would withdraw the exploratory parts of its network and thicken the connection with the newly discovered block. Within days, the network completely remodels itself beyond recognition. Such work takes great ingenuity, and it is such ingenuity that allows mycorrhizal fungi to form promiscuous relationships with plants and other fungal networks to build vast, complex, and circulatory underground networks that enable the transfer of nutrients, water, bacteria, toxin, and infochemicals about the health of plants and dangers in the environment. As "brokers of entanglement able to mediate the interactions between plants according to their own fungal needs" (Sheldrake, 2020, p. 162), fungi participate in complex and dynamic networks, whose behaviors are difficult to predict from the knowledge of the constitutive entities; they are also highly adaptive because they constantly reorganize into new forms and behaviors in response to changing circumstances. Indeterminacy and improvisation are central to fungi's ability to constantly wander outside and beyond and to relate across plants, networks, and ecosystems.

Unpredictable encounters are the outcome of forging and maintaining relationships across boundaries of various kinds—species, categories, spaces, and times. When we learn to notice fungal life-making projects that make up our worlds, we begin to see surprises, accidents, and transformative encounters as the norm. Anna Tsing (2015) draws on the example of matsutake, a prized mushroom favored by Japanese epicures, to discuss uncertainty and precarity as the norm for life enabled by cross-species coordination and to show us how indeterminate encounters, driven by contingencies, transform us unpredictably.

Matsutake mushrooms are famous for their ability to change shapes in relation to their encounters. They are impossible to cultivate because of their highly specific and capricious ways of forging partnerships and attuning to environments. Their flavors readily change when they come into contact with metal knives or butter. In Tsing's account of learning to prepare matsutake from a Japanese friend, the mushroom tastes the best when cleaned by hand and grilled without oil. While pines, matsutake's preferred companion trees, lose their competitive edge to their broadleaf counterparts in warm, moist, and fertile soils, they flourish with the help of matsutake in the most daunting places that boast cold temperatures, high altitudes, and barren, rocky soil. Humans participate in the scene through disturbed landscapes. When humans cut down commercially valuable trees for timber, firewood, or fertilizer, they create eroded hillsides and open fields that pines are quick to colonize with the help of their matsutake friends, who mobilize nutrients from rocks and help pines fend off harmful fungi and minerals. In association with fungal and animal companions, pines colonize disturbed landscape, which humans create without the intention of cultivating or supporting such collaborative survival. As such, pines, humans, and matsutakes are mutually transformed through their unpredictable encounters with each other.

Examples of such unintentional design abounds in many parts of the world, such as the now abandoned center of industrial logging in the pacific west of the United States, where fire suppression was used but failed to preserve and regrow commercially valuable timbers. One unintended consequence of modern forestry is the longevity of lodgepole pines, which easily succumb to fires but rely on fires to spread their seeds. Thanks to fire suppression, lodgepole pines get to enjoy newly found longevity, making them cordial and reliable hosts for matsutake to mature into fruition. Industrial forestry leaves behind disturbed landscape, which accidentally opens "the terrain for transformative encounters, making new landscape assemblages possible" and allows the pine-matsutake partnership to move into otherwise occupied landscape (Tsing, 2015, p. 160). The budding presence of the mushroom in these regions is the unintended consequence of coalescing historical trajectories of industrial forestry practices that created and sought to remedy disturbed landscapes. As Tsing (2015) argues, "Ways of being are emergent effects of encounters" that are indeterminate and multidirectional (p. 23). Patterns of unintended coordination develop in assemblages of humans with different commercial, scientific, and aesthetic interests in the forest. Fungi, as "cosmopolitan bodies, a place where lives meet" (Sheldrake, 2020, p. 82) coalesce into partnerships with taxonomically distinct and distant organisms to build life forms capable of entirely new possibilities. Life through transformative encounters vibrates with multiple historical trajectories; spans geological, biological, and geopolitical boundaries; and defies efforts to control and regulate relationships.

At the center of such coordination are historical contingencies and unpredictable, sporadic, yet consequential encounters. The joining of the historical trajectories of pines, mushrooms, animals, and humans, albeit profoundly transformative of landscape and history, is the outcome of "unintentional design" (Tsing, 2015). These unintended partnerships play out against the contingencies of history, including the apparatus of capitalist tree production model that does not allow pine to coexist with profitable timbers, the booms and busts of the logging industry, the vicissitude of Indigenous forestry traditions, the fluctuation of labor movements, and state regulations for forest preservation. Such collaboration, which entails working across uncertainties and differences, is a precondition for the survival of every species. Entangled in the various forms of world-making projects, each agent provides and receives help from another with or without intent. Pines, matsutake, and humans all cultivate each other unintentionally and are each transformed by their encounter with the other in intended and unpredictable ways.

Recognizing that collaboration across differences changes things, an entanglement perspective sees life not as the achievements of self-interests or individual intentions but as the outcome of transformative encounters. It encourages attention to the full range of phenomena, complete with mess, mismatched expectations, and unintended outcomes, rather than patterns of coordination, often portrayed as harmonious and coherent within an imagined boundary. In these scenarios, intersecting historical processes produce ecologically and culturally heterogeneous, singular, and idiosyncratic intricacies of (un)intended coordination. In this open-ended entanglement of ways of being, various trajectories could gain hold on each other, but indeterminacy, manifesting in surprising discoveries, unpredictable encounters, unintended coordination, and unexpected detours and departures, matters.

Because indeterminacy is the "outcome of the divergent, layered, and conjoined projects that make up our worlds because patterns of unintentional coordination develop in assemblages of entangled livelihoods" (Tsing, 2015, p. 24), we need to move beyond limiting analysis of one creature situated in one space-time configuration in one set of relationships; instead, we turn toward open-ended gathering of multiple ways of being. Such a perspective invites us to notice the amazing agility and attunement through which organisms come into being with and through each other. Dwelling on surprises allows me to notice how careful planning, tested strategies, researched practices, and sustained caring constantly and ultimately made way for surprises, innovation, and negotiations as multiple voices, perspectives, and historical trajectories of writers and readers are woven into entanglement. The pleasant and alarming surprises surface in multilingual writers' efforts to connect and engage with others, to notice their own emplacements in semiotic and material environs, and to work through linguistic, cultural, and rhetorical differences. It is by dwelling on surprises that I notice the multilingual processes as indeterminate/innovative and predictable/durable. Intended coordination and unpredictable encounters across boundaries are the norm; open-ended, shifting relationships are its outcome. Writers' emplacement in, traversing through, and encounter with open assemblages generate visceral sensations, intellectual insights, and powerful affects that bubble through spontaneous spurts and sustained contemplations. They gain indeterminate mobile potentials and become tangled in past, present, and future endeavors to produce utterances, meaning, and knowledge. Because the production and interpretation of the writing is not fully under the control of the writer, their friends, instructors, reviewers, or tutors, negotiation is the name of the game as they all "strike compromises, resolve trade-offs, and deploy sophisticated trading strategies" (Sheldrake, 2020, p. 136). At the center of entanglement is ongoing negotiation that depends on what is taking place around the constant efforts to make or break relationships, weigh options, and make choices in ingenious ways. Dwelling on surprises therefore provides a lens to consider how multilingual writing emerges and transforms as the result of unpredictable encounters.

Chronotopic Figuring

> As they wander around collecting mushrooms, their steps tracing the underground form of a mycelial network, the women sing amid the sounds of the animals in the forest. Each woman sings a different melody; each voice tells a different musical story. Many melodies intertwine without ceasing to be many. Voices flow around other voices, twisting into and beside one another.
> —Merlin Sheldrake (2020, p. 24)

Mushrooms call for scholarly attention to the dynamic interplay of life worlds together. Scholarly curiosities toward multiplicities have given rise to "polyphony" as a useful metaphor (Tsing, 2015; Sheldrake, 2020). Polyphony is music in which autonomous melodies intertwine. In Western music, the madrigal and the fugue are examples of polyphony, with musical themes entering harmony and dissonance with similar or different themes played at different scales. Such musical forms are bountiful in Indigenous cultures as well. As Merlin Sheldrake (2020) relays, as Aka women wander and gather mushrooms, each woman sings a different melody and each voice tells a different story, with these melodies "intertwin[ing] without ceasing to be many" and the women's voices flowing around, "twisting into and beside one another" (p. 54). These musical forms may seem archaic or exotic to modern, Western listeners who are familiar with musical composition held together by a unified rhythm and melody. The symphony, for instance, aims for a unified harmony by drawing various musical instruments into the same musical theme along a unified coordination of time. Whereas the goal of symphony achieves a single perspective, polyphony is the feature of musical forms such as jazz, when each musician listens for, responds to, and improvises in reaction to the performance of another. To appreciate a jazz performance, listeners are invited to notice moments of dissonance while attending to separate, simultaneous melodies. This kind of listening entails the willingness and ability to hear the multiplicity of voices, perspectives, and contours.

Anna Tsing (2005) draws on her ethnographic observation of life in the Indonesian forest to discuss polyphony as a metaphor to account for the generative mess of entangled lives. She describes the arrival of the fruit season after heavy monsoon rains, where a wide variety of tropical fruits such as durian, mango, lahung, langsat, and rambutan ripen en masse. Fruits are generously shared with neighbors and passersby, and their seeds are thrown into the bushes surrounding the house, where they settle, sprout, and grow. The shifting houses, occupied by farmers and made of bamboo and thatch, decay quickly and may themselves become fast-growing secondary forests. As villagers move into new shifting houses, with the only clue to the existence of the old ones being a shady young forest of fruit trees encircling the old house. The fruits whose seeds the villagers deposited will grow among many self-propagating herbs and trees. Furthermore, the young forest and many forms of human-initiated farming, spiritual, and medicinal practices co-evolve through the convergence of multiple trajectories of farming and harvesting. If we add other ecological relations, such as the life cycles of pollinators and cultural and religious rituals, temporal rhythms multiply further.

Indigenous farming in the Indonesian rainforest shows us the generative capacity of temporal polyphony. The dynamism of the polyphonic world is usefully contrasted with the singular rhythm of the commercial plantation, which effortfully cultivates the coordinated harvest of a singular, segregated crop whose growth is regulated to ensure simultaneous maturation. The colonial sugarcane plantation is a telling example of a scalable project that achieves the domination of a singular temporal rhythm through the engineered coordination of cloned planting stocks, alienated labor, and conquered land. While the plantation's regulated growth, premised upon the elimination of messy yet productive companion species, led to unprecedented profit, inspired global expansion, and informed models of industrialization, it also perpetuated the violence of scalability, which "reduced a once surrounding ocean of diversity into a few remaining puddles" (Tsing, 2012, p. 523), dispossessed vulnerable people of land and home, proliferated pathogens, and left the land in ruins after the departure of capitalist interests (Mitman, 2019). In striking ways, matsutake mushrooms, famously capricious creatures that resist efforts to cultivate and regulate their growth, push against the violent logic of scalability that undergirded colonial models of modernization and industrialization. While industrial farming and forestry, which rely on scalability to search for certainty, deprive the social and natural world of agency, matsutake mushrooms provide a polyphonic lens to examine how the multiple life worlds of pines, insects, farmers, and fungi take shape through the coordination of multiple attunements through which each organism comes into being. In their ability to flourish through collaboration across categorical differences, transform through unpredictable encounters, and innovate in response to polyphonic contingencies, fungi invite us to consider collaboration, contingency, and change as key features of entangled living.

For writing researchers, temporal polyphony encourages us to not only notice what is happening in each moment with a particular actor but also attend to writing as unfolding through the contingent, transformative encounters of multiple actors that bring into convergence trajectories of cultural, natural, literacy, and interactional histories. As such, temporal polyphony invites our attention to how historically developed narratives, repertoires, memories, and experiences intertwine to animate moments of literacy activities, which then fuse, connect, and branch into new trajectories of making meanings. The conceptual affordances of this concept, in its capacity to account for the messy and uneven ways temporal trajectories intertwine to generate dissonant and resonating meaning, productively engages with composition scholars' use of chronotopic lamination (Leander, 2002; Prior, 1999; Prior & Shipka, 2003) to explore how writers manage complex affects, identities, and consciousnesses through layered orchestration of multiple activities across space-time relations. Building on Bakhtin's (1981) notion of chronotope as a typified and dynamic envelope of spatial and temporal meanings, Prior (1999) grappled with the theoretical distinction between representational and embodied chronotopes, which offered the conceptual grounding for exploring how situated, dispersed, distributed, and mediated literate activities are chonotopically laminated to give meaning and shape to emergent literate activities. This notion was later articulated by Prior and Shipka (2003) to observe writing as dispersed

> not only across the loosely bounded acts of sitting and working with the text versus standing with the laundry, but also across a series of writing episodes... in a longer and blurrier chain of textual invention and production (p. 181)

They detail how experienced writers strategically manage their writing process by punctuating episodes of writing with household chores, which provide spaces for the mind to wander, for old ideas to resurface, and for new goals to emerge. As Kevin Roozen details, an engineering student's ability to work with graphic tables resonates with experiences of solving logic puzzles, performing everyday scheduling, and schoolwork with tables (2020). From this perspective, writing emerges across many moments as writers traverse activity spheres and conceptual bodies of knowledge. Such traversals rarely follow predictable pathways.

Scholarly efforts to further develop chronotopic lamination has drawn on metaphors of cymbal-making and roping (Holland & Leander, 2004) to articulate the iterative process of blending semiotic materials to create new and qualitatively different meanings that a single, undifferentiated piece of material would not produce. Lamination, as used in making a cymbal, is never a one-time process using a single mold with a single sheet of one metallic substance. The layering of distinct castings along a shared axis helps to create the grooves that are central to a cymbal's musical articulation. This emphasis on layering helps us explore how embodied activities and representational resources are routinely produced and hybridized in literacy practices, such as when students, teachers, and adults laminate multiple embodied and imaginary encounters with historical figures during the Civil Rights Movement to reflect on their pilgrimage trip (Leander, 2001). Participants layer multiple chronotopes of the home, imagined vacation, and Martin Luther King's assassination to make sense of the group's visit to Reverend Samuel "Billy" Kyles to anticipate an imagined future when photos of the meeting arrive, and to pay tribute to leaders of the movement. Similarly, De Fina et al. showcase how competing chronotopes about migration are complexly juxtaposed to produce conflicting narratives of transnational migrants as heroic travelers, victims to be rescued, invasive aliens, or threats to national security, which are differentially foregrounded or backgrounded in service of different rhetorical and political arguments (De Fina et al., 2020). While such conceptions are useful for considering how semiotic resources are hybridized to create new meanings, the metaphor of congealed lamination by layering metal castings along a shared axis or pressing a thin wood board onto a fiberboard core, suggests a settled, linear, and causal logic that fails to account for the messy and exploratory ways in which bits and pieces of ideas, narratives, artifacts, voices, and practices mobilize, energize, and detach from one another.

I offer chronotopic figuring as an alternative for exploring the ongoing, open-ended, multi-actor, and dynamic process of writing as becoming through resonance across materialities, activities, and spacetimes. To better account for the messy, uneven, and haphazard ways in which heterogeneous activities and histories are knotted across moments of intra-active becoming, I turn to Donna Haraway's theorization of string figure, the ancient game of manipulating strings on, around, and between the fingers of multiple players (2016). I remember playing string figures with my cousin when we were young. She would start the game by looping a long stretch of tied cotton twine around her wrists, picking up a loose section of the string, and twining it around her middle fingers. In a sequence of twisting, crossing, and twining, the string would transform into the basic pattern of a sled, with four parallel lines held up with the help of her thumbs, pinkies, and index fingers. I would then proceed to pick up sections with my index fingers, temporarily loosening the string from her hold, crossing the parallel lines, and forming and holding the new pattern of a star. Taking turns, we would find creative ways to partially "undo" each other's patterning and to bring the string into new patterns of a tree, temple, ladder, broom, and snail. When I failed to memorize routine moves for making a pattern, I would randomly pull and twist the thread to make something new. While we argued about proper names for these improvised patterns, they were difficult to replicate because of the contingent sequence of patterns and patternings leading up to them.

According to Haraway, string figure is a metaphor for learning to stay with the trouble of living and dying in response-ability to each other, which entails a "thick, ongoing presence, with hyphae infusing all sorts of temporalities and materiality" (2016, p. 2). Haraway describes figuring as one way to engage with the act of "promiscuously plucking out fibers in clotted and dense events and practices" (p. 3), which allows us to follow and track the messy ways in which the threads are temporarily held, tangled, and rearranged into patterns. Central to the game of string figure is reciprocation and anticipation, as each player receives the string pattern presented by the other player, which one then manipulates into something creatively and imaginatively new. String figuring is particularly appealing with its imaginary possibilities promised by the process of noticing new patterns, soliciting and anticipating response, reacting, and extending emergent patternings. Instead of evenly pressing molded sheets against each other into a laminate, string figure entails noticing, reciprocating, improvising, and "passing back and forth patterns-at-stake, sometimes conserving, somethings proposing and inventing" (2016, p. 34). In this sense, string figuring is the practice and process of becoming with each other in unpredictable and thrilling relays of making and unmaking, tying and untying, picking up and dropping threads. As such, string figure echoes the call by Prior and his colleagues to develop a "robust ontology of moments that illuminates the textures and consequences of experience within and across moments," attention to the "bio-cultural-historical weight of environments and practices," and careful tracking of "dialogic resonances across chains of moments" (Prior et al., 2023, pp. 10–11) as we conceptualize coordination, communication, and recognizable patterns of practices as the outcome of intra-active, dispersed, diffracted, and dialogic becoming. In contrast to lamination, string figuring articulates a disposition toward open-ended inquiry into temporaneous and uncertain knotting, the energy and skill to examine multi-actor collaboration, the willingness to work with contingency, and the readiness to move with and be moved by the mess of multiplicities.

Chronotopic figuring entails what Haraway calls "tentacular" thinking, which recognizes that myriad tentacular feelers' ability to feel and try to "make attachments and detachments," "to make cuts and knots," "to weave paths and consequences but not determinisms," and in doing so to sustain open and knotted patterning of material semiotic worlds (2016, p. 31). The attention to tentacular thinking resonates with the propositions of fungi scholars (Sheldrake, 2020; Tsing, 2015), who have argued for the importance of following and wandering with fungal hyphae as they fuse and fork to explore the underground expanse. Haraway (2016) offers tentacular thinking to not only account for the tentative, exploratory ways of becoming with others but use this trope to point to the multiple and complex pathways of sensing, acting with, and reacting to others. Noting the Latin roots of tentacle, "to feel" and "to try," I engage with tentacular thinking as a way to theorize the messy, exploratory, and tentative ways in which writers relate to, live with, and stay in becoming with natural, cultural, and literacy others, such as trees, flowers, rivers, squirrels, friends, mentors, and audiences, through unexpected associations and collaborations, risky partnerships, relentless contingencies, interlaced trails, improvised solutions, and emergent spacetimes. Tentacular thinking points me to the spontaneous and tentative ways in which semiotic fibers reach, feel, tangle, thread, probe, and move through material and semiotic practices. This mode of thinking is helpful in exploring how semiotic fibers (ideas, memories, jokes, notes, cultural tropes) accumulate meaning and become tangled to make meaning. It provides a lens to examine how semiotic fibers are twisted, tangled, loosened, or unknotted to produce new patterns with qualitatively and symbolically different possibilities. It points to the simultaneous intentional and improvisational nature of collaborative, emergent design, as semiotic fibers pass, reciprocate, and extend across spacetimes and in response to new peculiarities and exigencies. It allows us to consider the possibility of things losing traction and disappearing, ideas failing to connect, knots becoming untied, relationships breaking, and tension arising.

Materializing through unpredictable encounters, tentacular associations, and indeterminate contours, chronotopic figuring helps me work through the mess and complexity of writers knotting multiple life worlds together. First, chronotopic figuring invites the writing researcher's willingness to wander with writers, whose contours might be simultaneously strategic and exploratory, goal-driven and indeterminate, predictable and irregular. Sheldrake (2020) suggests that to follow the mycelial network is to resist the impulse to follow a single path/rhythm. That is, the researcher is to "become less focused and more distributed" in order to strategically listen for how multiple rhythms coalesce into a song that does not exist in any one of the voices alone (Sheldrake, 2020, p. 55). Following a single path might beguile the fact that writers weigh multiple connections and leads, assess the viability and feasibility of each, and make decisions reflective of multiple streams of hearsay advice, inspirations, intuitions, and feelings. In other words, an entanglement perspective argues that research methodology is better equipped to engage in open-ended and emergent wandering and be better prepared to account for the threaded fashion in which multiple actors across species and categories engage in intra-active articulation of the world-in-becoming (Barad, 2007).

Moreover, chronotopic figuring prepares us to notice the contingent ways in which ideas and partnerships are woven together in response to old and new exigencies. Wandering invites me to follow and drop semiotic threads, such as ideas, jokes, conversations, narratives, and practices that leave traces in the minds and bodies of multilingual writers. Picking up the material traces of these threads, such as an entry in a private journal, a social media conversation that is saved and shared, or a draft littered with annotations, allows me to notice the relentlessly contingent ways in which these leads form attachments and detachments, arise from or further generate visceral reactions, draw additional voices and perspectives into dialogue, and inspire new imaginative possibilities. As I will illustrate throughout this book, materials of multilingual writing, such as a thought, a personal story, a memory, a passing comment, or a screenshot, are not fixed layers that are pressed together into sentences and paragraphs that follow coherent and predictable hierarchical orders. Rather, they inspire, evoke, bounce off, coalesce, and dissipate through dispersed episodes of reading, drafting, conversing, note-taking, reviewing, revising, and reflecting. Although they sometimes coalesced through accumulating drafts and help to crystallize and stabilize ideas, how they emerge from and around writing was never settled or driven by a fixed axis.

Polyphonic sensitivity toward the working of multiple temporal trajectories resonates with Jay Lemke's argument (2000) that each intra-activity, a heartbeat, a breath, or an utterance brings into convergence evolutionary and historical trajectories of organisms with hearts to beat, words to utter, and breath to take from and to an atmosphere that they had all participated in producing. Extending Lemke's contention that "all human actions . . . takes place on one or more characteristic timescales" (p. 273), which seems to present an image of life unfolding on separable and fixed planes of existence, chronotopic figuring instead paints a picture of eco-social arrangements that involve the dynamic knotting and figuring of multiple spacetime relationships across scales. That is, moment-to-moment happenings emerge from the entanglement of writing-related resources, knowledge, and practices acquired along multiple historical trajectories. A keystroke, a spoken utterance, or the decision to pursue or abandon an idea takes a moment to create; the drafting of an essay extends over many such moments of articulating meaning; learning to write is a lifetime project that involves extended streams of literacy practices across languages and modes; one's writing enters into dialectical relationships with language and discourse patterns of multiple spheres of disciplinary, academic, and fandom practices that have developed over still longer times. If we temporarily abandon the single rhythm of instructional plans tethered to calendars, lesson plans, and due dates, we might notice how old and new friendships, sidebar conversations, backstage scenes of writing, and personal, familial, and interactional histories enter assemblages to create spaces for coordination, attunement, and negotiation. Brice Nordquist (2017) well illustrated how students' ability to complete schoolwork on the subway complexly intersects with quotidian rhythms of extracurricular activities, work obligations, train schedules, and Wi-Fi connections or dead zones entailed in their daily traversal. His research with high school seniors on their daily commutes from Queens, the Bronx, and Brooklyn to a public school in Lower Manhattan (Nordquist, 2018) reveals how material and embodied mobilities co-emerged with students' literacy practices, as they use their smartphones and time in transit to complete most of their reading and writing for school, collaborate on schoolwork across languages and media, and maintain and expand transnational social networks. From this perspective, the temporal rhythm of writing is negotiated with the vicissitudes of daily routines, project timelines, growth pulses of ideas, routinized writing processes, and a wide array of personal, social, and professional pursuits. Students' experiences, uses, and relationships with spacetimes are considered due to converging personal, classroom, institutional, disciplinary, and cultural histories.

An Entanglement Framework

Entanglement, as a theoretical metaphor, allows me to engage with transformative encounters, curated and emergent partnerships, indeterminate outcomes, conceptual trespassing, and negotiation and innovation as core features of multilingual writing. This view problematizes the myth of the singular author by pointing to the role of reciprocal partnerships in open assemblages. It invites us to observe writing and the writer as co-emergent in open articulation of the world along with natural, cultural, and literacy others. It focuses on negotiation across linguistic, cultural, and rhetorical differences as the norm and invites the researcher's efforts to follow the weaving and figuring of meaning through the mediation of semiotic repertoires and spatial-temporal configurations. It encourages an intentional departure from the modernist preoccupation with coherence, pattern, and clarity and instead provides a lens toward the slippery, ephemeral, and messy aspects of the world in becoming through the intra-active open articulation of multiple players and dwellers. It embraces surprises and improvisations as the norm of coordinated, collaborative survival; it places the writer in the world, knotted within and emerging through historical trajectories and contingencies.

These propositions encourage me to stray into the peripheries of the narrowly construed locale where the writing phenomenon is purportedly to unfold and to explore the emergence of writing as bubbling with competing histories (Tsing, 2015). In the chapters that follow, I provide details from ethnographic case studies to examine multilingual writing as simultaneously haphazard and coordinated efforts to write multilingual lives into meaning. Following multilingual writing in entanglement, I argue, presupposes an intentional departure from theoretical constructs that reinforce boundaries between nature and culture, individual and social, global lingua franca and languages on the periphery, and spacetimes that are simultaneously contingent and historical. Such efforts push back on my own impulse to seek out predictable patterns, transferable strategies, and intentional design as the only sites of meaningful inquiry and pondering.

2
Becoming With the River

Spatializing Nature in Multilingual Landscape

Writing in entanglement envisions writing as unfolding through the weaving and unweaving of material, semiotic, and social practices across mutable, permeable, and porous spatial boundaries. Such a view compels the writing researcher to follow a fuller spectrum of multilingual writers' literacy and social activities across linguistic, communal, and cultural boundaries as well as the various institutional and idiosyncratic forces that keep ideas, meanings, and texts (im)mobile. The complexity of life outside the classroom are inextricable from the complexities of life within the classroom; reading, writing, and digital literacies performed outside the classroom are affectively, imaginatively, and conceptually moved by literacy tasks inside the classroom. An entanglement perspective invites renewed attention to the literacy landscape as encompassing material and semiotic environs that are simultaneously natural and cultural. This literacy landscape is dynamically produced through material and discursive practices, such as walking from one class to another, relaxing on a riverbank while contemplating possibilities for writing, or entering a digital space to share inspirations through encounters with nature. These practices produce material and embodied forms of spatiality,

https://doi.org/10.7330/9781646427628.c002

such as classrooms, dorms, riverbanks, library corners that are "directly sensible and open, within limits, to accurate measurement and description" (Soja, 1996, p. 66). Socially produced, materially embodied, semiotically marked and represented, and affectively experienced spaces are both the medium and the outcome of human activity, behavior, and experience.

My thinking is informed by scholarly attention to how spaces acquire real and imagined forms and meanings through the entwined working of material and semiotic practices. Scholars have observed how routine classroom practices, such as worksheet distribution or implementation of an IRE (initiation, response, evaluation) sequence (Sheehy, 2004), spatial arrangement of objects such as desks, podiums, and black boards (Wang, 2017), or students' embodied acts of facing or shunning each other (Leander, 2002) could be read as spatial practices that produce real, geographic effects. Classroom geography acquires material shapes through routine practices (e.g., seating charts, team assignments), which shape interactional patterns among students, channel the flow of information, and limit or open ways to participate. Classroom geography can be highly contested partly because spatial practices embody and mobilize historical and geographical meanings teachers and students have developed with literacy, schooling, and social interactions in and outside the writing classroom. As I have explored elsewhere (Wang, 2017), Chinese international students draw on spatial memories of a traditional Chinese classroom and use self-selected seating to reify the teacher's authoritative identity, position students sitting in the front as experts, and spatially demote unengaged peers. Students' decisions about where to sit, with whom to sit, and how to manage access to resources involve ideological fixes of material spaces, index spatial histories, and co-evolve with identity aspirations. In these scenarios, spatiality is political enterprise, which enables certain forms of embodied experiences, meaning making, and interpretation through the physical objects, narratives, and imaginaries about space (Leander, 2002). Spaces are not only shaped by relations of production that operate with modes of reasoning, signs, knowledge, and codes for deciphering spatial meaning but are socially produced human geographies that enable and constrain forms of physical and imaginary traversals (Leander & Sheehy 2004; Soja, 1996). Such a lens enables attention to how spaces can be hybridized, laminated, and negotiated to create and articulate contested spatial meanings in an ongoing project to condense and stabilize identity and literacy practices.

I share the curiosities of scholars such as Janet Emig (1964), Sondra Perl (1979), Hannah Rule (2018), and Stacy Pigg (2014), who have explored embodied patterns in composing by detailing how writers' (un)intentional, embodied, and emergent interactions within their ambient environs powerfully shape, stabilize, and direct the contours of writing tasks at hand. What Hannah Rule calls "writing's room" vibrates with such "inconsequential details" as the furnishing of the space (e.g., desks, chairs, plants, decor on the wall), ambience (e.g., sunlight, aromatic candles, music), and bodily sensations (e.g., the calming effects of a drink). Similarly, Prior and Shipka (2003) and Rule (2019) have encouraged us to see pets as important writing companions who readily participate in scenes of writing through rapidly animate movements and the multi-organism interactions they initiate. As I am writing these words, my pet companion, Banana the cat, has emerged from his favorite nap spot, an empty shoebox, to patrol my writing desk. He chafed against my cheek, communicating to me the permission (and demand) to rub his back and head; as my focus on the writing made me slow to respond, he walked over my keyboard, blocked my gaze, and rested his head on my arm as he laid down in resignation. Beyond his bodily warmth and the soothing purr, his active body changed my writing space, as I waved his tail out of my face, deleted the random passage he co-wrote with his paws, worried about a cup of hot tea that he might spill, and repeatedly retrieved my notepad that he intentionally pushed off the desk. Here the writer and other players (Banana the cat, tea, notepads, laptop) are symbionts to each other as they participate in the ongoing becoming-with each other at all sorts of sizes and scales, through diverse kinds of relationalities, and with varying degrees of openness to opportunistic assemblages (Haraway, 2016, p. 60). The writer is merely one factor in the composing process and part of an emergent assemblage.

These components could configure into ritualistic, rhythmic practices that stabilize writing activities; they could also coalesce in unexpected ways to generate surprises and inspirations. Such "material minutiae, often falling outside of [the] purviews of writing researchers," provides much insight into the ways that objects, tools, journals, and furniture animate the intellectual and physical labor of writing (Rule, 2019). Jay Jordan (2015) usefully complicates the notion of "human-centric agency" by exploring how professionals engaged in translingual negotiation through symbiotic clusters of artifacts, smells, pathogens, and affects. The fertile material surrounding the Egyptian cheese importer and Danish exporter permeate translingual negotiation, as the two collaboratively negotiate the meaning of "blowing" cheese. Rather than focusing on multilinguals' language negotiation, Jordan suggests that we attend to the fermenting cheese not as a passive resource that the human interlocutors describe and recruit as the basis of linguistic innovation but instead as the cheese, "blowing" odorous chemical compounds, having powerful effects on the merchants' visceral experiences. Such theorizations move in closer alignment with ecological studies by attending to language work as implicated by the ambient auditory, olfactory, tactile, and visual communication between the cheese, bacteria, pathogens, chemical compounds, and merchants, changing the way the body reacts in the moment, business decisions based on such communication, and paths they find themselves channeling through.

These ideas of material environs and spaces, as contested rather than immutable, inhabited but given, open ways for discussing writing practices as inherently heterogeneous, particular and complex because they are entangled in "the dispersed, fluid chains of places, times, people, and artifacts that come to be tied together in trajectories of literate action" (Prior & Shipka, 2003, p. 181). Writing emerges with space through relationships and mobilizes meanings located across historical trajectories. These ideas inform my own thinking about spaces multilingual writers traverse daily as simultaneously being matter and meaning, real and imagined, inhabitable and transformative. Students' spatial contours are teeming with symbols and "vitally filled with politics and ideology, with the real and imagined intertwined ... [to] concretize the social relations of production, reproduction, exploitation, domination, and subjection" (Soja, 1996, p. 68). Therefore, the literacy landscape of multilingual writers is contested and has the potential to produce counter spaces for those arising from their subordinate, peripheral, and marginalized positioning. From such a perspective, lived spatiality is a strategic, political location from which institutionally ascribed identities and ideologies can be disrupted and destabilized through the imaginative reconfiguration and hybridization of spaces. Multilingual writers constantly interpret spatial meanings, articulate spacetime relations, and weave multiple spacetimes into material-semiotic grounds that continue to co-evolve with literacy activities. Spaces are not imagined as static containers bound by walls or backgrounds against which literacy activities unfold but as a nexus of relationships and trajectories that are continuously made and remade during social processes. Because spaces such as classrooms, digital learning spaces, and informal writing spots are sites of "perils as well as possibilities, [and] radical openness" (Soja, 1996, p. 68), it is important to observe how reading, writing, and digital practices draw on semiotic repertoires located across spatial configurations and how such practices are transformative and generative processes that are teeming with affects, symbols, and narratives; they mobilize geographic meanings and imaginary possibilities across interconnected spaces we inhabit.

Guided by these ideas, I approach the lived "human geography" of multilingual writers as dynamically produced multiplicities of relationships, layered with historical meanings, and connected across physical and digital spaces. More importantly, an entanglement perspective invites renewed attention to nature as an important sphere of multilingual students' literacy landscape. As the world of mushrooms shows us, nature is much more than a static entity, location, reference, or source for human activities. Rather, nature, as all matter, is "dynamic [material] articulation/configuration of the world" as much as the discursive practices, which are also material configuring of the world through which determination of boundaries, properties, and meanings are differentially enacted (Barad, 2007, p. 151). Compositionists have noted "the permeability of social and biological worlds as well as the inextricable positioning of the researchers within those worlds" (Fleckenstein et al., 2008, p. 394), which compels the researcher's own active involvement in and contribution to a research ecology that spans natural and cultural worlds. To research ecologically is to be immersed in a multilevel, multifaceted environment by fusing the knower, the known, and the material environs of the acts of knowing. Doing so means that the researcher is encouraged to actively participate in the production of ethnographic understanding by tracing messy linkages and attending to ephemeral and elusive feelings, affects, and bodily sensations arising from encounters with natural and cultural worlds.

Indeed, my ethnographic work has led me to discover many moments when literacy work emerges through the writer's entanglement within ambient and atmospheric natural and cultural environs—beautiful falling leaves that remind the writer of a poem and evoke feelings of nostalgia, a roaring river running through campus, a view of a street that resembles a scene in a Japanese anime and thus inspires feelings of reminiscence, a quiet corner furnished with a plush chair in a campus building, where the writer habitually seeks solace, or the circular drive in front of a campus parking structure that comes alive with the bellowing noise of revving engines. As I will show in this chapter, these materially emplaced encounters are charged with discursive and material impetuses—they inspire multiple forms of writing; fuel academic, professional, and class aspirations; call on specific ways to orchestrate linguistic and semiotic resources; and shape how professional networks and social relationships are co-constituted. Writing is *"never not emplaced*[,] composing processes *only* happen through things, spaces, time, action, and bodily movement" (Rule, 2018, p. 404; italics in original). As I will elaborate on in this chapter, Morgan's intimate relationship with a campus river produces a lived spatiality that is productive of new imaginaries that assign the river with geographical and affective meanings that contravene relations of dominance, subordination, and resistance manifested in official discourse of the river.

Meeting Morgan

Morgan is a multilingual writer who routinely performs a wealth of literacy activities across multiple languages and dialects (Chinese, English, Sichuan, and Internet dialects). At the time of my research, Morgan was a sophomore finance major, member of the honors college, candidate for a prestigious student scholar program in her college, and recipient of several merit-based scholarships. Despite such academic achievements, Morgan struggled to fulfill the expectations for academic writing in her honors FYW course.

Her experiences as an international student in a large public university were emotionally tumultuous. In addition to the daily stress of taking 15 credit hours per semester and the pressure to earn solid grades, Morgan struggled to navigate the unfamiliar academic and institutional culture of the university. During earlier interviews, Morgan recounted an ongoing confrontation with a biology professor, who responded to her request for help to navigate a challenging curriculum with unmasked hostility. Morgan was asked to explain how she secured admission to the university given her struggles to comprehend English. Reading her frequent visits during office hours and her insistence on detailed explanations of her test results as efforts to "bargain for a better grade," the professor politely advised her to study on her own rather than seeking his help. Compounding such daily struggles were also challenges in navigating institutional procedures that constrained her academic mobility. In her first semester, an assigned academic advisor placed Morgan in my bridge language course despite her protests and the fact that her TOEFL score was above the required score for FYW placement. As a result, Morgan did not take FYW like most of her peers and was not eligible for Honors College admission by the end of her freshman year. To Morgan, however, membership in Honors College was highly desirable because it served as an official recognition of her status as a high-achieving student and could propel her academic and professional mobility. Morgan worked hard to negotiate her way into Honors College.

Through two academic years (2015–2016), I followed Morgan as she migrated from the bridge writing course into an honors FYW course, with additional longitudinal data collected during the subsequent 5 years, as she took her first job in a commercial bank in Florida; attended a graduate program of finance with scholarship; transferred to an Ivy League university, where she received her graduate degree; and began her career as a trader in a Chicago-based financial investment firm.

My analysis begins with the ethnographic snapshot of an unexpected encounter with the Red Cedar River, which moved Morgan physically, affectively, and imaginatively. The ephemeral encounter was so powerful that it invited Morgan into intimate partnership with the river, which traveled into her drafting and revision of a FYW writing assignment. By tracing the movement of the river across drafts and genres, I detail Morgan's ongoing efforts to attune her semiotic and rhetorical repertoire to write the river into meaning; I also explore how the river continued to gain expressive purchase by staying emergent. In following the river's becoming throughout Morgan's multilingual writing process, I explore how writing researchers might usefully engage with entirely new possibilities when we turn our analytical gaze toward entanglements through which writers become with natural, cultural, and literacy others. In the same way that ecologists attend to complex, synergetic combinations of fungi, plants, and animals that sustain multiple life forms, I attend to how natural, cultural, and literacy beings and worlds are contingently woven together to give shape and purpose to Morgan's literacy practices in and beyond the honors FYW class.

Encountering the River

During one of our informal observation meetings, Morgan explained to me,

> I was feeling miserable about my participation grade [in FYW]. I was rushing to get to BCC [Business College] for my finance class, trying not to think too much about my problems in FYW. I ran into a friend. She stuck her hand in my face, teasing that I was so buried in my thoughts that I didn't even see her. She had a handful of beautiful, colorful fall leaves. We chatted a bit. She is such a lively character. After we parted our ways, I found myself suddenly awakening to the stunning beauty of the riverside trail lined with maple trees. The sight of the trees and their reflections in the river took my breath away. You know I am from a huge, crowded city, right? The streets are always exploding with sounds of people arguing, peddlers

yelling to attract customers, wives chasing their husbands from Mahjong shops—you don't find peace and quiet in my city. At that moment, I finally understood what Gu Cheng was trying to say—simple things can take your breath away. I always complain about how boring it is here, or how ridiculous it is that Hubbard [a twelve-story residential hall] is the tallest building in this town. For the first time, I realized that a rural campus could be amazingly beautiful. When I used to pass American students relaxing on the riverbank, I had always felt they were wasting their lives away. After class today, I found a spot on the riverbank and just sat there, bathing in the warm sun. I felt better about everything.

This encounter, which surfaced during an interview and was visually recorded through a WeChat post, was significant to Morgan because it captured a broader range of struggles she experienced in her FYW class. As an avid reader in Chinese, Morgan struggled to fulfill the expectation for close and critical reading in her honors FYW class, where the instructor used reading quizzes to support (or, rather, monitor) students' engagement with reading assignments that ranged from autobiographical narratives to treatise on topics of American history. Despite Morgan's assiduous engagement with course readings, especially autobiographical essays by authors such as Maya Angelou (*Why the Caged Bird Sings*) and Amy Tan (*Mother Tongue*), she had scored poorly on reading quizzes (Wang, 2019a). While Morgan enjoyed the readings, she struggled to develop strategies that could help her succeed in reading quizzes that aimed to assess students' grasp of factual details. On this very day, Morgan approached her instructor to inquire about her standing in the class; she was advised to improve her performance by "speaking up more in class" and "getting the facts right [for her quizzes]." Feeling demoralized, Morgan embarked on her routine commute between classes, when a chance encounter with a friend opened her eyes to the stunning natural beauty of the campus river.

Still affectively moved by the encounter after class, she collected a handful of leaves in different shades of green, yellow, and red, arranged them on a desk at her favorite campus quiet spot, took a picture, and created a WeChat post. Using two photos capturing the beautiful foliage change along the riverside trail, Morgan provided a visual illustration of one stanza from "At My Front Door," a poem by her favorite Chinese contemporary poet, Gu Cheng. The post recorded a moment of her suddenly "awakening to the stunning beauty of the riverside trail lined with maple trees." The sight "almost took [her] breath away" and reminded her of the poem she had memorized by heart.

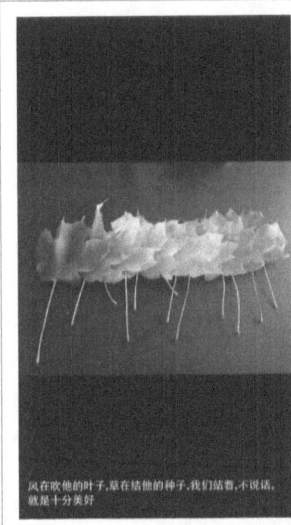

AT MY FRONT DOOR

By Gu Cheng

The wind brushing through his leaves
The grass yielding his seeds
We stand there
Without talking
Everything is idyllic

FIGURE 2.1. Morgan's WeChat Moments Remix of "At My Front Door"

This literacy event took shape in a figuratively cosmopolitan space where multiple life forms met and fused across taxonomic differences. These life forms brought into intersection distinct temporal rhythms and spatial arcs, such as the routinized spatial contour of Morgan's daily commute on campus, the photosynthetic processes of maple trees changing color in conjunction with seasonal temperature variations, the life cycle of maple leaves visually captured through her photo, and spatial lining of aesthetically appealing trees along a riverside walk bridging important hubs of residential and instructional buildings. The entanglement of these temporal and spatial contours created a unique, temporaneous articulation of the world-in-becoming: a gleeful friend offering comfort to a student in dismay. Additionally, the post represented an imaginary encounter occurring as the result of Morgan's multilingualism—a Chinese contemporary poet's country shed contrasted with the hustle and bustle of Morgan's hometown to emerge as the backdrop of Morgan's initial critique of the "rural" university campus and her sudden reckoning of its beauty. These multiple spatialities are literally, linguistically, and visually remixed and layered to give rise to a powerful affective experience.

Morgan turned this unexpected encounter into a multimodally orchestrated performance of her literary sensitivity. The visual and linguistic modes work in concert to create a meaningful remix of the Chinese poem. She fully explores the meaning potential of both modes, with the naturalistic themes in the stanza providing an anchor to the images and the spatial arrangements of colors and shapes in the visual mode enhancing the poem's theme. The two images are carefully aligned to create a categorical representation of leaves, with their carefully orchestrated lineup metaphorically displaying their life cycles in various stages and the photograph of the maple tree from which they grew and fell, show it in its natural state. Here we observe Morgan's meaning production as shaped by what Jody Shipka calls semiotic remediation practices, which encompass "the various ways that semiotic performances are re-presented or re-mediated through the combination and transformation of available resources (human, nonhuman, and natural)" (2011, p. 131). More importantly, the WeChat post encapsulated powerful feelings inspired by an ephemeral entanglement of friendship, nature, literary texts, and feelings of nostalgia and awe.

Embraced as a symbol of the university, the campus river embodies rich cultural meanings, institutional histories, and signature undergraduate social experiences. The university's website often highlights photogenic spots along the river, which indexes the university's legacy as a land grant university; introductory biology classes utilize the river as a research site to help students explore scientific procedures for gathering water samples, observing microbe density and variation, and analyzing scientific data; students gather on the riverbank, sunbathing, studying, and socializing; the riverbank is home to iconic animal companions, including bold squirrels, a family of local ducks, and proud Canadian geese constantly parading the riverside trail designed for human pedestrians. Morgan's first impression of the river was intimately entangled with her first experience with a tailgate party, which took place on the riverbank. As she remembered it, the riverbank erupted with fans cheering for the university's football team and vibrated with a campus a cappella group leading enthusiastic tailgaters in yelling verses from the university football team's fight song:

> On the banks of the Red Cedar,
> There's a school that's known to all;
> Its specialty is winning,
> And those Spartans play good ball;
> Spartan teams are never beaten,
> All through the game they fight;
> Fight for the only colors:
> Green and White.

Go right through for MSU,
Watch the points keep growing,
Spartan teams are bound to win,
They're fighting with a vim!

Rah! Rah! Rah!
See their team is weakening,
We're going to win this game,
Fight! Fight! Rah! Team, Fight!
Victory for MSU!

As such, the river is a simultaneously natural and cultural being that weaves the multiple life worlds of trees, waterfowl, students, classes, disciplines, and sports teams into patched and partial articulation of university life. More specifically for Morgan, the river's meaning remains in open articulation. Having taken the introductory biology class that brought her into the river, Morgan grimaced with disgust over a visceral memory of what she described as its "freezing cold water" and "putrid smell." Additionally, she had been critical of idle students sunbathing on the riverbank "wasting [their] lives away." On this day, however, chanceful encounters brought into shifting entanglement many agential forces to transform the river into a sanctuary for Morgan. The river suddenly acquired much affective meaning. The unpredictable encounter "awakened" Morgan to the aesthetic, expressive, and emotional possibilities of her being with the river. In her act of claiming her own spot on the riverbank, she "adventured into simultaneous worlds of the real-and-imagined" (Soja, 1996, p. 54). What used to be an ordinary path that led her from one instructional building to another was spatialized into her social and literacy world, joining a host of other secret campus spots to become one of her favorites to sit, contemplate, and idle. Weather permitting, she would spend time unwinding alongside the river at the end of a busy school day. I was drawn into this entanglement when Morgan invited me to meet her on the riverbank for one of our interviews on a Thursday in early September. Our experiences with the river were powerfully mediated by its ecological ambience, which was the product of polyphonic sounds of all those traversing through and inhabiting it. Morgan and I soaked in the soothing sound of the rushing water against the backdrop of the university's marching band practicing nearby, the ducks quacking, carillon bells playing on the hour from the iconic campus memorial tower, students jumping with joy when the iconic, daring squirrels claimed scraps of food from students' extended hands, and lively gossip we couldn't help but eavesdrop.

An entanglement perspective calls into question a representational logic that marks modern, humanist knowledge-making projects (Barad, 2007). A humanist perspective would conceive the river and the multilingual writer as ontologically separate entities, with the latter weaving together semiotic and material resources to experience, name, and exploit the former. Whereas representationalism positions the river as passively waiting to be studied by biologists, recorded by photographers, and written into fight songs, Morgan's multisensory experiences with the river unfolded through material practices of sitting, listening, touching, and feeling, which matter because they enabled certain forms of material engagement with the river, gave it a specific material form, and changed the nature of the river as well as our understanding of it. From this perspective, Morgan's knowing of the river is the outcome of the specificity of material entanglements in their agential becoming enabled by a haphazard patchwork of her emotional turmoil, chance encounter with a friend, sensory and aesthetic appeal of a pleasant autumn afternoon, and her material practices of absorbing and being absorbed into the ecological ambiance. These arhythmic adventures outside her everyday routine tangled into a particular way of feeling, experiencing, understanding, and relating to the river.

The river spatializes into various configurations through material practices (e.g., planting aesthetically appealing species of trees or plotting the riverbank for tailgate parties) and semiotic practices (e.g., singing the university fight song or remediating and featuring digitized images of the scenic river). The complex ecological networks of aquatic microbes, waterfowl, trees, and humans constantly redraw the boundaries of the river and assign it with properties that are salient and significant for certain actors. Interestingly, the river's temperature variations and seasonable changes of contours spatialize the duck family's resting and frolicking spots; the annual migratory trajectory of the duck family redraws the temporal and spatial contours for humans as well. In the thick of winter, the duck family would seek sanctuary in a small atrium in the building where the writing department is housed; an annual ritual has been made by the caring staff members to open the atrium door and initiate the ducklings' return to the river in late spring. The Canadian geese graze and defecate on the grass, changing the appearance and accessibility of the riverbank to students; their constant patrolling of the riverside trail often results in standoffs that temporarily stall the physical mobility of human pedestrians. Our enmeshment with the river is not a mere fact of "being specifically situated in the world" but "rather of being of the world in its dynamic specificity," where specific aspects of the river become intelligible through contingent working of relationships (Barad, 2007, p. 376). Rather than seeing Morgan as enacting a new form of reckoning with the river, we, the multilingual writer and the writing researcher along with ducks and squirrels, were all caught up in the river's open-ended articulation.

As illustrated here, an entanglement perspective provides a way for attending to boundaries between nature and culture as dynamically configured and reconfigured through practices that are simultaneously material and semiotic. Such a view is not calibrated to the writer; rather, it positions the writer in relation to other creatures, living and nonliving, in making sense of the world with the writer in it. The river is no longer seen as ontologically separate from the writer, waiting to be discovered and represented. Rather, it is a powerful agential force that transforms the writer, enables certain types of experiences, understandings, and relationships, mobilizes memories and sensations, changes perspectives, and inspires multimodal, multilingual writing. The river, as matter, is not a "fixed essence of property of things" but is "produced and productive, generated and generative" (Barad, 2007, p. 137).

Writing the River Into Meaning

Morgan's unpredictable encounters produced the river with unique materiality and spatiality, which was both the medium and outcome of institutional histories and cultural meanings intersecting with her material and semiotic practices. The river as lived spatiality was "a historical unfolding, an evolving sequence of changing geographies that result from the dynamic relations" (Soja, 1996, p. 77) between humans, plants, animals, and their cultural and natural environments. But lived spatiality is not just socially produced, empirically engaged, and physically traversed; it takes shape through Morgan's affective, imaginary, cultural, and semiotic renderings of it. Such is the case of Morgan's multimodal rendering of the river in dynamic relation to her poetry reading, cosmopolitan imaginaries, and semiotic repertoire. In this section, I further explore how Morgan assembles a dynamic repertoire of writing and rhetorical strategies to write the river into meaning. I contextualize Morgan's approach to the Memoir assignment, for which the river resurfaced as a powerful emotional anchor. In so doing, I provide a detailed analysis of how the river acquired differential meaning along with the Memoir through Morgan's efforts to navigate genre, rhetorical, and dialectal nuances. Moving away from Morgan's material entanglement with the river, I explore how her routine traversal through her linguistic landscape presented multiple opportunities to sample, assemble, and attune writing and rhetorical knowledge and practices.

The honors-designated FYW class Morgan enrolled in shared the curriculum of FYW, which unfolded in a sequence of five writing assignments (Learning Memoir, Cultural Artifact, Disciplinary Literacy, Remix, and Final Reflection). The Memoir, the first assignment in the sequence, "invites students to consider their experiences with learning in and out of school to encourage them to reflect on the relationship between their learning histories and present lives" ("About the FYW curriculum"). The memoir embodies an important learning objective of FYW—positioning students' own knowledge and experiences as important resources for generating new understandings of rhetoric, literacy, and culture. In Morgan's class, the assignment was also used to develop students' ability to use creative writing techniques. Such learning objectives were achieved through instructor-facilitated reading and discussion of autobiographical narratives previously mentioned.

Morgan's first draft was a patchwork of ideas gathered from in-class free writing, informal exchange with classmates, a lunch conversation with me, and an outline of topics. Drafting allowed her to explore conceptual connections among learning events in relation to her insight—persevering through pernicious attacks from peers and interrogation from professors during her first year. She opened her essay with a vignette of her being teased for selecting challenging classes during a guided course enrollment workshop. The narrative proceeded to portray her confrontation with her biology professor, which shattered her confidence. The opening scene focused on depicting feelings of helplessness and self-doubt; it then took a turn toward an optimistic outlook, describing an accomplishment, when Morgan leveraged knowledge acquired in a nutrition science class to help her grandfather adopt a healthier lifestyle. The essay ended with a statement on the reflective insight, as Morgan affirmed her belief that perseverance was key to achieving academic success. One rhetorical strategy Morgan used remarkably well, which three peers who reviewed her essay noted, was her ability to utilize sensory details to convey feelings of anguish, loneliness, and elation. Figure 2.2 shows an excerpt from the opening of her essay.

As the excerpt from Morgan's draft shows, she used several strategies to create vivid imagery, including a flashback constructed through dialogue showing the "questioning exclamations from my friends," a carefully constructed

Becoming With the River : 71

> —"You serious?! Don't you know it is just the first semester?"
>
> —"Oh! Jesus ! Wish you good luck to be a nutritionist !"
>
> —" You crazy fool ! "
>
> Besides the ebullient cheers of " Go Green ,Go White" and the murmur of rushing Red Cedar River, actually, these exaggerated exclamations lingered in my freshman year.
>
> I would never forget the day when I entered the computer lab to enroll course schedule. A crow of assistants and advisers walked through the room frequently in order to answer those ceaseless questions from students. However, I was just like a square peg in a round hole, because I almost finished schedule enrolling in no more than five minutes. Wondering why others came up with so many questions, I heard those questioning exclamations from my friends.

FIGURE 2.2. Opening Scene in Morgan's Memoir Draft

parallel structure consisting of three auditory details, and simile and idiomatic expression (comparing her to a square peg in a round hole), to reveal the emotional turmoil ensuing a guided course enrollment workshop, where her academic ambitions were met with ridicule from peers. Morgan's deployment of these rhetorical devices reflected an ongoing effort to grapple with conventions of the narrative genre, which was embodied by a range of writing techniques introduced in her FYW classes, including parallelism, flashback, metaphor, and sensory details. Such genre expectations were further communicated in her class through instructor-facilitated identification of writing techniques in course readings, testing of students' mastery of the reading material through quizzes, and language in the project description—"employ creative writing techniques that make your stories compelling and engaging."

In particular, she used one sentence that followed the opening dialogues to create an emotional space for her essay. She creatively mixed noises variously attached to the river to broadly encapsulate her feelings of excitement about attending her first football game, elation over her discovery of the university campus's beauty, and anger toward pernicious remarks from her peers. The sentence was organized with a carefully constructed parallel structure consisting of three auditory details—"exaggerated remarks," "ebullient cheers," and "murmur of the rushing Red Cedar River." Morgan used the murmur of the river, dialogues that replicated exaggerated remarks, and reference to the school cheer to comment on the emotional journey she undertook during her first semester. In the "Chinese draft in [her] head," she used a Chinese idiom 潺潺流水 (*chan chan liu shui*, meaning flowing, bubbling water) to capture the ambience of the river. 潺潺 (*chan chan*, bubbling), a duplication construction, is a Chinese onomatopoeia imitating the lively, bubbling sound of flowing water, which, for Morgan, also carries the feeling of comfort and relaxation, "like when you escape to a lively, bubbly stream in the mountains after a long, hot working day in the chaotic city." The river surfaced in resonance to her extended, embodied experiences with the Red Cedar River, which she articulated through personification—while she confided in the river, the river reciprocated with "murmurs" of comfort during stressful times.

It is worth noting Morgan's strategic construction of this sentence and her creative use of rhetorical strategies. Her drafting of this sentence emerged from the entanglement of multiple languages, writing-related theories, strategies, and practices developed in multiple literacy trajectories, and knowledge of the Western narrative genre and Chinese rhetorical tradition. The Western narrative genre was embodied by a range of writing techniques introduced in WRA 1004, the bridge writing class she took with me the previous semester and in her FYW class. As she reflected,

> I had an earlier draft. The introduction paragraph had a ton of inspirational quotes from a Brazilian revolutionist, Steve Jobs, and Chinese classical authors. But it was dry and boring; it wasn't a story. It was a five-paragraph essay. I kept thinking about an essay we read in [WRA] 1004. I kept thinking about the anecdotes Russel [Baker] used, about how his little sister bargained with a cheating grocery store owner, or when he kept saying "That's right." when his mom answered questions for him. The repetition does a good job in showing that he was intimidated. I enjoyed reading it because these details invited me to imagine the backstory. That's how you keep the reader interested. I abandoned my draft and started over. I then decided to write about my meeting with my biology professor, with a focus on how mean and harsh he was and how much I struggled to control my feelings. That is a good story.

Morgan's contemplation surfaced a rather nuanced understanding of different genres of academic writing. Her previous draft, which was a loose collection of stories of struggles decorated with inspirational quotes, was in alignment with expectations of argumentative writing, which relies on discussion of personal experiences, use of inspirational quotes, and analysis of multiple streams of evidence, perspectives, and opinions to make a point. Her ongoing grappling with the personal narrative genre drew on her experiences of learning to read and write essays in high school (with its emphasis on five-paragraph essays for high-stakes tests), the bridge writing class (WRA 1004), and the honors FYW class. Contrasting personal narrative with the five-paragraph essay, she noted one specific attribute of personal narratives: the use of descriptive language to create an imaginary space where readers and writers alike engage with reflective discovery of personal truth. Reflecting on reading assignments including *Growing Up* by Russel Baker and *Welcome to St. Paul* by Lorene Cory, she named a few strategies that she could use to move her writing from a "tedious and boring" speech to an engaging narrative. As shown in her draft, the opening paragraph of her essay displayed her efforts to use anecdotes, maxims, and dialogues to develop compelling characters with distinct personalities and behaviors. Whereas the previous draft was a loose collection of stories and anecdotes highlighting her struggles, the present draft centered around one carefully crafted moment of an emotionally charged confrontation with her biology professor, which encapsulated a broader range of social and academic struggles she experienced during her freshman year. In doing so, she demonstrated rhetorical awareness through her willingness to abandon a draft for failing to "keep the reader interested" and her capacity to retool rhetorical strategies to fulfill new genre-specific expectations. Such considerations continued to unfold during Morgan's drafting and revision during the subsequent weeks, when she incrementally moved the draft to a closer approximation of the Western narrative genre modeled and expected in her FYW classes.

In addition to showcasing her ability to manage rhetorical strategies typified in what she considered a Western narrative genre, Morgan also integrated colloquial English to demonstrate her growing cultural and linguistic expertise. In using phrasal verbs such as "came up with," colloquial exclamations such as "Oh! Jesus!" and idiomatic expressions such as "square peg in a round hole," Morgan worked to move her writing toward what she considered "authentic" US English and the monolingual norm. Indeed, Morgan worked assiduously to cultivate her repertoire of colloquial and vernacular English. She sought out opportunities to chat with American classmates and roommates, whose everyday speech was riddled with slang words that sounded authentically American, especially in contrast to the "textbook English" she had studied in China. On one occasion, Morgan reported with exuberance about a cultural lesson she received from a neighbor, who explained the difference between "date" and "hook up" with telling examples. To Morgan, authentic, colloquial US English represented native-like proficiency; it was elevated as a privileged dialect, access to which was uniquely afforded by her physical and intellectual proximity to it in a US university.

Here we observe Morgan's multilingualism becomes "truncated" (Blommaert et al., 2005), where multiple languages and dialects are "structured and regimented by spaces and relations between spaces" (p. 205). That is, Morgan's pursuit of higher education in a transnational context has led to a drastic reordering of the various linguistic resources at her disposal, with the multiple varieties and dialects of English becoming increasingly centered in her academic and social life. While English previously remained locally bounded (mainly as a subject matter presented through outdated texts in isolation from dynamic changes to the language), Morgan's life in the US has led to an expanding repertoire of English dialects and varieties across social (engaging with roommates and classmates), academic (access to academic and disciplinary material), and transnational (WeChat) spaces, making it increasingly nuanced and complex. Others in her transnational network also contributed to the restructuring of the language regiment. Morgan felt stressed by continuous "pestering" from family and friends, who expected her to drop English phrases in everyday conversations and sought language help by asking her to translate business correspondence from English to Chinese. Feeling pressured to speak authentic US English, Morgan was invested in incorporating colloquial English into her semiotic repertoire. Her use of "came up with" and "square peg in a round hole" (an idiomatic expression she carefully translated from a comparable Chinese idiom) could be seen as an effort to construct discursive proof of her linguistic and cultural expertise—she was in close contact with authentic, vernacular forms of American culture. However, she had yet to discover that her attempts at idiomatic expressions were in tension with expectations for precision, formality, and concision in edited, standardized written English.

Morgan's strategic fusion of genre features and dialectal varieties provides evidence for Horner et al.'s argument that negotiation across differences is a central feature of writing (2011). Morgan's understanding of the Western genre of personal narrative took shape through transformative encounters and collaborative relations. Transformative encounters with varieties and dialects moved Morgan to an appreciation of US English as an inherently dynamic and varied construction rather than a homogenous construct as previously represented in textbooks. Her understanding of the genre also drew on a web of reading and writing techniques honed across languages, each promising certain affordance. Morgan's grasp of the genre specifically and her ongoing effort to master the language broadly emerged through multilingual living: newly forged associations with these bodies of knowledge, shifting relationships with American professors, and day-to-day encounters with peers provided access to facets of the language-in-use that was not available from textbook English she learned in China. The river's ability to travel into her essay was afforded and limited by the competing expectations for vivid descriptions and insightful analysis, authenticity and formal language, rhetorical flourishes, precise language, clarity, and concision.

This excerpt from her draft is also a prime example of indeterminate meaning. Morgan continuously assessed tested strategies and entrenched understandings in dialectical relationship to creative impulses and risky experimentations with new strategies. Creative and risky endeavors manifested in linguistic slippages, such as uneven shifts across registers, awkward grammatical structures, and misinterpretation of culturally inflected nuances and connotations. Many tend to read such slippages as evidence of Morgan's lack of linguistic dexterity to marshal different language varieties. As I continue to explore in Chapter 3, Morgan's teacher and peers often noted such linguistic oddities by simply underlining them, marking them with a "?," and describing them without offering concrete suggestions for revision (e.g., inserting a comment in the margin such as "awkward phrase"). Her use of the word "murmur" to describe the campus river—which is conventionally rendered as a masculine presence in association with college football—received sustained inquiry and critique, eventually leading to the loss of its meaning. These slippages were often eradicated; "solved" as problems; or revised in accordance with familiar, established linguistic and cultural norms from which the author had been presumed to unknowingly deviate. A perspective informed by entanglement, however, suggests how such linguistic oddities might be read as evidence of Morgan finding her footing in an increasingly expanding and nuanced language ecology, where she enters coordinated relationships with peers, classmates, and teachers, each offering access to and engendering encounters with many dialects and variations of English used across dynamic social situations. That is, Morgan and her linguistic repertoire transformed in association with literacy others, manifesting in conversations, feedback, informal teaching, and cultural exchanges. As the important stuff of life on earth happens in those transformative encounters, Morgan's transformative language repertoire was the outcome of "livable collaborations" across differences, which led to contamination and manifested as linguistic slippage and oddity (Tsing, 2015, pp. 28–29). For Morgan, assembling genre conventions and writing strategies within a single language involved agentive and active efforts toward weighing, attuning, and testing language use against subtle and alarming differences.

Becoming With the River

Morgan's multilingual writing is entangled with the river. Becoming with each other is the name of the game. The river, Morgan, and multimodal texts, which moved the river toward meaning across visceral experiences, images, and writing in Chinese and English, are ontologically heterogeneous partners that become who and what they are in relational material-semiotic worlding (Haraway, 2016, p. 13). Nature (trees, waterfowl, maple trees) and culture (football songs, tailgate parties, students' ways of inhabiting or traversing the riverbank) do not predate their intertwinement. Similarly, it is difficult to distinguish the subject and the object of the scenario. While Morgan's affective engagement with the river seems to result from a moment of inspiration, the river, with its putrid smell, soothing babble, scenic view, and sociality, which already involved students, microbes, ducks, squirrels, and trees, had the capacity to draw, repel, stall, and change Morgan. Morgan was not simply in the world; she was part of the world in one version of its contingent patterning, imaginary possibility, and tentative articulation. Unpredictable encounters might have served as an impetus to draw Morgan and the river into entanglement, but histories of class activities, daily commutes, previous ponderings, feelings of homesickness, and reading across languages and genres were ready to be tangled into ongoing patterning of the world. These beings have teamed up to make each other capable of something in the world of relationships. The temporaneous tangle seemed whimsical. After all, the entwinement of the river and Morgan was fleeting (I was not even there when it happened); its affect seemed insignificant (one sentence out of the entire essay referenced the river); the probability of a similar encounter erupting with comparable energy was slim and certainly not replicable. Yet each time I trace "a tangle and add a few threads that at first seemed whimsical but turned out to be essential to the fabric" (Haraway, 2016, p. 29), the effort to stay with trouble allowed me a glimpse into Morgan's multilingual writing as history in the making. Indeed, Morgan's habitual visit became part of my own ritual on warm and sunny autumn days. The river became a part of her memories and subject of many social media posts we each created. My writing and thinking about multilingual writing contain vestiges of the textual history of the essay-in-becoming-with-the-river as well.

Theorizing multilingual writing in entanglement entails attention to collaborative survival, which is achieved through coordinated efforts of agential forces, both human and nonhuman. Entanglement compels efforts to dislodge binary notions that award determinacy and permanency to boundaries that mark the limits of nature and culture, subject and object, human and nonhuman, writer and researcher. Such a view begins with a reconsideration of entrenched assumptions we make about writers, rivers, and trees as operating with intrinsic boundaries, determinate properties, and available resources. As post-humanist theorists have argued (Barad, 2007; Tsing, 2015; Sheldrake, 2020), developments in modern medicine, such as organ transplants, and microbial sciences have shaken the notion of the individual to the core. Where one individual stops and another begins is no longer taken for granted. We are ecosystems, composed of—and decomposed by—an ecology of forty-odd trillion microbes that live in and on our bodies, facilitating our digestion of food, producing nourishing minerals, guiding our immune systems, and protecting us from diseases. As we are not exempted from symbiosis as "the ubiquitous feature of life," attention to the individual no longer makes sense (Sheldrake, 2020, p. 17). Indeed, the boundaries of writers, rivers, waterfowl, and maple trees become blurry as we attend to the shifting entanglement they cojoin to render specific and contingent articulations of the world-in-becoming. Morgan's literacy activity involves significant boundary-(re)drawing practices through which she differentiates herself from her environment and thereby makes sense of her world. Such boundary-drawing practices are materially and discursively enacted through vivid memories that highlight the contrast between the clamor of her metropolitan hometown and the serenity of the college town, her decision to insert herself onto the riverbank, which was perceived as a space for idling students unlike herself, or the world of the Chinese poet in juxtaposition of the transnational, multilingual writer. In Barad's words, "it matters to the world how the world comes to matter" (2007, p. 380).

It is even more important to observe how boundaries, properties, and relations are rewritten through multilingual writing in entanglement. Morgan's effort to write her multilingual life worlds into meaning is enacted through material and discursive practices. Her ephemeral, embodied, and sensory experiences with nature are discursively recorded, complicated, and negotiated through multimodal and multilingual writing, which in turn shapes her understandings of and experiences with the river. Evidenced in this analysis is the entangled co-becoming of the multilingual text and the multiple life worlds that were differentially enacted materially, semiotically, and culturally. The metaphor of entanglement allows us to observe the indeterminacies of textual meanings. As it is important to attend to the microbial relationships and symbiotic associations that make us functioning ecosystems, it makes sense to explore how symbiotic and semiotic associations writers forge with other living organisms, semiotic repertoires, and digital infrastructures change our experiences of our own bodies, the places we inhabit, and our positions in the world. Importantly, the river is always becoming with historical trajectories of social-material-natural worlds of the university's land grant history, its football culture, the landscape and geography of the campus, and the movements of its students. These histories partially determine how locally improvised textual meaning enters an extended stream of conversations, how brokers position themselves and participate in language work, and how literacy shapes natural, social, and cultural lives.

Attention to Morgan's ephemeral and indeterminate encounters with the river necessitates the effort to de-center the human for possessing the capacity, apparatus, and concepts to generate knowledge *about* the world. It points to knowing as inextricably entangled with being, feeling, and doing *in* the world. From this perspective, entanglement enables a textured analysis of the "ecological properties of written discourse and the ways in which ecologies, environments, locations, places, and natures are discursively affected" (Weisser & Dobrin, 2001, p. 2). Although the river offers much imaginative and expressive potential, it is through material and discursive practices, such as sunbathing, squirrel-feeding, sitting, thinking, talking, wading, swimming, and smelling, that the river gains differential meanings for ducks, tailgaters, biology students, the multilingual writer, and the writing researcher. This detailed attention to the co-constitutive existence of the writer, multilingual writing, and the natural and semiotic environ gives us a glimpse into the ephemeral and haphazard ways in which writing arises from and gives rise to Morgan's encounter with the river, her contemplation of this encounter, and her ongoing effort to articulate her sense of self in the world and in relation to the river. In doing so, this analysis resonates with Weisser's contention that our identities, and how they are manifested through writing, are inextricably linked to the larger biosphere that we live in and emerge through our orientation to nonhuman others (2001). Morgan and her writing are ecologically grounded in the materiality of spaces and negotiated around, beside, and in accord with her shifting relationships with organisms that share and co-construct such materiality. Entanglement therefore allows us to envision Morgan and her writing as "socially constructed and sustained in community with an enormous number of interconnected others along with their ecologies and habitats" (Weisser, 2001, p. 87).

Morgan's multilingual writing stayed emergent with lived spatiality that she traversed daily, life forms wittingly and unwittingly woven into her literacy landscape, and mobile semiotic and rhetorical repertoires evolving with multilingual living. The contingent weaving together of these components moved Morgan physically, affectively, and imaginatively. An entanglement perspective shifts my attention away from the writer as the designer of determinate meaning; it reveals how dynamic, temporaneous, and improvised acts of relating to natural, cultural, and literacy others direct the contours of Morgan's multilingual life-in-becoming-with. Placing shifting possibilities of the writer becoming with others at the center of analysis invites attention to unintended coordination, unpredictable encounters, and indeterminate meanings. As much as indeterminacy manifests in fungal hyphal tips that fork and fuse in their search for a friendly tree root, I see bountiful examples of Morgan drawing and being drawn into precarious, surprising, and productive associations with trees, rivers, friends, and teachers. A chance encounter with a friend, a sudden "awakening" to beautiful fall colors, and improvised connections with friends turned into literacy brokers; these are the small, anomalous adventures I follow and explore. These adventures hardly fit into rhythmic routines that fall within the purview of my ethnographic gaze by design, but they surface as fertile grounds where vibrant literacy activities take root and sprout. These unpredictable encounters, I argue, set into motion dynamic semiotic repertoires and writing-related knowledge, strategies, and practices; reciprocally, the mobility of resources, practices, and texts propels encounters across lines of difference and for literacy, social, and professional purposes. Multilingual life becomes with and through such encounters.

3
Turning Toward Thickets of Relationships

Translation as Rhetorical Practice

Morgan's effort to write the river into meaning has surfaced multiple layers of translation involving negotiation of nuanced meanings across language, dialectal, and rhetorical conventions. The complexity of such translation labor mirrors findings from interdisciplinary streams of research into multilingual writing, which has unraveled the role translation plays in meaning making. In second-language writing, researchers have extended a long tradition of analyzing translation as a venue for multilingual writers to practice cross linguistic problem solving, develop metalinguistic knowledge, enhance cohesion and coherence, develop vocabulary and syntactic complexity, and achieve clarity and depth of ideas (Cohen & Brooks-Carson, 2002; Cumming, 1990; Kobayashi & Rinnert, 2013; Murphy & de Larios, 2010; Qi, 1998). More recently, scholars have pointed to the limitations of such research tradition, which has relied on single-task-per-condition design and analysis of students' writing products in response to timed writing tasks, for not fully exploring the complexity of naturally occurring translation practices closely mirroring writing tasks performed in university writing classrooms. Calling for attention to translation as recursively and cyclically organized through

https://doi.org/10.7330/9781646427628.c003

layered reading, writing, and revision activities, scholars have called for research into how multilingual writers traverse highly developed and evolved symbolic systems to express and negotiate meaning within and through form (Atkinson & Tardy, 2018, pp. 87–88) and to reveal "stories about how, why, and what [multilingual writers] write and what they know and believe about their writing" (Casanave, 2005).

Moreover, a broader conceptual turn toward translanguaging (Li, 2018) and translingualism (Horner et al., 2011) in rhetoric and composition, applied linguistics, and literacy research has recognized language as inherently dynamic, evolving, and varied historical codifications, while directing our attention to fluid and innovative ways language users draw on a holistic communicative repertoire to make sense/meaning of the world across linguistic, cultural, and geographical borders. A translingual, practice-based view of language shifts our attention away from models that assess language knowledge based on an idealized monolingual user, and instead focuses on the holistic rhetorical repertoire of the social individual, often noting the agentive ways in which multilinguals engage in linguistic innovations when working through language ambiguities for strategic gains (Canagarajah, 2011; Genoz & Gorter, 2011; Lorimer Leonard, 2013).

This conceptual turn has engendered increasing interest in translation as a lens to capture, study, and support observable acts of multilingual writing. Recent theorizations of translation critique a mechanical view for reducing translation as attempts to identify semantic equivalents in meaning and form between discrete, bounded, and structurally comparable languages. Such a view has manifested in researchers' attention to translation as the effort "to equate expressions in their two languages," which requires "a priori mental equation of semantic, lexical, syntactic, and pragmatic categories across languages" (Cumming, 1990, pp. 494–496). A mechanical view reduces the intense physical, intellectual, and emotional labor of performing translation by theorizing it as a process of trading "cross-linguistic equivalents" between distinct language systems that are assumed to share a similar linguistic foundation. Such a view therefore attributes difficulties of translation to various forms of deficit in multilingual writers' proficiency, knowledge, and strategies, thereby contributing to its reductive and pejorative role in traditional language teaching (Pennycook, 2008; Horner & Tetreault, 2016).

A renewed view of translation posits that all language acts involve rewriting, negotiation, and translation. Translation, a process marked by ongoing negotiation of differences and boundary crossing, is a special form of writing that embodies core qualities true to all writing, which is always implicated within the "traffic in meaning, a passing to and fro of ideas, concepts, symbols, discourses" (Pennycook, 2008, p. 34). From this perspective, translation is a core process of multilingual (and monolingual) writing, and the emerging products of working with, through, and against internally diverse, interpenetrating, and fluid languages (Ayash, 2019). As Laura Gonzales (2018) argues, translation is not "a task that happens only after content is created or developed in one language, . . . but is an iterative activity that happens constantly within specific cultures and communities" (p. 57). Rather than bridging similarities, translation produces differences, which are an inevitable outcome of populating historical meanings and discursive conventions with new intentions.

The intellectual, physical, and emotional labor involved in translation has been compellingly illustrated in empirical studies of translation practices and pedagogical ways to leverage them. Scholars have named translation as an important part of bilingual children's linguistic repertoire implicated with intense legal, social, and emotional consequences (Orellana & Reynolds, 2008) and documented migrants' use of linguistic, cultural, and social translations to not only enter communities but disrupt social relations (Inghilleri, 2017). Laura Gonzales (2018), in her research on professional and everyday performance of translation, has revealed the complex ways in which professional translators navigate digital material tools within their specific communities, seek feedback, and adjust their practices to meet the constantly evolving ways through languages represent the realities, values, and ideologies of the cultural, rhetorical contexts. Conceptualized as culturally situated and constantly shifting rhetorical practices, translation is never a "one and done" event but involves iterative and cyclical instances of negotiation and localization distributed across individuals, languages, and platforms (pp. 59–60). Such work entails creative intellectual work as translators manipulate and coordinate multiple modes, digital platforms, and digital algorithms within their knowledge of the multiple languages, cultural logics, and values and needs of their communities.

As illustrated by such research, translation is achieved through dynamic, cyclical, creative, and rhetorical practices, which entail great labor that is often shared, negotiated, and collaboratively worked through in response to competing norms, values, and practices of cultural communities. Given the high stakes of a writer's ability to deploy accurate and effective translation to navigate bureaucratic, legal, and social structures of migration; to access cultural linguistic resources; and to manage social encounters across differences, it is even more important to examine how multilingual writers draw on an extended network of semiotic resources, relationships, and digital and materials tools to perform translation labor. And yet translation is often so naturalized that it becomes invisible to those who use and benefit from it, therefore creating pedagogical imperatives to surface and leverage the vast repertoires of linguistic skills and strategies entailed in translation (Martínez et al., 2008). Across grade levels, teacher researchers have shown the pedagogical benefits of sustained discussion, performance, and reflection of translation tasks in developing students' understanding of languages as linguistic, cultural, and rhetorical structures (Kiernan et al., 2016); expanding students' linguistic repertoires and metalinguistic and metacognitive awareness (Jiménez et al., 2015); providing opportunities to practice shifting voices for different audiences (Martínez, et al., 2008); and recognizing the value of translation skills in academic writing (Orellana & Reynolds, 2008). Together, such research has highlighted the creative and rhetorical nature of translation—speakers configure a repertoire of linguistic and semiotic resources to produce texts-in-becoming, constantly shifting their voices, grammatical choices, registers, and vocabulary in light of communicative contexts, audiences, and purposes.

In this chapter, I explore how analytical attention to thickets of relationship could enrich our understanding of the emotional, intellectual, and physical labor of translation and help unravel the nuanced purposes of translation through which multilingual writers in Morgan's literacy network continued to mobilize the river and articulate its meaning during an extended drafting, reviewing, and revision process. I continue to trace how the river, with its radical possibilities, actively participated in the becoming of Morgan's multilingual writing, and I examine how each textual, linguistic, and affective passing of the river from one writer, language, draft, and digital platform to another, is fraught with opportunities for innovation as well as power struggle.

A close analysis of the continuous entanglement of the river, Morgan, and a transnational network of literacy brokers she drew into her multilingual writing process provides compelling evidence of how boundaries and binaries that arbitrarily separate nature and culture, writers and brokers, and English and Chinese are constantly redrawn. The meaning of the river as well as Morgan's relationship with it are subject to open negotiation through collaborative efforts to manage cross-language relations, develop affinities, and retool semiotic repertoires. I analyze their entanglement by exploring how the river—teeming with symbols and potentials that affectively and imaginatively moved Morgan—continued to gain layers of reflective and affective meaning through rhetorical translation practices (Gonzales, 2018; Wang, 2020) performed by Morgan and the literacy others entangled with her. The imaginary and textual passing of the river from one draft, person, and language to another entailed cyclical, sustained translingual negotiation. Detailing her translation of the word "murmur" as unfolding through an emergent assemblage of digital tools, semiotic repertoires, and writing-related strategies across language and rhetorical traditions, I observe entanglement as the medium and outcome of complex negotiation of relationships broadly construed, including Morgan's evolving relationship with the river, cross-language relations between Chinese and English, competing relationships between rhetorical traditions, and various personal and professional relationships she maintained with literacy brokers in her transnational network.

Translating the River Into an Intimate Friend

After her draft was completed, Morgan carefully orchestrated a sequence of self-sponsored review and revision to make sense of her embodied and imaginary engagement with the river. The analysis I present in this chapter drew from data I gathered during one informal observation of Morgan's drafting session, which took shape primarily through Morgan's translation of a "Chinese draft in [her] head" into English. During a 45-minute drafting session in a campus dining hall, we both ate lunch, worked on our writing projects, and spent time chatting and discussing our writing processes. This was Morgan's first effort to formulate her ideas in English, a process filled with pauses as she used digital tools to translate from Chinese into English. The sentence below, containing vivid description, required extensive translation labor.

> Besides the ebullient cheers of "Go green, go white" and the murmur of rushing Red Cedar River, actually, these exaggerated exclamations lingered in my freshmen year.

The sentence was organized with a carefully constructed parallel structure, which depicted two ambient sounds that emblematize Morgan's adventures on the university campus as a natural and cultural space. These emblematic sounds contrasted with the critical voices of her peers as an important part of an otherwise exciting first-year semester. The overall insight was communicated through her use of three auditory details—"exaggerated remarks," "ebullient cheers," and "murmur of the rushing Red Cedar River." Morgan's deployment of these rhetorical devices reflected her ongoing effort to grapple with genres across linguistic and rhetorical differences. But her effort to mobilize such rhetorical strategies across languages presented significant challenges, specifically in terms of identifying words with precise meanings, appropriate connotations, and grammatical properties. She explained:

> I had to pause frequently to look up appropriate [translations of] words and phrases. It took me a long time to find the translation for 潺潺流水 (*chan chan liu shui*, translated as a bubbling noise of a running stream). The words they gave me from my search sounded awkward. It was a four-character idiom. Obviously, there was no easy way to translate an idiom, unlike when you translate simple words like "apple" or "banana." Baidu translation gave me words like "gurgling water," "purl," and "the murmuring of flowing water." But translation was creating more problems than solving them. I had to Google "gurgling" and "purl." Did you know "gurgling" was the noise your stomach makes? I was like, "This won't work!" I had no way of knowing what kind of noise "purl" was. "Murmur" seemed to be the only possibility. I back-translated "murmur," and the Chinese translation was 喃喃细语 (*nan nan xi yu*, translated into a low whisper). That's great. Even better than 潺潺流水 (*chan chan liu shui*, translating as the bubbling noise of a running stream). It is like the river listens to me and speaks to me like a friend. That was a pleasant surprise. Seeing the "ing" words like "gurgling" and "murmuring," I could hear my high school English teacher yelling, "Gerund, gerund is a noun; participle, participle is an adjective!" The nightmare of English grammar. As you can imagine, it takes me at least five minutes to research each word. I didn't get much done even though I worked on my essay from four to nine yesterday.

Using Baidu translation (the Chinese equivalent of Google Translate), Morgan worked assiduously to identify translation alternatives, which presented many options and even more challenges. Throughout her drafting session, Morgan followed the same process for translation: using Baidu translation to identify a pool of semantic possibilities, studying exemplary usage sentences to determine best options, surveying thesaurus to assess all available synonyms, and finalizing her choice based on her evolving theories about writing. A full appreciation of words that denote specific sounds, however, required embodied experiences and contextualized usage examples. Having little access to either, she assessed such options through careful study of usage sentences and back-translating them into Chinese. Therefore, the back translation provided a linguistic option that conveyed a subtle, emotional subtext she herself had not considered but seemed plausible. Such a connotation encapsulated the intimate partnership that she had forged with the campus river.

In addition to orchestrating parallelism at the semantic level, Morgan focused specifically on adjusting the part of speech of "murmur" (used as a gerund in the usage sentence "murmuring of flowing water") to its original noun form. This move allowed her to deliver syntactic parallelism between "murmur," "cheers," and "exclamations." In particular, she recalled "nightmarish" grammatical lessons in high school, when her English teacher invented a formula to help students distinguish between different verbal structures, specifically gerund and participle. Instruction of the "ing" verbal is a focal area of grammatical instruction in traditional English teaching in Chinese schools and typically unfolds through exemplification of usage sentences, multiple-choice problems that check students' understanding, and fill-in-the-blank exercises that assess students' ability to use appropriate verbal forms. Morgan noted she often had trouble distinguishing participle adjectives and gerund nouns, which led to problems in her writing. Morgan's difficulty with "ing" verbal is a site translingual negotiation. Managing inflection of verbs to give them new grammatical properties is a feature absent in Chinese, Morgan's home language. The Chinese equivalent of "murmur" can be used as a noun and a verb. The word itself does not undergo inflection changes, in contrast to English, where verbs undergo tense and plurality inflections in accordance with various syntactic constraints. Furthermore, morphological changes to the verb by adding the "ing" inflection to give it syntactic flexibility as a noun or an adjective was a linguistic phenomenon absent in her home language. Morgan noted that she often had trouble identifying the grammatical property of "ing" verbal, as it was its placement in relationship to other syntactic components that determined its part of speech. Jokingly characterizing her high school English teacher drilling on "participle as adjective" versus "gerund as noun" as nightmarish trauma, Morgan nonetheless mobilized linguistic knowledge imparted through such drilling to help her make her decision. Her attention to the parts of speech of "murmuring" versus "murmur" therefore pointed to her ability to position translation as a site of inquiry, where her linguistic knowledge and metalinguistic awareness were reconciled with creative and expressive intentions (Kiernan et al., 2016; Jiménez et al., 2015).

In addition to juggling translingual differences, Morgan's choice of "murmur" over other translation alternatives also surfaced her ability to juggle rhetorical differences between the Western narrative genre and classical Chinese rhetorical styles. The immediate resonance she discovered with "murmur" was powerfully mediated by her literacy trajectory as an avid reader and aspiring writer in classical Chinese essays and poetry. Her choice of murmur, which personified the river, allowed her to articulate subtle feelings of intimacy. Undergirding this choice was her literary sensitivity, which was cultivated through guided literary analysis of classical Chinese poetry. As she explained,

> Western authors are good, but they are not as sophisticated as classical Chinese writers. You know the rhetorical strategy of 寓情于景，情景交融 (yu qing yu jing, qing jing jiao rong, translated to embody emotions in scenery; fuse emotions with scenery)? Say you were a governmental official in the Tang dynasty and you were demoted for speaking your mind to the emperor; you were traveling to your new post in a poor, remote province. Disappointment and sorrow were eating you alive inside, but you couldn't openly criticize the emperor by calling him stupid; that is if you wanted to keep your head. You found yourself on the edge of a precipice, standing next to a lone pine tree. You put your feelings into the pine tree, with the howling wind and the rushing rain attacking it resembling the unjust treatment you received. You then put the pine tree into you by saying something like, "This lonely pine tree manages to stand tall, withstanding the wind in noble spirit." The pine tree becomes you. You speak through it.

Morgan's decision to personify the river through her use of "murmur" gave her an opportunity to practice a Chinese rhetorical strategy called 寓情于景，情景交融 (yu qing yu jing, qing jing jiao rong, or embody emotions in scenery; fuse emotions with scenery). As she suggested, the rhetorical strategy was taught in high school language arts classes through guided literary analysis of Chinese classical poetry. Morgan recalled a passionate lecture led by her favorite Chinese literature teacher on the verses of Du Fu, a renowned classical poet, who wrote about the evils of war by personifying flowers as shedding tears of sorrow (morning dew on petals) and mourning the destruction to homes. Having taken such lessons to heart, Morgan personified the river to express her feelings of intimacy and optimism. She compared her efforts to those enacted by classical authors, who would rather express their admiration of a lone pine tree standing on the edge of a precipice than discuss their own frustrated political aspirations.

What surfaces here is Morgan's sophisticated understanding of rhetorical styles and strategies as culturally developed and stabilized through rhetorical devices, literary tropes, and references to canonical texts, knowledge of which were expected of sophisticated writers like her. She recognized these rhetorical styles as dynamic and mobile structures that could be fused with other strategies in response to new rhetorical exigencies. On the one hand, Morgan relied on literary devices introduced in her FYW writing class and guided reading of Western authors to navigate the rhetorical exigency of the Memoir, a high-stakes writing assignment. Her efforts to manage parallelism through rhetorical, cyclical translation was an example of her seeking alignment with genre conventions entailed in writing instructions offered. On the other hand, she mobilized literary sensibility and rhetorical strategies honed through studies of classical Chinese to elevate her writing and to achieve what she considered a more sophisticated and subtle style. The fusion of the two rhetorical styles was a creative and risky endeavor. As I have observed elsewhere, Morgan's participation in high-stakes writing contests had helped her develop a disposition that embraced curiosity and risk-taking, as she strategically departed from platitude and habitually experimented with innovative ways of enacting, parodying, and extending conventional tropes (Wang, 2020). Experiences with several regional writing contests taught Morgan the importance of demonstrating her knowledge of and skills to extend canonical tropes in new and exciting ways. Her effort to personify the river was but one such move to retool a tested rhetorical strategy within the parameters of genre conventions that she expected her audience to navigate with ease.

A fine-grained analysis of Morgan's translation practices complicates one's interpretation of the sentence. The auditory details (murmur, cheers, voices of gossiping peers) should not be interpreted simply as efforts to fulfill Western genre expectations; they evoke a rhetorical tradition that allowed Morgan to articulate aspirations, feelings, and desires that were difficult to describe otherwise. It also brought Morgan's embodied history with the river into the writing along with vivid memories of encountering and dwelling with the river and feelings of thrill and intimacy, which the use of "murmur" helped to articulate. Each sound embodied an aspect of her emotional experience during her first year. The critical voices of her peers echoed her self-doubt when she received unsatisfying test scores; school cheers encapsulated the excitement of first encounters with social events on campus; the bubbling stream embodied moments of Morgan experiencing the pleasure of simply being *with* the river, which was a synergetic, listening friend who provided opportunities for healing and reflection. Working in concert, these auditory details helped Morgan project an overall optimistic outlook on her first-year experience. In her own words, the critical voices were but a small interlude that briefly disrupted the main theme of her first-year experience—working hard to achieve her goals and embracing an exciting life filled with new adventures and challenges.

Morgan's practice provides a telling example of translation as rhetorical acts. The translation of the Chinese idiom not only moved her in closer approximation of genre expectations but also provided rich opportunities for continuous discovery and invention of meaning. Translation is "not merely a distinct form of writing" or a "neutral bridge . . . connecting discrete, stable, internally uniform [languages], but a feature and outcome of all writing—a feature that entails difficulty and friction—labor—and that produces rather than bridges or erases difference" (Horner & Tetreault, 2016, p. 14). Morgan's translation practices unfolded in a transformative entanglement of languages and writing-related theories and knowledge that were fused, reconfigured, and retooled to maximize the writer's ability to craft compelling memories and affects with the river, an important natural other, into meaning. Such entanglements continued to shift and evolve, opening up new problem spaces, presenting viable solutions, and enabling unexpected connections. Although drafting in Chinese provided a space to assemble and formulate ideas, translation was an equally important inventive space, as translation and back-translation of "murmur" brought her writing in resonance with powerful memories of and affective meanings associated with the river. Observation of Morgan's embodied, fluid practice challenges a mechanical view of translation as a one-way movement of meaning from one language to another, as in Morgan's observation of translation as commonly misrepresented as the simple task of finding a semantic equivalent of the word "apple" in another language. It makes visible the extraordinary cognitive (identifying, assessing, and verifying linguistic choices), emotional (working through feelings of intimacy, uncertainty, and reassurance), and physical (managing multiple streams of affects, memories, norms, and information across times and spaces) labor, which makes it necessary for ongoing retooling and repurposing of writing-related knowledge in light of new rhetorical exigencies. Successful translation is only possible with an attitude of open inquiry into language differences, which brings into convergence an evolving repertoire of linguistic, metalinguistic, and rhetorical knowledge.

However, such a writer-centered reading loses sight of the messy, indeterminate, and contingent ways of multilingual writing. Morgan's translation allowed her to explore what Hass and Witte (2004) theorize as being experientially derived, material, and embodied knowledge of "the world of the senses, the world of affect, and the world beneath words" (p. 416). From an entanglement perspective, translation was a discursive practice that enacted an agential "cut," which produced/blurred boundaries and defined/dismantled properties (Barad, 2007). That is, the intra-action of memories, visceral feelings, words translated across languages and dialects, and literary and rhetorical sensitivity and knowledge differentially foregrounded and backgrounded certain semantic and expressive potentials of the river. Boundaries between embodied experiences and semiotic configuring became blurry. Had the river always felt like an intimate friend who "murmured" back words of comfort? Could it be that the surprising discovery of "murmur" through translation triggered memories of a particular bodily sensation or affect, thereby prompting the writer to remember and see the river in a certain way? The river continued to become through the dynamic interplay of memories, feelings, and words to describe and name it; simultaneously, semiotic configuring of the river across language and rhetorical differences created new possibilities to feel and experience the river. Morgan's semiotic configuring of the river into partially determinate meaning, an intimate friend who listened and offered comfort, emerged through indeterminate translingual work. Such work was not the outcome of pure writerly invention but stayed emergent through constant weighing of the expressive potential of English and Chinese words for naming visceral, affective meanings that remained treacherously elusive and creatively generative.

The more I think about the river as an important part of Morgan's social and literacy landscape, the more difficult it becomes to take an anthropocentric stance that centers the writer as the self-contained, distanced knower who approaches the river from above or outside. I am compelled to echo Karen Barad's postulation that humans do not simply "assemble different apparatuses for satisfying particular knowledge projects" but rather are "themselves specific parts of the world's ongoing reconfiguring" (2007, p. 341). That is, the river is not a passive material entity, its beauty waiting to be discovered by an otherwise preoccupied student, its materiality ready to be imprinted with cultural and historical significance, its purposes open to human design and exploitation. Rather, the river, living, breathing, and transforming, plays an active and generative role in its ongoing materialization in relation to Morgan's discursive and material practices orchestrated through her efforts to know and relate to it. Morgan's multilingual performance of the river encodes a form of knowing about the geography, cultural and historical traditions, and disciplinary knowledge-making practices that spatialize the river materially and imaginatively. Attention to Morgan's multilingual writing in entanglement makes it clear that she is part of the material configuration of the world in becoming, her struggles to name, articulate, and imagine all being part of its emergent process.

Translating the River Across Coordinated Life Worlds

The river continued to entangle with Morgan's multilingual writing as she shared her draft within a transnational network of literacy others. Writing and revising the Memoir assignment gave Morgan the opportunity to discover and articulate the emotional, imaginative, and expressive potential of the river. Her revision of the essay is nothing short of a remarkable achievement. Within the short time frame of three weeks, Morgan managed to produce eleven drafts and multiple outlines, which were variously shaped by three writing center consultations, one teacher conference, three peer reviews and a short conversation with one of her reviewers, nine digitally mediated peer-review sessions with two friends (Jessie and Ryan) in variant lengths (three minutes to one hour), one three-hour-long revision/hang-out session with a friendly neighbor (Nicole), and four observation meetings with me. It was in this entanglement of persons, texts, and writing technologies that these multilingual writers mobilized intersecting assemblages of semiotic resources, writing-related knowledge, and literacy identities to invent and transform the river across language and cultural differences.

Three literacy others, Ryan, Jessie, and Nicole, actively participated in Morgan's self-sponsored drafting and revision practices. At the time of my research, Jessie (Chinese and English bilingual), was Morgan's high school best friend and a rising sophomore attending an elite private university in the United Kingdom. Jessie was known for her expertise with English, which was honed through years of expensive, private tutorials with native speakers of English. Having attended the university a year earlier, Jessie was better socialized into the academic discourses of the university and used such knowledge to broker Morgan's transition. Jessie and Morgan chatted daily about their romantic interests, vacation plans, and academic affairs. Morgan referred to Jessie as her 闺蜜 (*gui mi*, best [female] friend) with whom she felt comfortable exposing her fragility in moments of crisis.

Ryan (Chinese and English bilingual) was a junior attending an elite Chinese university and planning to pursue a juris doctor degree in the United States. Morgan met Ryan through a mutual friend and was impressed by Ryan's charisma, professional aspirations, language expertise (Ryan achieved 98th percentile on the Graduate Record Examinations), and literacy achievement (Ryan had published a collection of humorous essays via an influential social media platform). While Ryan approached Morgan for her insights on US university life, Morgan consulted Ryan on issues regarding writing and career development.

Nicole (monolingual English speaker) was a rising senior who attended the same university and lived in the same apartment building as Morgan. After receiving Nicole's help with Internet installation upon arrival, Morgan reciprocated with frequent visits and small presents. Their friendship was strengthened when Morgan took Ryan's cultural inquiries to Nicole, which intensified their exchange and led to Morgan's discovery of Nicole's status as an honors student, a young professional who had completed several internships, and a strong writer (having scored 4.0 in the honors FYW class). Morgan carefully cultivated her friendship with Nicole, which led Nicole to provide her with writing assistance.

While my analysis in the previous section reveals how determinate meaning is articulated through encounters across life forms, languages, and rhetorical styles, it is important to note that such meanings remain indeterminate and open-ended when they play out against competing expectations for delivering ideas, imageries, or feelings with clarity and precision. In this section, I further illustrate how transnationally dispersed negotiation around Morgan's translation of 潺潺流水 into "murmur" offers opportunities to explore how shifting entanglements enact an "agential cut that produces determinate boundaries and properties of 'entities' within phenomena" (Barad, 2007, p. 148). That is, multilingual writing in entanglement involves specific material configurations that constantly redraw boundaries, redefine properties, and remake meanings. Each passing of the word from one person, language, and document to another enacts a new material cut and gains differential meanings. Freshly drawn boundaries could be easily redrawn; new properties could become salient. Tracing the collaborative translation of "murmur" within a transnational network of literacy sponsors reveals

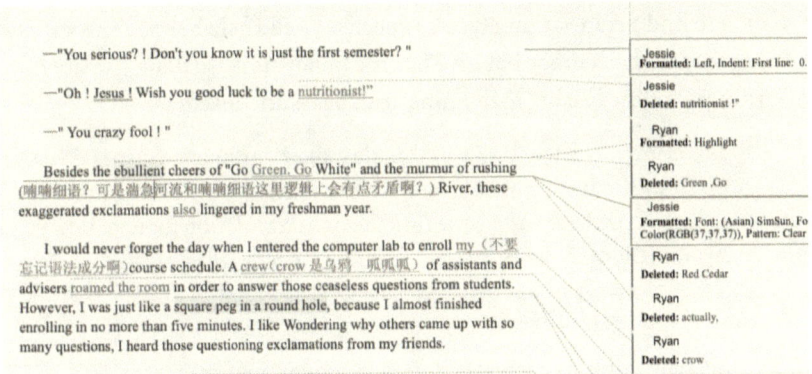

FIGURE 3.1. Peer Review Annotations (Jessie and Ryan)

perspectival, open articulations of the world-in-becoming.

After completing her first draft, Morgan solicited peer review from Ryan and Jessie. In the two days that followed, the three writers wove together an assemblage of intertextually connected documents riddled with in-text annotations, side comments, and edits, which were followed by a series of conversations via WeChat voice memos and voice calls.

Figure 3.1 shows Morgan's draft with comments and edits generated through two spatially and temporally dispersed but intertextually connected peer reviews. Multiple languages, comments, and edits are visibly entangled in the text; writing/editing practices and voices of different authors converged and intersected. Ryan completed his review in the morning of September 8, when he used in-text Chinese comments to raise questions, explain his reasoning, and use jokes to ease his criticism or correction. For instance, he corrected a spelling error by changing "crow" to "crew" and provided an in-text joke ("crow is [the bird], squawk squawk") to help Morgan recognize and respond positively to what she herself called a "stupid error." In addition to underlining "murmur" in the text, Ryan inserted a Chinese comment, alerting Morgan to the lack of consistency between the imagery evoked and the idiom used for descriptive purposes—"An intimate whisper? But the rushing river and intimate whisper logically contradict each other?" Here, Ryan supplied his interpretation of Morgan's use of "murmur" by back-translating it into 喃喃细语 (nan nan xi yu, intimate whisper). Then Ryan focused on what he perceived to be an inherent logical inconsistency—the "rushing river" produces roaring noises that embody speed and force, whereas "an intimate whisper" is evocative of a gentle, meandering stream. Morgan drew Ryan into a brief conversation when she made a specific request for Ryan to find a translation. Ryan's expertise would help her not only articulate her idea with accuracy but give her the opportunity to demonstrate how "charming Chinese can be" to her American peers and teachers.

> MORGAN: How did you know I was thinking about "intimate whisper?" You are a living dictionary! What I had in mind is actually "bubbling, flowing water." You have to help me find the right translation for it, to how charming Chinese can be. 你怎么看出来我想说的是喃喃细语？你真的是个活字典啊！我其实本来想的是潺潺流水，但是我翻不出来。你一定要把潺潺流水帮我写出来呀，显示中文的魅力.
>
> RYAN: I don't think it's necessary. It is more important to express your ideas as simple and clear as you possibly can, just so that the Americans get it. To me, things like feelings and emotions, [you don't want to] push it too far. Unless it's in a certain rhetorical situation that calls for exaggerated representation of feelings, you then need embellishments and flourishes. 其实我觉得也没有必要，把你想要表达的意思简单明了地表达出来让美国人能看懂我觉得更重要。这种情绪的东西我感觉是要点到而止，除非是特定的语言环境里，需要你渲染气氛，你才需要华丽的词藻.

These exchanges provide a telling example of iterative, cyclical management of distributed translation as sites of translingual negotiation. Ryan noted instances of logical inconsistency. Indeed, attention to logical connections marked a significant area of Ryan's expertise, as he highlighted six similar concerns throughout the draft. Morgan attributed such expertise to Ryan's extensive undergraduate training in writing in the sciences and his recent success in taking the LSAT (Law School Admission Test), which focused on assessing analytical and logical reasoning. Morgan recognized Ryan's back-translation of "murmur" into "intimate whisper" for partially capturing the affective meaning she intended to express. Complimenting Ryan's grasp of English vocabulary with her comment that Ryan was a "living dictionary," Morgan reiterated her request for translation help. Morgan noted that one area of Ryan's strength as a writer and a reviewer lay in his sophisticated understanding of nuances in meaning, which manifested in seven instances of Ryan suggesting alternative word choices and inviting her to unpack her reasoning, which moved her toward productive consideration of connotations or subtexts. The semantic nuances that Ryan and Morgan worked collaboratively to surface often existed at the interplay of historical meanings, cultural subtexts, and local exigencies. Such nuances were often lost in translation because of the lack of fundamental similarities between the languages—while seemingly similar semantic equivalents might exist in both languages, the imagery and connotations each embodied were rarely the same.

Ryan and Morgan's WeChat conversation was particularly productive because it enabled the back-and-forth traffic of meaning through dynamic negotiation of multiple options (e.g., Chinese synonyms, English alternatives), with connotations of each weighted against Morgan's intention. Morgan admitted to the challenge of such work, noting that the more deeply she delved into such nuances the more she came to recognize that her linguistic choices were rooted in cultural and experiential knowledge that her audience might not share—an issue that can potentially jeopardize the clarity of her writing. Ryan's comment furthered Morgan's ongoing effort to juggle nuanced literal meanings, feelings, connotations, and imagery embodied by idioms and words within and across languages, and the two students become increasingly aware that the interpretation of such words often relies on a shared understanding of rhetorical traditions and conceptual and experiential knowledge cultivated through being in a culture.

Moreover, Morgan considered translation specifically and her writing generally as a venue to perform linguistic pride, which assumed particular importance in the context of her FYW class, when she was visibly the ethnic and linguistic minority. Her need to outshine her American peers manifested in the request she put forward here and was echoed in her evaluation of Western authors' styles as being less sophisticated. Ryan, however, demonstrated rhetorical dexterity as he encouraged Morgan to adapt to the needs and expectations of her American audience, noting that clarity should be prioritized over rhetorical flourishes. Such sustained negotiation across differences allowed these writers to not only recognize nuances but also connect local issues of word choice to broader concerns of rhetorical situations.

Following Ryan's peer review, Morgan forwarded the document with Ryan's edits to Jessie through WeChat File Share, which Jessie opened 12 hours later to add her comments. "Murmur" did not surface as an area of inquiry for Jessie, who highlighted two words/phrases, "ebullient" and "a square peg in a round hole" to indicate concerns for word choice. These highlights became an invitation for further conversation. Instead of providing in-text explanations, Jessie sent a WeChat text message along with her edited draft to invite Morgan's inquiry. Taking up the invitation, Morgan drew Jessie into a digitally mediated, hour-long revision session, when she accepted edits by checking off track-change comments and sought clarification for problematic ones. To help Jessie navigate the document, Morgan shared screenshots of the document using her phone, noting comments she wanted to address. "Murmur" surfaced during this conversation, compelling Morgan's effort to unpack its meaning and therefore further enhancing her emotional bond with Jessie. Jessie engaged Morgan in the short exchange below.

> JESSIE: Murmur sounds a bit odd here? [I have] never heard anyone using it to describe a river? (Murmur好怪吗这里？从来没有听过人用这个词形容河水呀？)
>
> MORGAN: It's not like that. I am trying to say the river is like you, my dear, my *gui mi* [translated as the best female friend of an unmarried girl]. [It's] like the river is a trusted listener. (不是吗，我就是想说小河就像你啊亲，闺蜜啊。就好像说河是值得信任的倾诉对象。)
>
> JESSIE: [It's] so mushy! I don't think the Americans would get it.... Such a high-end rhetorical strategy, sarcastic laugh. (好肉麻哦，我觉得老美会看不懂。。。高端修辞呵呵呵。)

This exchange made visible the fact that material and embodied experiences that informed Morgan's linguistic choice became increasingly clarified as the text continued to move. The friction between authorial intention and reader interpretation, surfacing in Ryan's invitation for reconsideration, began to thicken. To Morgan, the sound of the flowing water evoked feelings of comfort and relaxation and compared the relationship she shared with the river with her friendship with Jessie. She used 闺蜜 (*gui mi*, translated into best female friend of an unmarried girl), to refer to Jessie and the river, both being trustworthy confidantes; she felt comfortable exposing her fragility to them in moments of crisis. Whereas Ryan's observation pointed to the importance of logical reasoning, Morgan's choice was motivated by the need to establish emotional affinity between her, her readers, and important actors (friends, the river) in her literate life. Although her use of an endearment that personified the river as a close friend led to Jessie's tease of her being "mushy," this exchange created a space for Morgan to surface her embodied experiences as an asset for writing, which allowed her to address the issue underlying Ryan's observation-writing to appeal to emotions versus reason. Indeed, the short exchange positioned Jessie as a reader and a friend, with emotional affinity between the two as an important rhetorical resource to be leveraged to achieve comprehension and empathy. Logical reasoning comes secondary to the production of affinity and intimacy.

The analysis illuminates how multilingual writing emerged through messy entanglements of "cultural, rhetorical, and technical skills [developed] through lived experiences" to transform meaning across persons and languages in powerful and intersecting ways (Gonzales, 2018, p. 11). Instead of seeing multilingual writing as materialization of an individual writer's authorial intention, I would rather see multilingual writing as collaborative discovery and invention of meaning across perspectives, voices, and rhetorical traditions. Key features of such "collaborative survival" (Tsing, 2015) are relationships materializing through and with coordination, transformative encounters, and indeterminate, open-ended inquiry and negotiation. Morgan's self-sponsored peer-review sessions brought into entanglement intertextual associations that allowed writers to speak with and against each other. Morgan's relationships with Jessie and Ryan were quite resemblant of Tsing's discussion of symbiotic relationships as "outsourcing," when trees outsource their need for nutritious minerals to fungi and fungi conversely outsource their need for lipids and sugars to trees (2015, p. 144). Whereas Morgan's request for help from Ryan and Jessie was certainly dependent on her friends' expertise and willingness to invest their time, she fully reciprocated such favors by providing Ryan with tales of her college experiences and a taste of academic writing expected at US institutions of higher education. With Jessie, review sessions were often mixed into other aspects of their friendship. Discussion of writing was always mixed with tales of romantic encounters, venting about the frustrations of living in a new culture, lessons learned about writing and literacy, gossip about a shared friend, and planning for vacation together. Multilingual writing was but one way of being in multilingual worlds.

The essay was materially transformed through relationships, where idiosyncratic approaches to reading, annotating, and reviewing materialized through simultaneously habitual and contingent assemblage of writing technologies and digital tools. Layers of annotations and edits built up on the page, leaving visible traces of multiple perspectives and voices speaking from unique positions of writing-related narratives, strategies, and dispositions developed across long literacy trajectories. Conversations revolving around a single word were efforts to access, invent, and valuate meaning. But it was not just the text that transformed through relationships. In this recursive process of decision-making, Morgan was given the opportunity to further discover meaning, unpack her reasoning, and reconsider her choices. The interanimating voices affirming, challenging, and questioning each other encouraged Morgan to retool and repurpose writing strategies and to navigate the writing assignment in simultaneously stable and innovative ways (Roozen, 2009a, 2012; Rounsaville, 2014). Such retooling was propelled by uncertainty, as different theories and approaches molded through intersecting learning trajectories occasionally came into conflict. What is important here is the fact that conversations remained open-ended, issues were discussed without being fully resolved, and differential affordances of following one route versus the other were evaluated without being dictated. Indeed, such uncertainty was not fully resolved, as all three students agreed about the need for the critical perspective of a language expert, as in Jessie's suggestion that Morgan check her choice of "murmur" with "the Americans."

These relationships are not simply mediated by digital technologies, they also produce innovative digital tools. Textual comments invited digitally mediated conversations through voice memos or voice calls. Jessie's comments created the need for new associations, which were enabled by new technological configurations—the boundary between Morgan and her cell phone was hardly impermeable. Her creative use of screenshots not only created a plane of conversation with spatially and temporally distanced writing collaborators but also scaffolded her ongoing effort to identify, inquire, and prioritize issues for revision. The spatial-temporal contour of the draft was a haphazard enterprise propelled by an improvised weaving together of daily routines and schedules of everyone involved. When entanglements continue to expand, it becomes increasingly difficult to just follow a singular author/text; it becomes important to trace the passing of meaning along with the contours of personal and professional relationships. As such analysis shows, "interspecies relationships draw evolution back into history because they depend on the contingencies of encounter" (Tsing, 2015, p. 142). In shifting entanglements, these relationships do not form a self-replicating system. Rather, they are always just "things that happen" that could lead to predictable patterns as well as unpredictable outcomes.

Entanglements Could Fail

Thus far, I have observed how cyclical, rhetorical translation evolved through and with relationships, which propel open articulation of multilingual worlds. Shifting entanglements afforded ongoing negotiation across differences as multilingual writers assembled and retooled writing-related knowledge and practices to navigate the intersection of authorial intention and audience expectation. Learning happened through entanglements that continued to redraw the boundaries of natural and social worlds, which created rich opportunities for words, texts, practices, and knowledge to move, connect, and dialogue. In the last section of this chapter, I explore how entanglements might also fail when ideas and drafts were stalled, when connections were broken, when voices were silenced. I do so by following the trajectory of the draft as it was taken up during a self-sponsored peer review with Nicole, instructor-facilitated peer review with three classmates (conducted on Eli Review, a digital review platform), and one teacher conference (paper and pencil).

Whereas comments from Jessie and Ryan made visible differences rooted in rhetorical and personal trajectories, the textual meaning of "murmur," as intended by Morgan, remained mobile and stable. Even though Jessie reluctantly withdrew her complaint after Morgan's explanation, she made her reservation clear by suggesting that Morgan check if "the Americans" would get her "high-end rhetorical strategy." Taking such advice, Morgan specifically asked for Nicole's help with her "Chinglish." This deficit stance, coupled with Nicole's confidence as a writer, led to Nicole taking a strong editorial hand by rewriting and reinterpreting the sentence.

> Snippy remarks were a common part of my freshman year. The echo of their judging voices grew to a decibel that covered the ebullient cheers of "Go Green, Go White" eventually completely drowning out the mighty roar of the rushing Red Cedar.

In contrast to Ryan and Jessie, who focused on lexical search and verification, Nicole was more concerned with enhancing the essay's flow at the sentence level, which was accomplished through complete reconstruction of the sentence: She crossed out chunks of texts, broke up the parallel structure, reorganized the auditory details, and supplied additional transitional strategies. Morgan was in awe of Nicole's change of the word "exaggerated" to "snippy," a word she had never heard of but that "sounded like authentic American English [听起来就很地道的美语]." Responding to Morgan's inquiry, Nicole explained that words like "murmur" were "quaint" and "cute" but might raise questions for an American professor. Feeling reassured, Morgan yielded complete editorial control to Nicole. While the revised sentence demonstrated several features that enhanced overall coherence (transition strategies, participle phrase, and complex sentence structure), such a revision came at the cost of affective meanings and visceral memories. Nicole's management of the syntax structure not only disrupted the carefully crafted parallel structure but also shifted the cultural frame of reference, which recast the river as a familiar cultural trope associated with the university's football team. Instead of positioning the three sounds and their symbolic/affective meanings as equally important dimensions of Morgan's first-year experience, the revision placed emphasis on the critical voices of peers, which were so overwhelming that they drowned out the ebullient cheers and the "mighty roar" of the rushing Red Cedar River. Nicole's revision enacts a different cut of the campus river, configuring it as an important part of the imaginary of the university's football culture. Her use of "mighty roar," directly mirroring the lyrics of the fight song, revealed the river's rich cultural history, particularly through the river's entanglement with the sport of American football, which erupted with thunderous energy and resonance during home games. No longer was the river an intimate female friend who shared secrets and provided support; it was no longer an open articulation of Morgan's multilingual life. The reference of the "mighty roar" reified the dominant, institutional discourse that sought to cultivate coherence through the rally of athletic competitions. The masculinity, embodied by the "mighty roar," now directed the audience's attention to the intensity of Morgan's struggles rather than the ongoing reconciliation of conflicting emotions. More importantly, the "main theme" of Morgan's first-year experience was no longer an overall optimistic outlook but one portraying her as a victim of judging voices. Morgan had lost the river as an intimate friend.

Along with my analysis of two other collaborative translation moments, Nicole's revamping of Morgan's writing showed how multilingual writing was a specific, material articulation of the world, which was always flavored with writerly idiosyncrasy and colored by embodied, rhetorical, and cultural histories. The river could be differentially enacted as masculine or feminine; it could be absorbed into the dominant, institutional narrative, which in this case had subsumed its meaning emerging from Morgan's multilingual ways of being in the world. The contrast between Nicole's revision is particularly revealing of the ways in which culture has been assumed as the driving force of change, when the river is discursively manipulated in alignment with college football to provide an orientation toward competitiveness and excellence ("warriors," "winning," "points [that] keep growing," and opponents as "beaten" and "weakening"). The mighty roar fuels the school spirit. The cultural fit between the campus river and university life, perceived and experienced through the lens of competitive sports (Rah! Rah! Rah!) is so seamless and comfortable that the idiosyncratic, intimately embodied, and emotionally

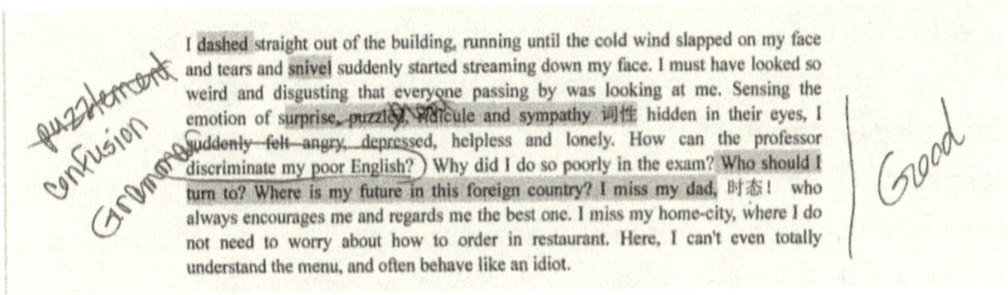

> I dashed straight out of the building, running until the cold wind slapped on my face and tears and snivel suddenly started streaming down my face. I must have looked so weird and disgusting that everyone passing by was looking at me. Sensing the emotion of surprise, puzzled, ridicule and sympathy 词性 hidden in their eyes, I suddenly felt angry, depressed, helpless and lonely. How can the professor discriminate my poor English? Why did I do so poorly in the exam? Who should I turn to? Where is my future in this foreign country? I miss my dad, 时态! who always encourages me and regards me the best one. I miss my home-city, where I do not need to worry about how to order in restaurant. Here, I can't even totally understand the menu, and often behave like an idiot.

(Margin annotations: "puzzlement / confusion", "Grammar", "Good")

FIGURE 3.2. Morgan's Draft With Instructor Comments

tumultuous relationship Morgan forged with the river becomes irrelevant and invisible. Meaning, as seen here, "is not a property of individual words or groups of words but an ongoing performance of the world in its differential dance of intelligibility and unintelligibility" (Barad, 2007, p. 149). Recognizing meaning as performed is important for multilingual writing research because it points to the inherent political nature of such work. Although intelligibility, manifesting in linguistic oddities, grammatical irregularities, and opaque meanings, is the necessary outcome of different ways of knowing and being in the world, it easily slips into unintelligibility when the frame of reference is shifted in service of dominant narratives.

Running parallel to Nicole's review were instructor-facilitated peer reviews and one conference with the teacher. The draft Morgan submitted for teacher conference and peer review retained traces of the rich translingual negotiation that had taken place during self-sponsored peer reviews. While she had made most of the changes by accepting or rejecting suggested changes by Ryan and Jessie, she highlighted major areas of change and attached a short in-text Chinese note containing goals for revision and questions to raise during the teacher conference. For instance, she highlighted a sentence that contained "surprise, puzzled, ridicule, and sympathy" (see Figure 3.2) and attached a sticky note on faulty parallelism, reflective of a condensed version of Jessie's review and a conversation with Ryan. Similarly, she included a note on tense in anticipation of her conversation with her instructor during the 15-minute conference.

Morgan's instructor spent much of the conference time scanning through the document, occasionally asking for clarifications. In response to her inquiry into the faulty parallel and parts of speech issue, the instructor offered the correction of changing "puzzled" to "confusion" without much explanation. Interestingly, the instructor also circled "discriminate my poor English," marking it as a "grammar issue." When Morgan brought the draft to our informal observation meeting, she raised the issue with me. Whereas I was able to explain with relative ease the usage problem with phrasal verbs by explaining grammatical construction of intransitive action verbs "discriminate" and preposition "against" rather than "discriminate," I could not help but wonder if the deeper issue that her instructor wanted to address was her use of a word loaded with ideological riffs unique to the political reality of the United States. I dwell on this detail simply to illustrate the wide range of issues her instructor attended to, which seemed so encompassing that little time was left for specific strategies for addressing any of the issues. Her instructor's notes on the margin included one comment on document formatting (reminding Morgan to use 1-inch margins), one on citation (requesting MLA [Modern Language Association] citation), four on clarification (using question marks and questions, indicating something is "unclear," and asking Morgan to "explain better"), three comments on word choice or grammar (underlining or crossing out words and supplying alternatives), and two with words of praise (using "good," or "well done" to note well-developed passages).

Morgan felt reassured about the strength of her essay in terms of global issues such as the narrative arc and insight, received guidance on specific usage problems, and was given prompts to further develop details and clarify ideas. However, the teacher conference did not materialize as a space to discuss strategies for revision based on goals Morgan had already identified through self-sponsored peer review. While the conversation supported her ongoing process to discover and invent meaning, it did not provide resources for addressing a wide range of language issues that posed unique challenges for multilingual writers. That is, pedagogical practices developed through a monolingual orientation, which did not require pedagogical attention to or provide pedagogical vocabulary to name language irregularities informed by language differences, fell short in responding to the productive mess manifested in Morgan's multilingual draft. Even less attention was given to odd translations, awkward word choices, and unfamiliar writing techniques that retained traces of writing in another rhetorical tradition. As I have discussed in previous sections, productive negotiation with such irregularities required the readers' willingness and capacity to meet the writer halfway.

The challenge of such translingual negotiation was further mirrored in Morgan's experiences in instructor-facilitated peer reviews. Her draft received favorable feedback from her peers on its global structure and effective use of literary devices, with various peers noting that her story was "relatable and about college, a large transition that everyone in our class has recently experienced," her ability to use descriptive details to "allow you to feel exactly how she felt," and the emotional impact of the essay on the reader, "I can only imagine how frustrating it was as an international student struggling to overcome language barrier." At the same time, all three peer reviewers identified addressing grammatical irregularity as a goal for revision, with variations of their suggestions ranging from "refining the language," "making corrections for missing 'a' or 'the,'" and addressing confusing sentences attributed to problems with "word choice and verb conjugation." Morgan read such peer review comments with assiduity and curiosity, bolding and italicizing certain parts of the text as she strategized for revision. Below I provide her annotation of Jnay's comments, adhering to her bolding and italicizing while supplying translation for her notes composed in Chinese:

> **BOX 3.1. EXCERPTS OF MORGAN'S ANNOTATION OF PEER REVIEW FEEDBACK**
>
> JNAY: 1. My first impression of the essay is that it helps me understand how hard it would be to study in a foreign country. Her stories of not being able to understand her professor made me feel very sympathetic for her because language was her barrier, not her ability, and I can only imagine how frustrating that would be. I think its strengths are the impact of the ending and the stories she used. The weaknesses of the essay are just **grammar mistakes and making the sentences flow together**. The paragraphs are split in her own unique way, but I think they flow fine. Her stories are well developed and her ideas are developed as well.
>
> *I especially like the paragraph that started with, "I dashed* (羞羞哒 *bashfully) straight out . . ."* because her progression through her feelings in that moment allow you to feel exactly how she felt. **You asked about American phrases at the end of your essay. I tried to help you out with the comments on the side** (没有找到? couldn't find them?) **by giving you ideas to make your sentences flow better.**

Morgan's annotation of Jnay's comments (see Box 3.1) was indicative of her investment in peer feedback. Despite her efforts to highlight suggestions from her peers' feedback to identify patterns of issues and bolding comments to set priorities for revision, she struggled to navigate these comments. First, the structured peer review directed students to focus on global issues, which her reviewers noted as an area of strength. Conversely, while all three reviewers highlighted grammar as an issue that hindered comprehension, they used "grammar" as an umbrella term to discuss a wide range of language irregularities with roots in semantic, syntactic, cultural, and rhetorical differences.

Although the concern for language irregularities was unanimous, they were operationalized at variant scales. One student's recommendation focused on specific issues of word choice and verb conjugation (tense) that echoed concerns emerging from self-sponsored reviews. Jnay, as seen here, used the umbrella term "language flow" to address two issues: awkward sentence structures and the need to use authentic "American phrases." Another student commented on specific examples of missing articles. While all three peer reviewers suggested that Morgan focus her revision on refining the language, none was able to offer concrete strategies for doing so, partially because of their lack of vocabulary to name issues ranging from odd translations, awkward sentence structure, lack of coherence, and various usage problems in connection to parts of speech, article placement, and punctuation. As such, peer review suggestions, oscillating between vague generalization and specific requests for proofreading, confused rather than helped Morgan. In one rare occasion of Jnay connecting her comments to a passage by means of a clear signal "the paragraph that started with 'She dashed . . . ,'" Morgan highlighted this comment, with additional changes of the fonts into purple to provide her personal reaction to this compliment (羞羞哒, xiu xiu da, translated into feeling bashful [from the compliments]).

Second, there was a lack of opportunity for students to engage in sustained and evolving conversations around their feedback. Each student was invited to read and respond to three essays during a 2-hour in-class meeting. Despite the instructor's recommendation that students take their time, most students rushed to complete the task during class. Little time was left to allow for clarification or inquiry. Taking the lesson from her conversations with Jessie and Ryan, Morgan requested her peers' help with American phrases, to which Jnay responded by supplying examples in her comments on the document. Morgan appreciated the personalized attention to her writing when adequate evidence was provided to justify the student reviewer's effort to recognize her strength, diagnose specific issues, and offer concrete strategies for revision. Unfortunately, she was not able to benefit from Jnay's suggestions because of her unfamiliarity with the digital platform used for peer review, which prevented her from accessing the side-comments that Jnay included in her review. Her effort to seek Jnay's feedback was further deterred when students were reshuffled into new discussion teams for the next class. Although Morgan managed to connect with Jnay after class, their conversation ended prematurely because both students were rushing to their next classes. Whatever meanings and feedback were generated during the

> "Don't you realize it is only your first semester, yet you selected six courses?"
>
> "You are a fool to enroll in ISB202! It is full of professional jargon!"
>
> I would never forget the first day when I enrolled the course schedule. I finished it very quickly, wondering why others found the process so daunting. I heard those questioning exclamations like ones above from other Chinese freshmen. Snippy remarks were a common part of my freshman year. The echo of their judging voices grew to a decibel that covered the ebullient cheers of "Go Green, Go White" eventually completely drowning out the mighty roar of the rushing Red Cedar. Being only an international freshman, little did I know that those first few months at Michigan State University would become one of the most significant learning-related events of my life.
>
> "She must be eccentric and dull, and I will never invite her to hang out together."
>
> "She pretends to be smart, but her GPA will prove she bites off more than she can chew."

FIGURE 3.3. Extract From Morgan's Memoir Final Draft

review stayed contained within the classroom and failed to connect in productive ways.

To address such concerns, Morgan took it upon herself to visit the writing center multiple times and recruited Nicole's help to engage in systematic "clean-up" of her writing. Having developed a sustained relationship with a writing center tutor through her previous visits required in her bridge writing class, Morgan made two half-hour appointments with the tutor and brought her essay to Nicole's apartment for a 3-hour chat, with intensive episodes of revision and discussion sandwiched between social activities such as dressing up, snacking, and gossiping. According to Morgan, this draft bore the hand-written edits from three individuals, the writing center tutor on two separate occasions, Nicole, and Morgan herself. As such, it was these messy, recursive, low-stakes, and inquiry-driven reviews that helped Morgan address issues on which she needed the most help.

By the time Morgan submitted her final draft, she had already gone through 11 drafts, with at least three of such drafts embodying a rich textual history and a polyphony of voices listening to and responding to each other across spaces and times, revealing moments of consensus and dissonance that are reflective of distinct literacy trajectories. The final draft, as shown in Figure 3.3, bore witness to the polyphony of these voices, perspectives, and trajectories. Words such as "ebullient" and "roar," now seemingly comfortably settled on the page, had traveled across languages, geographic spaces, times, technological platforms, modalities, and minds. "Murmur," on the other hand, had been eradicated, its translingual history evaporating without a trace. Considering the final draft in isolation from the extensive, knotted textual history, I argue, does not do justice to the thickets of relationship that made it possible to distribute translation labor, negotiate across differences, and share the affective labor of writing the river into meaning. The entanglement that gave the essay its richness and complexity was somehow edited out of its messiness and indeterminacy.

The contrast between the slow, recursive, and low-stakes peer reviews outside the writing classroom and the rushed, structured, and graded in-class peer reviews invites renewed attention to meaning making as a political enterprise. Meanings emerging from collaborative and individual translation could appear salient and significant for students who are emotionally and intellectually invested in the essay's evolution. Such meanings, often mobilized with the "perfect imperfections" so lively with idiosyncratic quirks, creative and risky choices, and polyphonic voices, could be negatively valued by power structures and normative values that orient toward monolingual norms. Such power structures shape how multilingual writers are intellectually, imaginatively, physically, and emotionally immobilized (Lorimer Leonard, 2017). School- and self-sponsored peer reviews are material configurations that operate with practices, tools, and norms that differentially enable and valuate language differences, which this chapter shows to be critical parts of the multilingual writing process. Even when multilingual writers pursue open-ended inquiry and negotiation energetically, the labor involved is often lost to the writing instructor. Indeed, in naming their own Chinglish, multilingual writers in Morgan's transnational network seemed to have internalized a deficit perspective, which led to them perceiving the linguistic irregularity manifested in Morgan's translation as "linguistically and socially embodying something other than 'the norm'" (Lu & Horner, 2013, p. 583) rather than as creative endeavors with rhetorical purposes. The metaphor of entanglement allows us to capture and examine certain rhetorical exigencies, technological affordances, and institutional workings that render the intense translation work irrelevant (in-class peer review), problematic (Nicole's revision), and meaningful (Ryan's and Jessie's comments).

Translating Through Thickets of Relationships

Entanglement happens through the movements and translation of meanings across persons, documents, languages, and modes. Morgan was physically and imaginatively moved by visceral and affective experiences with the river;

ideas generated in one spacetime became encoded and mobilized through digitally managed comments, highlights, edits, and chats; documents intersected across spacetimes, engendering resonance and dissonance. As seen here, the entanglement of the multilingual writer and the river created opportunities for textual meaning to move across persons and languages; it also drew into polyphony a wide range of writerly voices, practices, strategies, and theories, which were pooled from multiple, interrelated literacy life worlds, channeled through improvised assemblages of writing technologies, and woven into intertextual connections across permeable spatial, temporal, linguistic, and modal boundaries. Also in entanglements were the many idiosyncrasies, narratives, and theories garnered through a lifetime of successes and failures to write multilingual lives and worlds into meaning. Entanglement provides a way to consider how semiotic fibers are twisted, layered, and dropped through coordination and encounters or how connections and partnerships fail to forge. It provides a window into how writers continue to enact and test diverse referential systems, literary sensitivities, and rhetorical knowledge when meaning moves from one person, document, or spacetime to another. Life worlds are formed through efforts to move, connect, and transform.

Entanglement was made possible through relationships across semiotic, material, and ontological differences, highlighting the role played by an expansive repertoire of codes and practices leveraged by different writers. It offers a framework for examining rhetorical translation as distributed, collaborative, and indeterminate practice. By unraveling empirical details about the intellectual, emotional, and physical labor of translation, it challenges a mechanical view that reduces translation to simple acts of trading semantic equivalents across languages. Such analysis surfaces a wide range of micro-level translation strategies Laura Gonzales theorized through her research (2018), such as use of digital translation tools, storytelling, unpacking, and frameshifting, while complementing the current understanding of the problematics of multilingual composing by describing concrete moves involved in realizing meaning. Tracing the dynamic use of these translation strategies across drafts, languages, and writers helps us observe the exigencies, practices, and consequences of language negotiation in highly indeterminate, dispersed, and distributed processes. Observing micro-level strategies helps unpack the complexity of open inquiry into language differences and describes successful strategies for performing complex linguistic and rhetorical work.

An entanglement perspective further illuminates the translation labor that is so intense and complex that it demands coordinated distribution of labor—multilingual writers work in concert with digital tools and semiotic resources to infuse the translation process with polyphonic voices, heterogeneous activities, and mobile potentials, often requiring careful negotiation. The analytical affordance of entanglement lies in its ability to make visible dispersed chains of translation labor occurring in situated and embodied moments, which weave together contingent assemblages of materialities, activities, brokers, digital tools, semiotic repertoires, and strategies. Even those utterances in Morgan's final draft that appeared monolingual had undergone transformation through coordinated deployment of micro-level translation strategies, including identifying linguistic options, assessing alternatives, surfacing semantic nuances and connotations, situating language use in historical trajectories, managing conjugation, adjusting syntax to accommodate translation, and tailoring language to audience expectations. Successful deployment of such strategies is key to managing a continuum of linguistic, discursive, and cultural differences when textual meanings emerged with the multilingual writer's effort to make sense of the river for herself and her readers. To translate is to perform the challenging task of determining "what kinds of differences to make through writing, how, and why" (Lu & Horner, 2013, p. 585). Although Morgan's case highlights the distributed and mediated nature of language negotiation, the rhetorical and linguistic moves manifested here are common to all those working to navigate writing at the intersection of the author, reader, and text. Even monolingual writers, such as Nicole, engage in the complex task of assessing, validating, and unpacking linguistic choices they make based on the dynamic interplay of authorial intentions and audience expectations.

Evidenced in this analysis is the indeterminate co-becoming of the multilingual writer with natural, cultural, and literacy others, their material and discursive practices, and multilingual writing. The outcome of translation cannot be predicted by predetermined templates because each translation moment involves innovation, as each broker evokes their unique perspective to cast textual meaning in different lights. Meanwhile, multilingual lives entangled in messy, exploratory, and tentacular ways as each multilingual writer reinvent the words, phrases, and story in response to each other (Haraway, 2016), thereby unpredictably directing how idiosyncratic and cultural meanings mirror, amplify, and contradict one another (Stornaiuolo et al., 2017, p. 81). As illustrated here, the emergence of semantic, rhetorical, and affective meanings is transformative with specific, contingent, and shifting entanglements. Sustained inquiry from Jessie and Ryan not only surfaced writing knowledge operating on the backdrop of each choice, comment, and suggestion, it also caused significant friction because they unfolded at the intersection of the reader-writer-text dynamic, with meaning bouncing back and forth in the process of seeking comprehension, clarity, and consensus. The students collectively assessed lexical items (words and phrases), compared cross-linguistic equivalents, and reasoned about linguistic choices, with each passage mobilizing narratives, meanings, and emotions uniquely informed by different actors' educational and social pasts, such as Ryan's academic training in the sciences and the friendship between Morgan and Jessie. Whereas such exchanges enabled a productive distribution of the cognitive, emotional, and intellectual labor of translation, they also created layered frictions with each effort at articulating one's choice, providing reasoning for critique, offering suggestions backed by examples and personal stories, justifying decisions to adopt or reject a recommendation, or experimenting with rhetorical strategies. Such practices provided each writer with the opportunity to repurpose writing knowledge and strategies developed through previous literacy activities in stable and innovative ways (Roozen, 2009b). Intertextually connected, iterative, and cyclical translations are fundamentally frictive because they brought into convergence multiple social worlds "where discourses and knowledge are necessarily heterogeneous, and where multiple semiotic resources are so deeply entangled that distinct modes simply don't make sense" (Prior, 2018, n.p.).

Simultaneously, Morgan's effort to join the river in embodied articulation of the world is subject to evaluation. Although collaborative translation practices open multilingual writing as fertile ground for open inquiry into linguistic, cultural, and rhetorical differences, they fail to gain recognition in formal structures that sanction a singular rhythm for teaching, reviewing, and assessing writing. The passage of textual meaning from "murmur" and "whisper" to "mighty roar" across languages, readers, and rhetorical traditions is often not read as different ways of engaging with the material world but judged against a singular, dominant trope that deprives the river of its imaginative potential to enact changes in those who form associations with it. Such a dominant trope enforces boundaries and valuation systems that deem certain linguistic choices as exotic, emotional, cute, and quintessentially other. Figuring nature as wild also aligns with dominant Western ideologies of human-nature relations, which observe nature as wild, dangerous, and amenable to taming and exploitation. Indeed, the linguistic "irregularity" manifested in Morgan's use of "murmur" was differently questioned, diminished, and eradicated; it was interpreted as evidence of failure rather than innovation. Within those same terms, Nicole's endeavors, which disrupted Morgan's intent, were accepted for being in better alignment with linguistic, discursive, and referential norms of academic writing at the university, which is entangled with broader sociocultural and historical currents.

Entanglement offers a way to trace the explicit and subtle ways in which power structures and normative values shape how meanings are mobilized and contained. School- and self-sponsored peer reviews operate with practices to differently value and enable open inquiries into language differences, which this chapter shows to be critical parts of the multilingual writing process. Even when multilingual writers like Morgan pursue such inquiries energetically, the labor involved is often lost on the writing instructor. Indeed, in naming their own Chinglish, the students took a deficit stance toward their creative endeavors, which are interpreted through the lens of language irregularities underlined by lack of proficiency. Could multilingual writing and multilingual worlds, inherently heterogeneous, find their articulation despite theoretical binaries that tend to separate natural and cultural worlds, knower and known, experts and novices, Chinese and American cultural and rhetorical sensitivities? This chapter offers a glimpse into the tremendous challenges for writers and researchers alike, as our ways of being, relating, and making meaning recursively and iteratively unfold through moments, words, and encounters that are woven into polyphony through thickets of relationships.

4
Dwelling on Unpredictable Encounters

Looking for Unpredictable Encounters

Fungi are especially skilled in navigating labyrinths of messy connections, exploratory paths, and tentative solutions. Like fungi, multilingual writers are often skilled in entangling with sprawling, interlaced webs of literacy others, semiotic resources, and material configurations, improvising their way through the mess and mass of forms of living, being, and writing across language, rhetorical, and cultural differences. As I have discussed thus far, multilingual writing is often energized by unpredictable encounters. A chance encounter with an acquaintance or beautiful natural scenery might inspire impromptu acts of writing, a fledgling friendship might turn into a productive professional connection, a treasured albeit dormant memory might resurface through social media browsing and morph into an academic essay. Such encounters, often unintended, uneven, and fleeting, may or may not gain a foothold in writing and literacy processes that often revolve around set timelines, established norms, and expectations implicitly or explicitly articulated in a FYW class. A beautiful scenery might go unnoticed by a preoccupied passenger; a fledgling friendship might falter and dissipate when efforts to cultivate it lag; a treasured memory might remain dormant and

https://doi.org/10.7330/9781646427628.c004

fail to translate into a writing topic. Writing takes shape through ephemeral assemblages with multidirectional histories that may or may not connect into circuits through unpredictable encounters. Mushroom-pondering helps me consider the many surprises that I was not previously equipped to make sense of as I followed the contours and detours of multilingual writing.

Writing researchers have begun to explore indeterminacy, surprise, and improvisation as core features of writers' efforts to transfer writing-related knowledge across contexts. Alexander et al. (2020) use "wayfinding" as a metaphor to theorize the meandering paths of students finding ways to orient themselves as writers in a "bewildering ecology of writing challenges, tasks, technologies, and opportunities" (p. 107). To these authors, wayfinding is especially useful in accounting for the serendipitous ways in which individuals discover new avenues to explore opportunities for attuning and transferring writing expertise. Chris Anson (2016) provides an illustration of unexpected challenges and unpredictable outcomes of writing transfer through a study of his own difficulties composing game summaries of his son's football team for a suburban newspaper. Although the summaries he wrote demonstrated a level of writing competency, with features such as sophisticated vocabulary, expert control of syntax, smart phrasing, impeccable grammar, and skillful use of rhetorical strategies, the veteran writer struggled to mobilize such writing-related knowledge and practices into the transient and unstable community of sports writing. Part of his struggle arose from the fragmented social collective of the community, which passed along team routines and features of communication to shape the genre of the game summary. To his own surprise, the veteran writer experienced great difficulty in deploying writing knowledge and practices; such difficulties arose from the idiosyncrasies of a partially settled and transformative genre, the disjointed activity system in which the genre was used and produced, the ephemeral nature of transient groups of people making up the community, and unexpected reactions from family members and newspaper editors.

Unpredictable, ephemeral encounters surface even more forcefully in research into students' digital writing practices. In Ehret and Hollett's (2014) exploration of adolescents' embodied experience of composing with mobile device, the authors note how the moving and feeling bodies shape meaning making in unpredictable ways. They explore how two students' composing processes are differently shaped by their sensory experience of places, with unpredictable activities emerging as the result of how "the body feels and directly perceives the material environments through which it moves" (p. 432). Similarly,

Wargo's (2015) analysis of the ephemeral composition process of a high school student composing with Snapchat offers emergence as a lens to notice surprise and unexpected interruptions for mediating the unfolding of literacy activities. Christiansen (2019) provides a compelling account of open-ended, opportunistic improvisation as a key feature of massive participatory writing in her analysis of a viral event triggered by one rural Mexican family's video invitation to a quinceañera (15th birthday) party for a young girl. The family's video was posted on Facebook and reposted on other social media platforms and drew members in a transnational Mexican diaspora into a virtual and live carnival that produced continuous parody and remix of the video's agrarian ranchero lifestyle even after the family retracted the video and many uninvited guests attended the live party. No one gains control of the writing phenomenon, which could take on a life of its own, stringing parties of divergent interests into an ongoing articulation that nurtures, invents, and cobbles together ways of feeling, remembering, and celebrating. It is through the contingent, improvised gatherings of sociomaterial assemblage of body-technology that new meaning potentials emerge to steer composing activities indeterminately.

Fungi are useful thinking tools for exploring how entities across ontological differences encounter each other within entanglements, each time taking on new intentions and meanings that gain a momentary hold amid an evolving phenomenon. Ephemeral encounters and unexpected connections indeterminately steer writing. From an entanglement perspective, ideas for writing emerge through the writer's playful orchestrations of semiotic resources and unpredictable encounters with contingent circumstances. An experienced writer's repertoire evolves in uncertain ways with new genres of writing. The discovery of a video intended for a rural community by a transnational audience is partly whimsical; the formation of a writing community is as contingent and ephemeral as its dissipation; how a student writes on the move is as unpredictable as its effects on oneself and others. These encounters across political, language, cultural, and socioeconomic differences produce users, ideas, and jokes that hold together, develop, communicate, and form polyphonic conversations about such differences. Whether or not our idiosyncratic actions gain purchase in the broader scheme of things almost entirely depends on tentacular ways in which beings tangle into encounters. One certainty is transformation.

The focus on unpredictable encounters as a tool for inquiry makes it possible to account for inter- and intra-actions that steer literacy practices in powerful ways. The ephemeral experiences that arise from encounters across ontological differences, easily unnoticed, provide important insights into the ways writers are energized, motivated, and constrained by their efforts to move along, connect with, and relate to natural, cultural, and literacy others. Unpredictable encounters prepare and prompt me to attend to affectively charged moments that connect into the multilingual writing process, compelling me to foreground writers' entanglement with materials, people, and practices that "may oppress and discriminate as much as they liberate and amplify" (Stornaiuolo et al., 2017, p. 79), while pointing to how intensities that drive writing "are not only affective but also emerge as people manage multiple indexical fields amid complex intra-actional moments and as polyphonic histories animate those moments" (Prior et al., 2023, p. 32).

As I detail in this chapter, unpredictable encounters are transformative—they produce powerful feelings, inspire improvised acts of writing, call on unexpected players and memories, and facilitate the writer's effort to find his positioning in the world through writing. In this chapter, I explore how Leo's iterative encounters with a calligraphy story in its past, present, and future tenses enabled various forms of writing for different purposes and audiences. The intense sociality of informal writing, playful bantering, and collaborative interpretation connected the writer with the story and his audience in unexpected ways, produced unintended social consequences, and iteratively energized Leo's drafting of his Memoir assignment. Leo's willingness to wander with his story outside and beyond the temporal and spatial parameters of the writing assignment allowed the expressive potential of the story to surface through the *string figuring* (as I have discussed in Chapter 1) of past and present experiences, familiar and novel interpretations, and old and new relationships.

Meeting Leo

At the time of my research, Leo was a sophomore who had not declared his major but was seriously considering a career in business. Compared to Morgan, who tirelessly worked to assemble all available resources to achieve ambitious and well-articulated academic and professional goals, Leo approached life and learning at the university with ease and curiosity. He assembled courses in political science, philosophy, theater, and fine arts in his first and second years, dropping them when his grades faltered and excelling in them when they suited his interests and strengths. Leo led an active social life. As a person of many interests and talents, his WeChat Moments were populated with photos and video clips that depicted him as a performing pianist, amateur magician, street dancer, singer, and Kung Fu master. At the university, Leo was well liked by his professors and mentors. He stood out from his fellow Chinese international students as someone who was willing to speak his mind, take creative risks, and explore ideas different from his own. His personal relationships with his professors were so strong that quite a few of them attended his graduation ceremony and joined his family for a celebratory dinner afterward. Following the same research design I used to study Morgan's multilingual writing practices, I followed Leo through 2 academic years (2015–2016) as he migrated from the bridge writing course into an honors FYW course, with additional longitudinal data collected during the subsequent 5 years as he graduated with honors as a finance major, attended a highly selective graduate program in a prestigious university in the United Kingdom for a semester and dropped out, received his graduate degree in finance from the global campus of a US university in Hong Kong, and took a job in a state-affiliated think tank in China.

His decision to enroll in an honors section of FYW was another example of his adventurous and exploratory approach. Although his close friends, who struggled in regular sections of FYW, advised him against enrolling in a writing course with an even more reading- and writing-intensive curriculum, Leo chose honors FYW because of his interest in writing. He embraced writing as a venue to develop ideas and expertise, perform class and literacy identities, and explore professional aspirations and interests. Like Morgan, Leo was an avid reader and sophisticated writer whose essays were often read in class or submitted to writing contests throughout his educational career. To Jill, his instructor for the honors FYW class, Leo was unlike typical honors students she taught, who "are anxious about every tiny detail, worrying that some teacher is out there to get them for the smallest risk-taking." Instead, Leo strove to distinguish himself from those in his social, academic, and professional circles by taking bold, albeit carefully calculated, risks. As Jill relayed at the end of the semester, Leo approached the final presentation assignment with great creativity—he brought a liter of Coca-Cola and paper cups to teach his classmates about the Chinese cultural etiquette of toasting. His well-calibrated jokes, warm demeanor, and willingness to engage with his audience energized the entire class.

Leo's experiences with creative risk-taking, however, were not always positive. While some of his essays were read for how they provided new insights into conventional themes, others were chosen to warn his peers of the dangers of toying with writing prompts given for high-stakes writing tests. Leo named one instance when his middle school Chinese Language Arts teacher tore apart an essay he had hoped to submit to a regional writing contest. His teacher first read it aloud in front of his class and praised its demonstrated craft. Afterward, the teacher tore the essay apart with dramatic gestures, slowly spreading pieces of the torn essay around the classroom while discussing the consequences of risk-taking—creative ideas and beautiful craft were worthless when the focus of an essay deviated from the parameters set by the prompt. The teacher cautioned, "If your essay doesn't provide the inspirational insights that the judges want to see, all its rhetorical flourishes are worthless." This anecdote illustrates a broader range of paradoxes in Leo's social and literacy life: his desires for creative expression, social distinction, and material luxury and the felt need to exercise restraint, self-censorship, and strategic silence. As I will discuss throughout Chapters 4 and 5, such paradoxes arose from intensified anxiety of living with the privileges and perils of his class identity.

Below, my analysis begins with noticing the many unsettling and thrilling surprises that drove Leo's multilingual writing process, including an unpredictable encounter that invited musings about the serendipitous ways of life, a surprising discovery of a writing topic that involved intense affects, unexpected detours that distracted the writer from professed goals for a writing session, and unintended consequences of sharing one's writing with a heterogeneous audience. By tracing the emergence of Leo's calligraphy story, I unravel the haphazard nature of multilingual writing, which constantly departs from set plans, authorial intentions, and strategic design. I also explore how powerful feelings generated through his encounters with memories, facets of past and present experiences, and interactions with friends and family drove his writing in indeterminate ways. In the same way that fungi scholars turn to unintentional design, surprises, and accidents for enabling entirely new possibilities, I examine how following encounters across spatial and temporal boundaries allows me to uncover the resonating ways in which the story was repeatedly taken up in alternation or juxtaposition across real and (re)imagined times as Leo continued to discover and articulate its meaning.

Finding the Calligraphy Story

In contrast to Morgan's expansively distributed writing process, Leo's completion of his Memoir assignment did not involve much feedback from others during his invention and drafting stages. Beyond three teacher-facilitated in-class peer reviews, one 15-minute conference with his teacher, and three informal observations with me, where we broadly discussed his ideas, Leo only sought the feedback from a former teacher, an experienced ESL teacher who also worked as a writing consultant at the English Language Center's Writing Lab. However, his drafts remained significantly stable, with very few changes made throughout the drafting, translation, and revision processes. On the surface, Leo's discovery of a writing topic seemed to result from pure happenstance—he was scrolling through his old WeChat Moments one night before bed and rediscovered an interesting encounter that took place during the previous summer break, which resurfaced a childhood story about taking calligraphy lessons.

Leo's multilingual process, which turned the calligraphy story into an essay for the Memoir assignment, emerged through strong feelings of awe and nostalgia toward a childhood memory; familial teachings on the value of patience, humility, and perseverance; and Leo's contemplation of the value of serendipity. Incrementally, the story became layered with memories, affects, and insight through three WeChat Moments posts, which generated a strong reaction and much commentary from his transnational circle of friends; two extensive drafting sessions; and one consultation with his teacher at the English Language Center. As the calligraphy story continued to transform across languages, modalities, and purposes, it became densely layered with semiotic substances (descriptive details and imagery), affective materials (feelings of awe, fragility, and anxiety), and literacy and identity practices (certain details were erased when they were perceived as acts of flaunting privilege). Below, I focus my analysis around three WeChat Moments posts and social interactions around them (a July 11 post recording his meeting, a September 19 post marking his surprising rediscovery of the story, and a September 17 post recording Leo drafting his essay in English with my help) to provide a glimpse into the becoming of the story through unpredictable encounters. These WeChat Moments, created along a longer trajectory during which Leo experienced, recorded, interpreted, and rediscovered the calligraphy story in playful collaboration with his peers, accidentally contributed to his drafting of his Memoir assignment.

As shown in Figure 4.1, Leo created a WeChat Moments post on July 11, 2015, to record and reflect on a chance reunion with his childhood calligraphy teacher when he traveled back to China during the summer after his first year at the university. The post recorded one stretch of the social

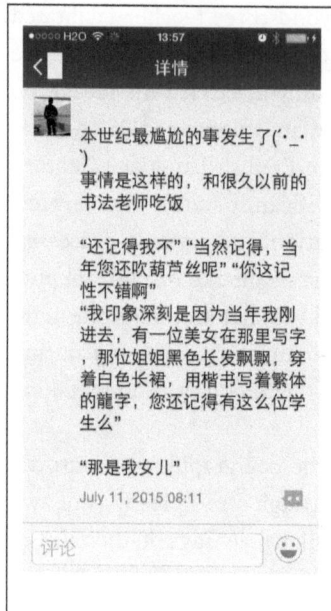

UNPREDICTABLE ENCOUNTER

The most embarrassing incident of the century just happened (embarrassment emoticon)

It went like this. [I was] having dinner with my calligraphy teacher from a long time ago.

TEACHER: "Do you still remember me?"
LEO: "Of course I do. You (honorific pronoun) used to play Hulusi (a traditional Chinese musical instrument)."
TEACHER: "You have a great memory."
LEO: "I remember [the calligraphy class] well because when I first joined the [class], there was a beautiful girl practicing calligraphy. Her long, black hair swaying in the air, she was dressed in a long white dress and writing the traditional Chinese word 'dragon' in Kai style. Do you remember having a student like that?"
TEACHER: "That was my daughter."

FIGURE 4.1. Leo's WeChat Moments of July Meeting With Calligraphy Teacher

conversation taking place between them over dinner, as they reminisced about shared experiences in and around the calligraphy class. The story itself encapsulated two unpredictable encounters that were interwoven across spacetimes to produce a surprising discovery. The first encounter unfolded when Leo ran into his calligraphy teacher and the two decided to gather for a light dinner. Chatting over dinner, Leo reminisced about his encounter with a beautiful young girl on his first day attending calligraphy class as a 10-year-old child. The beautiful appearance and calm demeanor of the young girl engrossed in calligraphic practice captivated Leo, leaving him awestruck by the aesthetics of the artistic form. The memory was so powerful that it compelled his current inquiry into the woman's identity and led to a surprising discovery—she was the daughter of Leo's calligraphy teacher and a talented young artist graduating from an elite French art institute, soon to join the most prestigious Chinese art institute as faculty. Feeling so imaginatively moved by this encounter, Leo used WeChat to surface this old memory, which gained new meaning and purchase: it invited Leo to contemplate the serendipitous ways in which chance rewrites one's experiences in and perspectives on life, a theme he subtly commented upon in his WeChat post and continued to pursue in his essay.

The memory of his encounter with the young woman was significant because it epitomized the classical aesthetics and practices of calligraphy, which seek to discipline and harmonize the mind and body. In Leo's words, calligraphy changed him by teaching him the importance of focus and tenacity. For one thing, calligraphy requires extreme focus from the practitioner, who manages to stay "calm and steady despite all the noises on the streets outside and all the distractions in the world." Calligraphy also taught him perseverance because repeated practice of simple brush strokes was key to maintaining and improving one's craft; lapses for even one day show through slippages recognizable to one's master. To Leo, the awe he experienced when he encountered the young woman marked his encounter and reckoning with the artistic form.

Connecting calligraphy to lessons he took in Tai Chi, which required vigorous training in tedious foundational moves such as maintaining a standing posture for hours on end, Leo reflected that his father had been especially supportive of extracurricular activities that taught him to practice focus and patience, attributes he showed to be lacking with his childish behavior at school. Although the young Leo protested his father's decision to enroll him in calligraphy because he saw it as punishment for his unruly behavior in school—he had been caught skipping classes and throwing rocks at a teacher from the rooftop of a faculty abode. In good humor, Leo poked fun at the fact that his naughty behavior had alarmed teachers across grade levels, who unanimously demanded parental intervention. Although he continued to mock the futility of parental efforts to use extracurricular activities to cultivate his character, he expressed retrospective appreciation for their support of his pursuit of a variegated range of hobbies, including lessons in Kung Fu, stage performance, magic tricks, street dance, debate, and singing. These experiences helped him develop a repertoire of skills and aptitudes necessary to lead a fulfilling and rewarding personal life. In particular, he now appreciated the calligraphy lessons for teaching him to embrace life with optimism, to practice tedious skills with patience, and to persevere through challenges. Leo had come to appreciate how his father, sometimes in consultation with him, had carefully orchestrated rich extracurricular activities to develop his character as a disciplined individual with various strengths and talents. This approach, which encouraged versatility over expertise, had shaped Leo's aspiration to stand out across multiple circles of social elites.

Unpredictable encounters are sites where new meanings and possibilities emerge in response to historical contingencies. The calligraphy story emerged from unpredictable encounters that resumed emotional ties with an old acquaintance, renewed feelings of awe toward a classical artistic form, and invited contemplation of the core values of familial teaching. The story co-emerged with historically developed streams of embodied practices (e.g., the physical acts required to practice tedious Tai Chi standing postures and calligraphic brush strokes), material artifacts (e.g., plaques and drawings with adages and proverbs displayed in the calligraphy classroom), persons (e.g., the young woman and his calligraphy teacher), and affectively charged and imaginatively moving memories. These experiences and the lessons they imparted became densely layered, brought to the surface through Leo's efforts to remember, narrate, and compose the calligraphy story into meaning. Iteratively imparted through family conversations, disciplinary actions, and extracurricular activities, values such as perseverance and humility became intimately entangled with the memory and readily surfaced to inform a reflective insight that Leo continued to ponder—the serendipity of life.

Leo's accidental discovery of the story was transformed by and with unpredictable encounters, which were the outcome of forging and maintaining relationships with acquaintances, memories, and philosophical perspectives across spatial and temporal boundaries. Reflecting on how matsutakes are capricious creatures that are impossible to cultivate, Tsing argues that "encounters are, by their nature, indeterminate" (2005, p. 46) and shows how collaborative living and being across differences take shape through intricate, opportunistic assemblage of variables. Similarly, the accidental discovery of the calligraphy story was driven by capricious contingencies that unfolded through the unintended, coincidental gathering of variables, such as the distinct daily itineraries that brought Leo and his calligraphy teacher together, a coincidental schedule overlap that allowed for a brief reunion over dinner, the meandering contour of casual conversation that brought up the story, and Leo's ability to recall details that resonated with the teacher. The story's ability to surface and stabilize was dependent upon fickle environments and dynamic circumstances. Would Leo's reminiscence of an encounter from a distant past provide enough substance to move the conversation forward? Was the bond between the teacher and the student, formed decades ago, strong enough to allow for the sharing of such intimate details? Did the reminiscence create an opportunity for a proud father to celebrate the accomplishments of his daughter or agitate anxiety over unfulfilled aspirations?

The story's meaning and significance were indeterminate. The story did not surface as the outcome of intentional pursuit. Rather, it surfaced as the result of well-versed conversationalists navigating the contingencies of a rhetorical situation that invited its participants to explore new connections, possibilities, and meanings.

UNEXPECTED DETOURS

The accidental discovery of the story invited multilayered and multiperspectival crystallization of its meaning, which Leo was eager to record and share through the WeChat Moments post he produced. Intense social interaction followed the publishing of the post (see Box 4.1), as his friends collaboratively engaged with Leo to discover more details about the story. Leo's July post on WeChat was followed by enthusiastic and playful comments from a steady circle of friends he met at the university. Whereas Leo's post celebrated the mysterious and serendipitous way in which life unfolded, his peers reinterpreted the plot of the story to be one of a boyish crush on a beautiful young woman. Leo's WeChat friends worked collaboratively to recast the story in alignment with tropes from genres of youth literature and popular culture.

As shown in Box 4.1, Leo initially indulged and relished his peers' playful efforts to rewrite his narrative, including Lyn's enactment of the love-at-first-sight trope from teen romance novels, Fish's extension of the romantic trope into the Western "cougar" girlfriend archetype, Sun's reimagination of the plot in alignment with the transnationally remixed horror movie franchise *The Ring*, and Little Feeling's reference to the Dragon Princess, a character in a Chinese martial arts novel classic, *Legends of the Condor Heroes*. Leo engaged in friendly banter with his friends, providing clarifications and jokingly dismissing alternative interpretations and enthusiastic encouragement for him to pursue a romantic relationship with his childhood crush. What is also noteworthy is that his friends were responding to each other's comments to Leo's post, including Sun building on others' ideas to suggest an alternative remix ("It could also go in the direction of horror movies—white-dressed girl turns around as Sadako"), Lyn's affirmation of Sun's proposal ("That's a good idea!"), and Fish being "in support of relationship with an older woman," which built on Leo's response to Lyn's proposal of a romantic relationship and his explanation of a significant age difference between the young woman and himself. Such moderated sociality was enabled by WeChat's screening function, which allows the content owner to sort his WeChat friends into groups and to moderate access to content and user comments based on group

> **BOX 4.1. COMMENTS ON LEO'S JULY WECHAT POST**
>
> Date of post: July 11, 2015, 08:11 PM
>
> *Friend Comments:*
>
> LEO: [I was pronounced] Dead. Died from verbosity. 卒。死于话多。
>
> LYN: Typical setup for a romance novel—Your teacher tells his daughter about this. It turns out she has always liked you. You end up together. 😊 言情小说的剧情一般就是从这里开始。你老师回去就给他女儿说了这件事，然后他女儿其实早就对你情根深种，然后你俩就在一起了。
>
> LEO REPLIES (LYN): That's enough! You! 你够了啊
>
> LEO REPLIES (LYN): She was a young woman already and I was just a little kid? 我小屁孩的时候那姐姐都多大了
>
> LEO REPLIES (ALL): Can't you all just change your ideas [perspective on this]? I was only 10; that sister would be 30 now. 😊 你们的思想能换换不，当年我才10岁吧，那姐姐现在得30了。
>
> LYN: Age [differences] is not an obstacle. 年龄不是距离
>
> LEO REPLIES (LYN): [I] wish you find a [boyfriend] of a grandpa's age. 祝你找位爷爷级的
>
> LYN REPLIES (LEO): I wasn't in love with an unknown old uncle many years ago after all. 😊 毕竟没有多年前钟情于一个不知名大叔
>
> FISH REPLIES (LEO): [I am] in support of relationship with an older woman. 支持姐弟恋！
>
> SUN: It could also go in the direction of horror movies—white-dressed girl turns around as Sadako. 可以转型恐怖片让贞子姐姐转过头
>
> LYN REPLIES (SUN): That's a good idea! 好想法！
>
> LEO REPLIES (FISH): I thank you! (Sarcastically) 😊 谢谢你咯
>
> LEO REPLIES (SUN): How could she be Sadako. 😊😊😊😊😊 哪里是贞子
>
> LITTLE FEELINGS: 后续：当年的小龙女现在仙居何处？
>
> SEQUEL: Where does this Dragon Princess reside now?
>
> LEO REPLIES (LITTLE FEELINGS): École Nationale Supérieure des Beaux-Arts, as the only Chinese student. Soon to be teaching at Central Academy of Fine Arts. 巴黎美术学院，全国一人。马上去中央美院任教

designations. Only friends within the same group could see and respond to peer comments. Such a function provided Leo with a certain degree of control and created feelings of intimacy among members of his audience, who were primarily classmates he met from the bridge writing class, whom he grouped by using the tag "bridge writing class."

As shown in Leo's response to his peers' playful comments (see Box 4.1), he exercised self-restraint and humility when responding to the comments. He initially withheld an important detail from his friends, which made his dinner meeting with his calligraphy teacher especially significant—he was surprised to discover that the young woman was one of only two Chinese nationals ever admitted to the prestigious École Nationale Supérieure des Beaux in France and was soon to join the elite Central Academy of Fine Arts of China as a faculty member. The prestige of these art institutes and the esteemed social status of a talented artist/professor were important markers of class distinction that motivated Leo's class aspirations (a theme I pursue in Chapter 5). To Leo, his connection to a prominent young artist he "discovered" as a child was important because it provided proof for his acumen and discerning tastes in artistic talents, an ability he took great pride in. In his WeChat Moments post, however, he withheld details about such prestige and refrained from mentioning his connection to this talented artist. He did not volunteer such information until an explicit prompt from Little Feeling, who asked, "Where does this Dragon Princess reside now?" to which he replied with information about the woman's educational credentials. Here Leo engaged in what I have come to see as strategic silence. He intentionally withheld details about the accomplishments of an acquaintance, the divulsion of which could be perceived as acts of flaunting his own class privilege (a theme I pursue in Chapter 5). At the same time, it is important to note the rhetorical effect of his play with this information. Instead of withholding the information through a vague answer, such as "she lives in Paris," he provided a fuller answer, achieving an intended, albeit calculated, dramatic impact.

Unpredictable encounters are sites where multiple voices, perspectives, and curiosities, cultivated through distinct historical trajectories, are juxtaposed and negotiated to produce entirely new possibilities for the writer and his readers on social media. Unexpected detours manifested in creative interpretations, playful banter, and friendly teasing that invited clarifications that Leo did not intend to share. These collaborative efforts to make sense of the story vibrated with the energy of multiple interpretations that clearly departed from Leo's understanding of the story's significance and his intention for sharing it. Indeed, Leo's friends engaged with the calligraphy story by retelling it through many different lenses. At the backdrop of such storytelling polyphony was the genre network of youth literature and popular culture, including Chinese martial arts fantasy novels that were adapted to popular movies and TV series, teen romance novels that Lyn always carried around and read before the bridge writing class I taught, Sun's curated list of transnationally distributed horror movies that he often reviewed for his readers on WeChat, and cultural jokes about older women dating younger men that Fish referenced. The voices of these readers never welded into a unified form. As Sheldrake observes about Aka women singing while gathering mushrooms, in polyphonic discursive scenes, "no voice surrenders its individual identity. Nor does any one voice steal the show" (2020, p. 43). Not even Leo, the presumed "owner" of the story, was able to dictate how the story was interpreted. In fact, Leo struggled to contain the creative energy and was also unable to channel the conversation in the direction he desired despite tireless efforts to debunk and dismiss competing interpretations. Leo's simultaneous amusement and frustration surfaced most vividly through his sustained efforts to invalidate playful remixes of his personal story and his response to Lyn's tease by suggesting that she find herself an older boyfriend, which Lyn forcefully refused, thereby silencing Leo's further efforts to unify the storyline.

Building on Sheldrake's analogy that connects each Aka mushroom gatherer's singing voice to a hyphal tip, which "[explores] the soundscape for itself," I note how each of the students' voices was free to wander in unintended encounters with each other. Each "take" of Leo's story built on and extended an interpretation provided by another, giving the story a distinct heterogeneity and historicity unique from but connected to Leo's original intent. Leo's voice was quickly drowned out, his intentions disrupted and undermined. Despite the casual and playful tone of his interaction with his peers, Leo expressed mild exasperation that he was never prepared to respond to how quickly these social media conversations spun out of control. Nonetheless, the story continued to gain semiotic and reflective meanings, as layers of affective energies, literacy histories, and inside jokes accumulated through collaborative play.

The dynamic exchange around the calligraphy story was a prime example of unintentional design. Enthusiastic response to and creative interpretations of the story were the unintended consequence of an improvised effort to collaboratively give meaning to an ephemeral encounter that inspired Leo's writing. Moreover, affinity between Leo and his peers grew as multiple streams of life experiences coalesced and conversations tangled to give rise to new opportunities for bonding and play. The polyphonic voices of Leo and his readers constructed the WeChat post's comment section into a discursive terrain for transformative encounters. The continuous, creative recasting of the story in the casual, low-stakes social media environ was the unintended consequence of coalescing historical trajectories of old and new friendships, infrastructural affordances of the technology to afford and limit types of sociality, and ongoing efforts to develop friendships at the university. For Leo, the calligraphy story was a way of being and becoming with others, which was the emergent effect of indeterminate and multidirectional encounters, as patterns of unintended coordination develop in assemblages of readers with distinct interpretive lenses, intellectual interests, reading preferences, and experiences with romantic encounters. Through informal writing, Leo coalesced into unlikely partnerships with his readers to build meanings capable of entirely new possibilities. The multilingual writer and the story evolved through these unpredictable encounters, which vibrated with multiple historical trajectories, spanned social, literacy, and class aspirations, and defied efforts to control the story's meaning.

SURPRISING (RE)DISCOVERY

Although the unpredictable encounter surfaced a childhood memory, which gained new meanings through playful interpretations by his peers, the calligraphy story was no more significant or memorable than dozens of posts Leo produced and shared during the 2 summer months he spent in China. Nor did the story naturally surface as a viable topic for his Memoir assignment as Leo completed various invention activities in and outside his FYW class in early September. One such invention activity took place during an informal observation meeting with me, when he built on an in-class brainstorming activity to create his own list of topics, such as learning Tai Chi, overcoming stage fright, and participating in a writing contest. Although he saw much promise in each of these topics, Leo was hesitant to commit to any given topic and left our meeting somewhat frustrated but not seriously deterred. A few days later, with the due date for a rough draft approaching, Leo rediscovered the calligraphy story by accident. In the evening of September 19, he was lying in bed and performing a bedtime ritual that he had come to call "WeChat time travel" as he scrolled through his old WeChat Moments posts in reverse chronological order to enable a form of imaginary "travel" back to the lived and imaginary realities of his past. As he stated,

> Sometimes things get difficult and life here is devoid of the usual entertainment we had in China, I scroll through my old posts to remind me of the good times with friends and to revisit the lovely, tucked-away corners in my city that only locals know. [I do this] to keep me going.

Indeed, such practices provided ways for Leo to reconnect with family, friends, places, and experiences, all in partial compensation for the feelings of alienation and isolation he felt at the university.

The July post resurfaced the calligraphy story during this bedtime ritual, presenting it as a viable idea for his writing assignment. Thrilled by this discovery, Leo jumped out of bed, turned on the light, and reopened his laptop to start drafting the opening scene for his essay. The opening paragraph of his essay, written entirely in Chinese, recounted the chance meeting with his teacher and the reminiscence that ensued.

> Ten years later, [I] met that teacher at a random dinner gathering. Slightly intoxicated after rounds of toasting and drinking, [I] couldn't help but share this past event with him, trying to obtain information about the young girl from him. After listening to my narrative, he broke into laughter.
> "Oh, that girl."
> "Uh huh?"
> "That was my daughter." (Translation of Screenshot A in Leo's WeChat Moments Post, September 19, 2015)

In this draft, Leo leveraged two strategic moves to reformulate the story. First, the opening paragraph provided minimal contextual information about the powerful encounter with the young woman, the dinner meeting with the calligraphy teacher, or Leo's curiosity that led to his inquiry. He eliminated the first sentence in the July post, which framed his encounter with his calligraphy teacher as engendering the "most embarrassing incident of the century" and set the tone for his July narrative. In the present draft, Leo practiced the principle of "showing rather than telling," as discussed in his honors writing class, to narrate the social event that led up to his discovery of the woman's identity, including rituals of Chinese social gathering that involved "rounds of toasting and drinking," his own intense desire to obtain additional information about the woman's identity, and the reaction of his teacher, who "broke into laughter." Such moves were effective in setting up expectations for his readers while creating suspense that he did not explicitly address until much later in the essay. Second, he simplified the conversation between his teacher and himself, which originally contained details about his teacher playing the Chinese musical instrument hulusi and descriptive details about the young girl's appearance (e.g., white dress, swaying long hair) and action (e.g., writing the character "dragon" in Kai style). In the present draft, Leo included a significantly simplified representation of three turns of dialogue, with succinct exchanges further dramatizing the impact of the surprising discovery. The three turns of dialogue contained minimal details about the girl and reduced the friendly banter present in the original

POSTING DATE: SEPTEMBER 19, 2015

Screenshot A: A screenshot of his laptop, with the screen displaying the opening paragraphs of his essay, written entirely in Chinese.

"十年之后，一次偶然的饭局上遇到了那位老师。杯觥交错间醉意涌上心头，情不自禁告诉他这段往事，企图从他的回忆里获取关于那个少女的信息。听完我的叙述，他哑然失笑。"

"啊，那位姑娘啊"

"嗯？"

"那是我的女儿。"

Translation: Ten years later, [I] met that teacher at an accidental dinner gathering. Slightly intoxicated after rounds of toast and drinking, [I] couldn't help but share this past event with him, trying to obtain information about the young girl from him. After listening to my narrative, he broke into laughter.

"Oh, that girl."

"Uh huh?"

"That was my daughter."

2015/9/19

Screenshot B: Screenshot of Leo's July 11 WeChat Moments post.

Written Note: Thank **you**. Never thought I would use **you** to write my essay. Pleading for blessing that points won't be taken off for no good reason.

FIGURE 4.2. Leo's September WeChat Post

post into simple verbal exchanges (e.g., the use of "uh huh" to prompt one's conversation partner to continue). When I asked him about such discursive moves, Leo simply explained that he was so thrilled and inspired by the accidental "rediscovery" of the story that these ideas simply flowed onto the page without much effort on his part. From a reader's perspective, however, the dramatic tension afforded by the provision of minimal details and overall absence of commentary were effective. These opening paragraphs sprouted from the thrill of surprise and vibrated with the improvisational energy of an inspired writer. These paragraphs set the stage for Leo's completion of a full draft in Chinese the next day. The three turns of dialogue, as seen here, stayed intact throughout his drafting, translation, and revision process. He argued that the story was so ready to be told that it took him less than an hour to produce a sophisticated draft.

The surprising (re)discovery of the story was yet another outcome of an unpredictable encounter between Leo's present and past selves, who continued to discover, interpret, and feel the story differently. The WeChat Moments post Leo created (see Figure 4.2) was a visual juxtaposition of two images, with a photo of his laptop displayed the opening paragraphs of his essay and a screenshot of his July post. The juxtaposition of the story there and then (Leo's account of the event after his dinner with his teacher during his summer) and the story here-and-now (Leo's effort to craft the encounter into the opening scene of his essay) was accompanied by a written note, in which Leo positioned his July post as "you," who deserved credit for inspiring his essay. The photo on the top in Figure 4.2 shows Leo's laptop displaying a Microsoft Word document with a few paragraphs of writing in Chinese already produced, which embodied the here-and-now of Leo making his first attempt to include the story in the rough draft of his Memoir assignment, written entirely in Chinese. The image on the bottom is a screenshot of Leo's July WeChat Moments post, which recorded Leo's meeting with his calligraphy teacher and inspired Leo's essay through his WeChat time travel. Both the photo and the screenshot are what Kevin Roozen characterizes as "inscriptions," which are temporarily stabilized artifacts that retained and mobilized material traces of a powerful memory, animating Leo's ongoing effort to make sense of the story as an object of academic contemplation and personal reflection (2021). These artifacts took shape through distinct inscription practices. The former was taken at the end of an intensive drafting session, when Leo typed paragraphs of writing on his laptop and used his phone to record his textual accomplishment. The screenshot was achieved through a function common to most smart phones. For the model of iPhone Leo used, a screenshot was created through the simultaneous pressing of the side button and the volume-up button, which generated a screenshot that was automatically saved to his photo stream. It was with this simple action that the previous inscription of the story, in the form of a written narrative he shared through his July post, was repurposed into another inscription, which allowed him to annotate his writing process driven by a powerful surprise. Both inscriptions, involving distinct productive processes, could be "touched[,] manipulated . . . and continue to exist as physical objects" that motivated an ongoing flow of semiotic activities (Wertsch, 1998, p. 30). These multimodal, multilingual artifacts figured powerfully into Leo's meaning- and knowledge-making practices, in ways similar to labels attached to racks of soil samples scientists gathered from the Amazon forest (Latour, 1999), maps and diagrams used to navigate a ship (Hutchins, 1995), oral narratives produced about a construction project gone awry (Kell, 2015), handwritten alphabetic prose, drawings, diagrams, numbers, markings, and objects that are promiscuously blended to texture the pages of architecture students' sketchbooks (Medway, 2002), or sketches produced to graphically represent organic molecules (Roozen, 2021). These inscriptions propelled writing with their materiality, achieved through different media and for different purposes. While such inscriptions are more noticeable because of their obtained materiality, they were as powerful as other inscription practices that did not leave material traces behind, such as ideas pouring into Leo's head as he scrambled to get out of his bed, notes fingered onto a foggy mirror, or words written on a sandy beach. Regardless of their lack of material permanence, as ideas could be forgotten and words could be erased by ocean waves or the process of evaporation, these moments played a powerful role in making writing happen.

From such a perspective, the photograph of his open laptop and the screenshot were indeterminately assembled to annotate two moments of Leo co-emerging with the story across multiple moments of remembering, discussing, writing, and sharing the story. These artifacts differentially embodied and enacted Leo's knowledge, memories, feelings, and relationships around the story, allowing them to move, connect, and layer across spacetimes and inviting innovative ways to remediate and repurpose it for different audiences and purposes. Leo himself was in dialogue with the original post, as seen in his annotation accompanying the visual juxtaposition: "Thank *you*. Never thought I would use *you* to write my essay. Pleading for blessing that no points be taken off for no good reasons." Recognizing the agency of the story, obtained through unexpected assemblages, Leo used the second-person pronoun "you" to address the screenshot of his July WeChat post as if it was a person with the capacity to listen, dialogue, and act.

As such, the story acquired its own historicity, its melodic theme and semiotic materials remixed in juxtaposition to the original form to provide it with new purchase. The fact that the screenshot assumed its own voice in the dialogue between Leo's present and past selves points to the inadequacy of a "representational logic" (Barad, 2007), which treats writing as mere "representation" of cultural and natural happenings and assigns agency to the writer for discovering, comprehending, and making meaning. Here the WeChat Moments were not an objective, mirroring image of Leo's life but powerful agential forces that set writing into motion, propelled its forward-moving trajectory, reanimated powerful memories and feelings, and created opportunities to discover and accumulate meaning across heterogenous activities. These screenshots were not separate layers of thin veneer mapped onto each other; rather, they dialogue across spacetimes, entangled densely layered semiotic and affective fibers, performed different rhetorical purposes, and gave the story polyphonic energies.

Traversal through and juggling of multiple times were salient features of Leo's multimodal and multilingual writing. Times were conceptually and visibly entangled through the juxtaposition of multiple time stamps in this WeChat post. In a chronological sequence, the first timestamp was system-generated, showing the publication of the original post at "8:11 PM on July 11, 2015." The second time stamp was created by Leo and placed at the bottom of his Chinese draft-in-progress, noting the time of his writing as "2015/09/19." The last one, which this visual representation does not show, was also system generated and indicated the post was published at "10:23 PM on September 19, 2015." Additionally, Leo explicitly signaled the passing of time in his draft, which opened with the prepositional phrase "ten years later" and proceeded to describe his encounter with the young woman. His post was a visual orchestration that pointed to writing as the outcome of imaginary time travel. The story took shape through the interplay of multiple times, as the here-and-now (Leo drafting in the comfort of his dormitory) in anticipation of a future here-and-then (Leo completing the essay for his FYW class) was chronotopically figured with the there-and-then (dinner with his teacher in his hometown the previous summer) and the further temporally distanced there-and-then (his encounter with the young woman a decade ago).

The temporal and spatial traversals I observed in Leo's multilingual writing resonate with Eva Lam and Sidury Christiansen's (2022) exploration of transnational youth's digital literacy practices, as they routinely used linguistic markers, imaginative role-play, photos, and videos to connect with family members and to insert themselves into the histories of their hometowns. As Lam and Christiansen argue, inscriptions such as photos and videos not only evoke memories but also create opportunities to contemplate social issues, generate new knowledge, and enact future changes. Indeterminate encounters between the past and present through the mediation of screenshots, therefore, allowed Leo to string figure memories, affects, semiotic materials, and knowledge into emergent assemblages to make sense of who he was.

Encounters as the result of polyphonic assemblages are transformative. Leo, the story, and his renditions of it were transformed through encounters, as they continued to attune to open-ended interpretations and relationships. The visual juxtaposition of the two takes of the story evinced the polyphonic construction of the emerging story, which relied on the imitation, alternation, and juxtaposition of the same theme to create a story that is simultaneously harmonious and dissonant. Although both screenshots were "imitations" of the same theme, they allowed the story to wander in different directions, one for the recording of a thrilling event and another for the invention of an academic assignment. Polyphonic gathering of these takes of the theme brought into entanglement autonomous tracks of affective energies (e.g., feelings of awe, thrill, and surprise) and meanings (e.g., value of patience and serendipity), creating unexpected coordination that made improvised writing happen.

With these inscriptions, the theme of the story also achieved an increasingly, albeit partially stabilized semiotic substance (e.g., dialogues, visceral feelings, imagery). This substance was then rearticulated and juxtaposed with other streams of meaning- and knowledge-making projects to help inform Leo's writing of the Memoir assignment. The story could be annotated to express nostalgia, invite commentary, give rise to parody, and provoke open-ended inquiry. Old memories and lively conversations were reimagined, retuned, and translated in accordance with genre-specific conventions for academic writing. It is through the multiple unpredictable encounters, which produced surprises and thrills, generated derivative interpretations, and motivated improvised iterations, that a childhood memory continued to gain intellectual texture and density.

UNINTENDED CONSEQUENCES

The last of Leo's WeChat annotation of the calligraphy story took place a week after his accidental rediscovery of and subsequent effort to draft the story for his Memoir assignment. I joined him in Phillips Hall, his favorite lunch spot best known for its all-day service of fish and chips, a comfort food we both loved and relied on to sustain us through another long weekday. During this informal observation that lasted 2 hours, Leo spent time translating a complete Chinese draft of the Memoir into an English draft, which he intended to submit the coming Monday. This translation session, when Leo paused frequently to contemplate the specific meanings of Chinese idiomatic expressions and to unpack the aesthetic subtleties he aspired to articulate, helped Leo interrogate and analyze linguistic choices and cultural assumptions that he had previously taken for granted. Whereas the observation surfaced interesting translation practices comparable to those illustrated in Chapters 2 and 3, I was particularly drawn to an "accident" that alerted me to another layer of the story's historicity driven by unpredictable encounters. More specifically, Leo's intensive engagement with his commenting peers following his social media sharing allowed me to recognize strategic silence as an important feature of Leo's literacy and identity practices.

During this meeting, Leo struggled with translation and consulted me when he felt stuck. As I gently reminded him that I could not help as a translator, Leo collapsed into the corner of the booth and turned to his phone, claiming he was suffering from a headache and needed a break. For the next 15 minutes, I tried and failed to reengage Leo, as he spurted sporadic chuckles and sighs of frustration. As detailed in my field notes below, Leo's multilingual writing was again indeterminately redirected by the reactions and actions of his friends on WeChat.

> Leo struggled with the difficult task of translating a well-structured draft in Chinese into English. He exclaimed, "This is already a beautiful essay in Chinese, but my translation of it is a bizarre monster that resembles neither English nor Chinese. My writerly voice is nondescript." He drew me into his translation of a Chinese word 怨怼 (*yuan dui*, loosely translated as grievance). I did not know or use this word. His explanation became more complicated as he delved into the origin of the word, which was rooted in a Japanese anime serial. As I conducted a search on my laptop to learn more about the word, he fell silent. For the next 15 minutes, he checked his iPhone frequently, chuckling and murmuring, sometimes slamming his phone on the table in mild exasperation, only to pick it up a few seconds later. As I offered my interpretation of the word, I felt mildly annoyed that he was so distracted by his WeChat activities that he ignored me. His writing also paused. When I inquired, he asked me to check my phone for his WeChat Moments, which, according to him, was "exploding with comments." I was able to see some of such comments because they came from former students of mine. Intrigued, I did not interrupt his WeChat activities for the next 10 minutes. When he finally put down his phone, he sighed and said that he had already deleted the post. When I asked if he deleted his post because of mean comments, he shook his head and said, "No, I just don't want to draw too much attention to me." When I asked him if it was

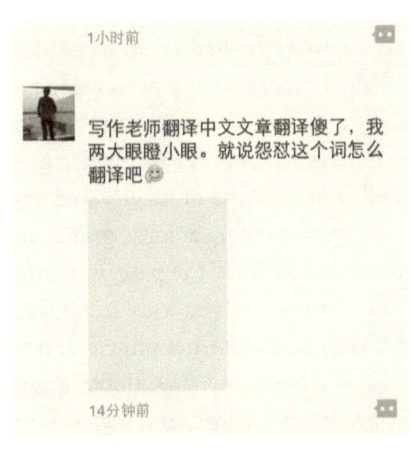

SEPTEMBER 27, 2015

Translation of Leo's Post: [My] writing teacher hits a wall when translating [my] Chinese essay. We stared at each other in mutual consternation. [You tell me] how to translate 怨怼 (*yuan dui*, loosely translated as a feeling of grievance, self-pity, and reluctance to let go).

Comments: LYN: You kids in Honors are writing essays in Chinese already? Too lofty, grand, and classy. 你们Honors 的孩子都开始用中文写作文了？太高大上了！

LEO REPLIES (LYN): I thought it would be fun to write in Chinese first, to show the teacher my writing skills. And then I couldn't put a brake on it. I finished it in Chinese, only to realize I am in big trouble. Nothing is easy to translate. 我用中文开了个头，给写作老师看一下我的写作技巧。结果刹不住车了. 写完傻眼了，没有一个好翻译的。

FISH: That's sick! 牛逼!

SUN: I kneel before the big Learning God!!!!我给大神跪了！！！

LEO REPLIES (SUN): Get out! 滚！

LYN REPLIES (LEO): Now I see the difference between Honors students and us commoners. Kneel before you!这下看出我们普通人和honors的差别了。给你跪了！

LEO REPLIES (LYN): 😂😂😂

YUAN: What the heck! There are procedures like this? 卧槽！还有这种操作？

LEO REPLIES (YUAN): Trilingual learning lord, give me a few tips on translation. 三语大神指导一下怎么翻译。

FIGURE 4.3. Leo's September WeChat Moments Post and Peer Comments

okay for me to keep the screenshot of his post and comments he received, he gave me permission to do so.

Figure 4.3 captures the exchange following Leo's post involving several students who had followed the calligraphy story from its July origin to the present, including Lyn, Fish, and Sun. The post itself featured a screenshot from Leo's laptop, showing the Microsoft Word document of his Chinese draft, with various words and phrases highlighted to indicate the need for translation. I was not able to capture this post because Leo had already deleted it when I was preparing to create a screenshot for data collection;

his peers' comments, however, were left intact. As seen here, Leo's friends expressed their surprise at the unusual approach he had taken to produce and translate a Chinese draft into English, a process many perceived to be time-consuming and labor-intensive. Lyn, with self-deprecating humor, drew a distinction between regular and honors sections of FYW, which most Chinese international students refrained from because of its elevated level of difficulty. In her comments, Lyn teased Leo for taking a "lofty, grand, and classy" approach to his assignment, noting sarcastically the perceived intellectual deficiency of "us commoners" in contrast to "you kids in honors." 高大上 (*gao da shang*, lofty, grand, and classy) is an Internet phrase derived from the acronym of three adjectives, 高端, 大气, 上档次 (lofty, grand, and classy), and is used to poke fun at events, behaviors, and styles out of reach for those placed on the lower end of the social strata. Lyn, a talented writer who strategically avoided honors FYW to maintain a solid GPA, used the phrase to tease Leo and to inquire about his experiences in the honors writing class. Leo responded with a sincere explanation, with a focus on his own struggles and his regret to have written his essay in Chinese. Lyn's use of the word "commoner" to include herself and everyone else in effect singled Leo out as a high-achieving student. Lyn's hyperbolic expression of admiration was echoed by Sun addressing Leo as a "learning god" (see my discussion of learning identities in Wang, 2017) and multiple students using the figurative expression of "kneeling before" Leo and his talent. Such expressions of admiration, laced with sarcasm and mockery, alarmed Leo, who argued comments like these masked mild resentment and jealousy he might have inadvertently engendered by "showing off" his multilingual writing achievements. As detailed in my field notes, Leo was initially thrilled but increasingly agitated by his peers' comments. After failed attempts to diffuse tension with explanations and jokes, Leo eventually deleted the post. He looked visibly relieved afterward.

In my experiences working with multilingual writers, the approach Leo took was very unusual. International students I taught routinely used digital dictionaries to aid their learning, including efforts to translate unfamiliar disciplinary jargon and instructional language, find an English equivalent for a Chinese word during drafting carried out in English, and perform inventive activities in a mix of languages. However, on the few occasions when I encountered examples of student writing whose tone, lexicon, and style were highly suggestive of the use of translation tools, such students vehemently denied that their essays were translated from drafts written in a different language as if their ability to articulate ideas in their home language revealed a detrimental deficiency. With equal passion, they protested that I would suspect that they recruited digital tools, paid tutors, or roommates to help them navigate writing tasks at hand; these usage of literacy tools and brokers, perceived as illicit and contravening expectations of the writing classroom, seemed to point to another layer of their linguistic, ethical, and moral deficiency. Such a deficit disposition enacts a multilingual ideology, which perceives the relationship between languages as separate and discrete, thereby rendering efforts to negotiate cross-language relations through translation efforts illegitimate. Such an orientation fails to recognize how all language acts are implicated with cross-language negotiation throughout the construction, reception, and circulation of mobile texts assembled through multiple semiotic resources (Canagarajah, 2013). Inherent in the students' rejection of their own practices of finding voice through the meshing of hybrid codes and voices is the working of a dominant ideology that perpetuates linguistic shame and fortifies language barriers (Young, 2009).

Never have I witnessed the endeavor Leo had performed here—an entire essay drafted in Chinese. The comments from Leo's peers seemed to provide additional evidence that such practices were not common. Leo, emboldened by the positive feedback to his attempt to integrate his home language and culture into writing across his ESL, basic, and honors writing classes, wanted to perform his writing craft to the writing researcher. His desire to shine resonated across many spheres of his literacy life, manifesting through his efforts to impress his social media audience with his talents in music, dance, and art and his unorthodox approach to presentations in his honors writing class. More importantly, it provided Leo with an opportunity to perform rhetorical knowledge and practices that had earned him both accolades and humiliation during his journey to grow into a talented writer. During this informal observation, he sought to highlight his linguistic and rhetorical knowledge by drawing me into reading his essay and inviting my feedback on phrases, tropes, and literary devices he crafted. On occasions when I did not immediately understand a sophisticated writerly move, he explained at length and teased me in friendly humor. In contrast to his peers, whose comments reified linguistic hierarchies that privilege English, Leo's draft demonstrated the hybrid, cyclical, and synergetic ways through which multiple languages were woven into contact with each other, their mutual influences upon each other carefully considered, their emergent meanings and grammars iteratively negotiated (Canagarajah, 2013, p. 40).

On the surface, the social media post and the interaction that followed seemed to create another opportunity to move the story toward stabilized meaning. It was through an iterative sequence of invention, drafting, and translation processes that the meaning of the story became increasingly crystallized and articulated across languages. These aspects of the writing remained within the purview and control of the author, as he modulated his writing process, made strategic decisions about details to include, and leveraged writing-related knowledge, practices, and strategies developed across language and life worlds to draft the story. Analyzed with the broader insight of the essay and Leo's vigilance toward others' reactions to his actions, the impulsive and idiosyncratic decision to delete the post was coherent with the lesson on humility and restraint that was imparted through familial teaching and pursued in the essay.

Moreover, Leo's decision to delete the post pointed to the unintended consequences of mismatched expectations of the writer and his readers. Leo's WeChat post, intended to channel his frustration and seek empathy, was received with curiosities about his approach to writing and his peers' relentless efforts to mark him as different. What I initially saw as harmless teasing, when his peers expressed exaggerated admiration for perceived distinction Leo had achieved through his demonstration of linguistic dexterity and intellectual superiority, visibly agitated him. Although Leo embraced his academic aspirations and took pride in his ability to navigate a challenging curriculum that the institutional hierarchy rewarded, he was not comfortable occupying a social position that isolated him from and placed him above his peers. Writing on social media, with its intensely social, emotionally charged, and highly interactive features, lent itself to such unexpected social consequences.

Leo used the series of social media posts of the calligraphy story to not only discover and rediscover the story but forge meaningful connections with important players in his literacy landscape. Such connections, originating from casual relationships formed in a shared learning space, evolved precariously through playful interactions on social media. These connections were dynamic, formed and reformed through conversations around slices of intimate personal details that also addressed shared struggles and triumphs of multilingual writers finding their ways at the university. Just as it is important to understand the "quirks and needs not only of the fungi—with their idiosyncratic reproductive systems—but also of the trees and the bacteria they live with" (Sheldrake, 2020, p. 39), it is important to understand the social and intellectual significance of the calligraphy story in connection to

Leo's relationships with important literate beings and the subtle variations in his natural, cultural, and literacy surrounds. Established relationships thickened through sustained following, friendly comments, playful banters, curious inquiries, and words of sympathy and comfort. But they could also cause pain, fracture friendships, and force writers into silence.

Unintended consequences are the "outcome of the divergent, layered, and conjoined projects that make up our worlds because patterns of unintentional coordination develop in assemblages of entangled livelihoods" (Tsing, 2015, p. 24). An entanglement perspective suggests that we move beyond limiting analysis of the writer situated in one spacetime configuration in one set of relationships; instead, we turn toward open-ended gathering of multiple ways of being through the lens of the writer, the evolving story, and readers.

Dwelling on surprises, manifesting in Leo's thrill and frustration over unexpected reactions of his readers and his impulsive decision to delete his post, allows me to notice how careful planning, tested strategies, and researched practices constantly made way for surprises, innovation, and negotiations as multiple voices, perspectives, and historical trajectories coalesced. The pleasures and alarms, triggered by surprises, surfaced in powerful ways in Leo's efforts to connect and engage through writing; to notice his own emplacements in the semiotic environs of social media and the university; and to work through linguistic, cultural, and rhetorical differences that were not immediately visible. It is by dwelling on unpredictable, transformative encounters that I began to notice the multilingual processes as indeterminate and innovative. Unpredictable encounters necessarily produce unintended consequences and invite open-ended negotiation of shifting relationships based on cultural affinity, class identities, and academic achievements. Leo's emplacement in, traverse through, and encounter with open assemblages of readers and texts across spatial-temporal framings generate visceral sensations, intellectual insights, and powerful affects that bubble through spontaneous spurts and sustained contemplations. They gain indeterminate mobile potentials and become tangled in past, present, and future endeavors to produce utterances, meaning, and knowledge. As the writer and his friends "strike compromises, resolve trade-offs, and deploy sophisticated trading strategies" (Sheldrake, 2020, p. 136), unintended consequences in turn invite ongoing negotiation that depends on what is taking place around the constant efforts to make or break relationships, weigh options, and make choices in ingenious ways. Unintended consequences, premised upon the need for ongoing negotiation and attunement, therefore provide a lens to consider how multilingual writing and the multilingual writer emerge and transform as the result of unpredictable encounters.

What Do Unpredictable Encounters Show Us?

The calligraphy story emerged through unpredictable and transformative encounters between the person and his acquaintants, between the writer and his readers, and between past and present efforts to relate to a meaningful experience. These encounters resulted from the polyphonic assemblage of multiple historical trajectories of Leo's multilingual life experiences accumulated in the past 20 years, new and old friendships, ways of feeling and relating to writing, and the improvisational rhythm of his WeChat activities. These encounters across spatial, temporal, cultural, and language differences gave rise to accidents and surprises, taking the writer to unplanned literacy work, on detours from planned writing labor, into extended interactions with unintended social and literacy consequences, and into moments of inspiration and unexpected insights. The multilingual process to discover and articulate the story unraveled the many failed attempts to stick to schedules and plans, modulate spontaneous conversations, steer alternative interpretations toward authorial intention, and regulate playful efforts to interact with the story.

The interactive, unpredictable scene observed here resembles the performance of a jazz band, with players listening for, interacting with, and reacting to one another. A great jazz performance is fluid, improvisational, and indeterminate as each player actively senses and responds to other players, whose thinking, feeling, and reacting ways create dynamic contingencies. Each musician co-emerges with fickle environments in unpredictable ways. The incredibly shifting, dynamic, and improvised scene of Leo's social writing and interaction resembles Sheldrake's discussion of the mycelial network as a swarm of probing, exploratory hyphal tips, which is conceptually slippery because it is simultaneously a multitude when viewed from the perspective of the probing tips and an interconnected, heterogeneous entity when viewed from the perspective of the network (2020, p. 47). It does not make sense to think of the writer, any given reader, and the writing sociality they co-construct solely from the perspective of one individual and their idiosyncratic ways because what each person shares and how one feels about and reacts to another are the results of the interconnected entity that evolves with each effort to respond, refute, bond, and agitate.

The writer, his readers, and the story itself are unpredictably transformed through encounters. Unintended consequences emerge from and evolve with precarious, adventurous living in interaction with and reaction to literacy others. Leo was thrilled, amused, and unsettled by his encounters with the story, his past self, other literate beings, and the unanticipated reaction from his peers, who at times celebrated his achievements, extended his story with playful and (un)desirable interpretations, teased his academic aspirations, or disregarded his frustration over a daunting writing task. Leo's decision to share, interact around, and delete his post were acts of "shapeshifting," which Merlin Sheldrake describes as a central feature of mycelial "developmental indeterminism," when "living, growing, opportunistic" mycelium, as bodily form of speculation, shape-shift to embed itself in irregular and unpredictable environments (2020, p. 51). Leo's self-sponsored writing on social media and the social interactions that ensued often promoted and redirected his writing process in indeterminate directions, with his peers approaching his post with variant perspectives, availabilities, and moods while tailoring their comments in reaction to the reactions of others. The story came into being through unpredictable encounters that produced and were produced by reactions and interactions in interanimating ways. Leo's feelings about his writing indeterminately morphed with the here and now of each encounter, in all its contingencies and surprises.

The perspective of unpredictable encounters encourages us to engage with the cascades of coalescing, changing, and dissolving assemblages. The calligraphy story draws us into the story of Leo's familial teaching, the vicissitudes and dynamism of his transnational literacy landscape, and the increasing affordances of digital tools for annotating, mobilizing, and amplifying personal content. These encounters create imperatives for various kinds of literacy work. In a dynamic discursive scene like this, pieces of information flow in multidirectional and uneven ways and affect, bounce off, and generate themselves as ephemeral assemblages and multidirectional histories forge and dissipate. The impromptu way in which Leo's last WeChat post emerged was as surprising as the impulsive yet resolute decision to erase it. Unless we look for surprises purposefully, the powerful affects that energized Leo's multilingual writing remain elusive. It might be mere chance that I noticed and recognized the need to capture the lingering traces of the ephemeral happening, but it was the methodological decisions that I made, to be with the participant in writing spaces open with opportunities, to embrace fluid positionalities of me as an observer, a teacher, and a friend, and to wander with and follow the trails of the hyphae in the writing landscape, that occasioned the observation. Despite Leo's resolute move to permanently erase its trace, I could not help but feel the powerful affective impact it had on everyone involved. My impromptu decision to retain traces of it then provided me with the opportunity to dwell on it as an example of how a seemingly nonliving, static literacy artifact could have a life and historicity because of its capacity to "assemble many ways of being in an affect-laden knot that packs its own punch" (Tsing, 2015, p. 52). It is therefore important to listen to the multiple thematic lines of the story, the writer, the interactional circle, the researcher, and their coming together in moments when they come into sporadic but consequential coordination.

As evidenced here, affective energies drive and derive from unpredictable encounters to add layers of texture to the story's substance. Here my observation echoes what Prior et al. (2023) has argued—"becoming is shaped not only by the intensities of moments, but also by the sustained, often backgrounded, bio-cultural-historical weight co-genetically embedded as affordances in emergent functional systems that generates resonances across beings, sociomaterial spaces, and timescales" (p. 32). That is, the calligraphy story was situated in a childhood encounter; the lesson it imparted was contemplated over time and juxtaposed with a range of extracurricular activities intended to cultivate his character. As the story was repurposed, translated, and reconfigured across spacetimes, it joined in complex relationships with Leo's social media audience to generate a mix of intrigue, surprise, incredulity, admiration, envy, caution, humility, and amusement. As social interactions erupted with surprising energy, traces of affect, memory, and meaning resurfaced and crystallized through Leo's effort to make sense of the story in collaboration with his audience. Although the form of the story seemed to incrementally stabilize when discursive moves were replicated faithfully across iterations (note how the three turns of dialogue had retained their original form and substance across drafts, languages, and modes), the simultaneous interplay of these iterations continued to transform the story, generating intended and unexpected insights and affects. These affects powerfully directed the contours of Leo's multilingual writing by inspiring impromptu acts of writing with thrill, inviting pondering about authorial intentions and audience expectations, and agitating trepidation over and appreciation of the power of words.

5
Following Chronotopic Figuring

As I have observed thus far, the calligraphy story emerged and grew through Leo's iterative and interactive attempts to remember and record it, capture and articulate compelling details, process its powerful affects, and co-construct its meaning with his peers. Such a process allowed Leo to recursively "perform" the story across multiple languages, modes, spacetimes, and audiences. Similarly, the dynamically surprising and creative scenes, where Leo's peers took up his calligraphy story and collaboratively remixed it in alignment with different genres of youth and popular culture, showed us how Leo's multilingual writing was always buzzing with the polyphonic voices, perspectives, and experiences of other literacy beings. These scenes mirror Merlin Sheldrake's description of the cultural and musical practice of "Women Gathering Mushrooms" in the forests of Aka, the Central African Republic, when they weave disparate melodic and lyrical lines into a polyphonic performance of harmony and difference. Similarly, the calligraphy story took shape in a polyphonic way, as multiple meanings of and emotions toward the story coalesced across multiple temporal trajectories of the person-, writer-, and story-in-becoming.

In this chapter, I complicate Leo's performance of strategic silence, a seemingly idiosyncratic writerly move, by observing how it gradually

https://doi.org/10.7330/9781646427628.c005

emerged as an important writing strategy he consistently deployed throughout his literacy and social life. I begin by contextualizing my discussion of strategic silence, which manifested in Leo's sustained efforts to practice self-censorship, manage and erase digital content, and silence his own voice and experiences, within scholarly inquiry into rhetorical silence. I then perform a chronotopic analysis of Leo's strategic silence as informed by familial teaching, which resulted from his family's effort to navigate the privileges and perils of their class identities. In shifting my attention away from multilingual writing per se, this chapter situates Leo's iterative performance of strategic silence within a broader range of identity practices central to his identity as a second-generation governmental official. Specifically, I use chronotopic figuring to connect Leo's idiosyncratic practices of strategic silence to familial practices for occupying one's class identity, which are shaped by social discourses of discontent and increasing public surveillance of social elites in contemporary China.

Rhetorical Silence

Scholars in rhetoric and composition have called attention to silence as an undervalued and under-theorized rhetorical act (Glenn, 2004). Theorization of silence and silencing as rhetorical acts challenges long-standing emphasis that has conceptualized speech and language as the authorized medium for achieving humanity, which provides the conceptual ground for viewing silence as simply the absence of speech. Such a conceptual binary between speech and silence has historically served to suppress the voice of disenfranchised groups, as silence was positioned as a "lamentable essence of femininity, a trope for oppression, passivity, emptiness, stupidity, or obedience" (Glenn, 2004, p. 2). However, scholars have also noted the rhetorical work entailed by strategic acts to maintain or break imposed silence. Belanoff (2003) suggests that silence allows those historically deprived of their voice to use reflection and meditation to push through constraints against their right to speak. Shimabukuro (2011) provides compelling analysis of how incarcerated Japanese Americans used *gaman*, an inherited cultural rhetoric for "enduring difficulty in silence," to survive rampant racism, enforced curfews, and forced relocations that made up the humiliation and hardships of the incarceration period. While the rhetorical practice of *gaman* seemingly encourages outward silence and quiet acceptance of oppression, it also allowed Japanese Americans in internment camps to verbalize a wide range of emotion-thoughts through politically resistant uses of literacy and writing to redress the racist logics used to justify their imprisonment.

Cheryl Glenn (2004) has noted how the keeping and breaking of public silences by women such as Anita Hill and Lani Guinier were the result of these women's negotiation of imposed power differentials, survivance, and social responsibilities. For Lani Guinier, the University of Pennsylvania law professor nominated to head the Justice Department's Civil Rights Division by President Clinton, silence was imposed on her following efforts by rightwing conservatives to politicize her nomination, condemning her into wordless silence and humiliation. By contrast, Anita Hill used silence not only to protect her from becoming a public spectacle but to raise her voice to help sensitize Americans to the pervasiveness and difficulty of sexual harassment. Silence—self-determined, deliberately imposed, or strategically broken—was read differently, as some celebrated Hill's breaking of her silence as a brave act to advance feminist civil rights while others condemned it as a conniving opportunist's futile effort to sabotage the appointment of a Supreme Court judge. Guinier's forced silence allowed the media to negatively portray her as a quota nominee and to destroy her political opportunities. In scenarios like these, silence, employed as tactical strategy or inhabited in deference to authority, "resonates loudly along the corridors of purposeful language use, . . . can reveal positive or negative abilities, fulfilling or withholding traits, harmony or disharmony, success or failure" (Glenn, 2004, p. 15). As rhetorical practice, silence can deploy as well as serve power. In so doing, these scholars have challenged conceptions of silence as surrounding discourse, subordinate to speech, and insignificant in terms of power and culture, instead arguing that silence and speech shape and generate each other in making meaning. Silence, as speech, fulfills different purposes—to threaten, show deference, resist, connect, judge, or agitate. It is differently motivated by the need to break a stream of conversation, signify an invitation for others to contribute, mark the exhaustion of a topic, punish and exclude certain participants, enforce social orders, or disrupt power differentials. Accordingly, silence is invested with power; its meaning and function depend on the specific power differential embedded in a rhetorical situation, partially directing who can speak or remain silent, who may listen, what can be said, and what those listeners could do (Glenn, 2004, p. 8).

This view of silence as inextricably entangled with speech, as power-invested, and as fulfilling dynamic rhetorical purposes, informs my thinking of silence as a site of knowing, composing, and generating meaning. When we enact silence as a strategic choice, we use it toward expressive, aesthetic, ethical, and political aims. This is particularly useful for contemplating the various forms of silence materializing in the pedagogical and personal spaces writers and writing teachers navigate. Anne Ruggles Gere (2001) points to public silence, manifested in students' refusal to disclose details of hardship, as resistance to participate in the exploitation of the vulnerable. That is, silence can be a transformative and revolutionary space that provides creativity, inspiration, and protection for writers feeling marginalized by their language and cultural differences, sexual orientation, racial and class backgrounds, and traumatic experiences. These students could leverage silence to shield themselves from the view of an attentive audience and to safely and tentatively make sense and meaning of experiences and language and cultural irregularities. Highlighting the strategic ways in which we deploy silence across modes (e.g., speech, languaging) and rhetorical situations (e.g., private, public, political), this perspective recognizes silence for fostering insight and nourishing ideas for writing and creates an argument for pedagogical efforts to help students deploy silence with its aesthetic, ethical, and political affordance and commitments. Together, these authors move us away from a conception of silence as crippling, chaotic, and passive and instead encourage us to recognize the productive, transformative, and empowering potentials of silence.

In this chapter, I echo these scholars' argument to not simply dismiss silence as evidence of passivity or absence of ideas and instead examine the power-invested norms that shape the aesthetic, rhetorical, and political purposes of silence in Leo's multilingual writing process. To meaningfully engage with Leo's strategic silence, I learned to listen to polyphonic temporal rhythms of his multilingual life, which brought multiple streams of literacy and identity practices and social discourses into sporadic but consequential coordination. These literacy and identity practices, cultivated and developed across Leo's lifespan, powerfully shaped writerly decisions I initially dismissed as impulsive and random. Chronotopic figuring, as a frame of analysis, directs my attention away from the various "contexts" of writing such as FYW classroom, social media, or private spheres; instead, I look for ways in which stories, insights, and practices reverberate with their own histories, rhythms, and melodic lines to inform writing-related decisions and strategies. On the surface, Leo's multilingual writing unfolded within a unified, instructor-coordinated rhythm of his FYW classroom, which leveraged a series of invention, drafting, reviewing, and revision activities to help Leo find his voice and commit his story to words. When we look beyond the pedagogical efforts to find voice, however, I notice the many intertwining enactments of silences that played out in Leo's cyclical, interactive, and indeterminate process of writing the calligraphy story and performing his class identity. Following Sheldrake's call to listen to the "archaic and strange" forms of polyphonic rhythms of open-ended gatherings, I learn to listen for moments of harmony and dissonance when individual, interactional, familial, and national trajectories were chronotopically figured to shape Leo's practices of strategic silence.

Performing Strategic Silence

Leo's life motto was to straddle the multiple worlds of the wealthy, educated, and talented social elites. He aimed to be "the wealthiest among the educated, the most educated among the rich, and the most talented among the rich and educated." Such views were reflective of his class identity as a second-generation government official. His parents were both first-generation, college graduates, and successful professionals who achieved upward social mobility through educational credentials acquired at reputable Chinese universities and memberships in the ruling Communist Party. His father, the executive head of a state-owned enterprise, and his mother, an esteemed surgeon at a local hospital, were busy professionals. In Leo's words, "The distribution of responsibilities was clearly defined in my home. Our live-in nanny took care of me and the apartment. I was responsible for having fun. My parents just worked and worked." In contrast to the archetype of the traditional Chinese parents who demand academic excellence and nothing else from their children, Leo's parents were more concerned with developing his character as a well-rounded individual.

When discussing his life aspirations, Leo also referenced his role model, Wang Sicong, an Internet celebrity and archetype of China's second-generation rich, whose constant wealth-flaunting and luxury brand name-dropping had drawn scathing criticism from the public. Leo criticized the Chinese public for focusing on Wang's scandalous behavior and failing to see how Wang's elite education in the humanities and social sciences (e.g., philosophy, political science) was key in preparing China's new generation of aristocrats consisting of heirs to emerging business conglomerates. To a degree, Leo organized his academic studies in emulation of Wang by taking courses in philosophy, theater, political science, and fine arts. To Leo, such coursework might not prepare him for a job but would equip him with the disposition and soft skills to join the social elite, who would continue to propel and benefit from China's booming economy.

As much as Leo actively molded his academic profile in alignment with popularized imaginary of China's future elite, his family teaching consistently emphasized the values of restraint and humility framed within traditional Confucius teaching:

> "Hide brightness and nourish obscurity" has been a motto my father emphasizes. He wants me to restrain myself and not to show off, especially under current political circumstances. Ever since my younger years, he has always said, "I don't want you to be a talent that everyone seeks out; [I] just want you to be a good person." In retrospect, sending me to practice calligraphy and Tai Chi were efforts to cultivate discipline and character—learn to practice restraint and smooth my sharp edges—that's how you go a long way.

Sustained familial teaching of humility and restraint provides a lens to consider Leo's deployment of a literacy practice that I describe as strategic silence. I use "strategic silence" to name a wide range of purposeful erasures, which could manifest in descriptive and conceptual gaps left unfilled in drafts, imaginative possibilities eliminated, details withheld, desires restrained, voices silenced, and aspirations unachieved. Moving physically and imaginatively with Leo throughout his writing process has alerted me to the fact that it was often things left unsaid, details failing to travel, and decisions to eliminate traces of multilingual living that unraveled complex backstories that held much intellectual and emotional significance for writers like Leo. The strategic decisions made to withhold, silence, and hide certain aspects of his experiences and identities were as revealing as visible practices to write toward coherence, clarity, and elaboration in approximation of standardized, edited writing expected in FYW.

Chronotopic figuring provides a useful lens for exploring the ongoing, open-ended, multi-actor, and dynamic process of the writer/person-in-becoming through resonance across materialities, activities, and spacetimes. Leo's family offered teaching on the values of humility, patience, endurance, and restraint through disparate streams of extracurricular activities such as Tai Chi and calligraphy, which cultivated the body and the mind through physical training with concrete, material implications (e.g., the physical pain from practicing a Tai Chi standing posture). Familial teaching also took place through intertextually connected family conversations that contained memorable mottos and sayings, likely motivated by childish behaviors that invited parental reprimand, and lectures on social norms and etiquette. Temporal polyphony invites our attention to how historically developed narratives, activities, practices, lessons, and experiences intertwine to animate moments of literacy and identity practices, which then fuse, connect, and branch into new trajectories of making meanings. Such familial teaching manifested in the reflective insight of Leo's essay: Humility and endurance are essential qualities for survival and success, especially when contrasted with arrogance and ostensible display of privilege.

The values of humility and restraint, as embodied by the aesthetic form of calligraphy, were so strong that Leo contemplated the integration of multimodal images into his essay to amplify his insight. Such a decision involved significant creative risks. Leo read the project description closely and consulted his teacher to ensure that his inclusion of multimodal images would not be penalized. As shown in Figure 5.1, his title page included two images placed in juxtaposition, each containing the words "endurance" and "inner peace" written in different calligraphy styles. The image on the left (see Figure 5.1) contained the word 忍, ren, which Leo translated into "endurance," along with a proverb that read 忍一时海阔天空，退一步风平浪静, translated as "restraint in the moment ensures space for exploration; small compromise ensures peace and harmony." The image on the right of Figure 5.1 contained the word 静, which Leo translated as "inner peace," along with the proverb 静以修身，俭以养德, translated as "cultivate your character in tranquility and your virtue in frugality." Presented visually, these images also materialized the aesthetics of Chinese calligraphy that Leo struggled to articulate in his essay, which opened with a dramatic scene depicting his father resisting the impulse to inflict corporal punishment when he was informed of Leo's infringement of school rules, followed by a scene of a frustrated young Leo suffering through his punishment by trying but failing to concentrate on calligraphic practice, and his encounter with the young woman, whose utter absorption in the art form moved him emotionally and imaginatively. The values, multimodally represented, served as the backdrop against which the meaning of the story could be comprehended and interpreted.

This visual display of calligraphic art not only worked to enhance the insight of Leo's essay, these images also string figured disparate trajectories of embodied activities, familial and Confucianist teaching, calligraphy as an art form, and his personal encounter into assemblage. The integration of Chinese calligraphy invoked moral lessons developed in a much longer

FIGURE 5.1. Multimodal Title Page for Leo's Memoir Assignment

historical trajectory of Confucianist teaching, which emphasizes virtues such as self-restraint, simplicity, and frugality with proverbs, poems, essays, and tales voiced by parents, teachers, and classical authors. In discursive scenes like this, the moment-to-moment happenings of Leo's essay-writing emerged from the dynamic knotting and figuring of cultural, literacy, and familial histories to inform the insight of his essay.

In addition to pursuing the values of restraint and humility as the focus of his essay, Leo also exercised restraint through his practice of strategic silence. As I have discussed in Chapter 4, the drafting of the calligraphy story was filled with erasures and losses. Such was the case when Leo deleted his WeChat post in reaction to what he perceived to be audience antipathy toward his academic achievement, linguistic dexterity, and access to resources, privileges that were out of reach for most. The deletion put an end to an episode of multilingual writing, erasing traces of playful interpretations and silencing curious inquiries. Such erasures gain new analytical significance when chronotopically figured with his decision to initially withhold information about the artistic achievement of the young woman, which could have enhanced the dramatic impact of the story. Leo's omission created ambiguity, invited inquiry, and left spaces for playful extensions, which led to the audience missing the story's significance. Viewed through the lens of chronotopic figuring, strategic silence took shape through heterogeneous activities and histories in messy, haphazard, and uneven ways, incrementally entering assemblages to create spaces for coordination, attunement, and negotiation and informing patterned ways of accessing semiotic and rhetorical repertoires in response to new contingencies. These moments of strategic silence should not be dismissed as consequences of idiosyncrasy or impulsive decisions but as windows into writing-related strategies, dispositions, and knowledge that Leo developed and mobilized across multiple spheres of his literacy and social life.

Masking Second-Generation Privilege

Strategic silence also manifested in Leo's much-pondered decision to eliminate an alternative idea for his Memoir assignment. After reading the project description repeatedly and seeking his teacher's affirmation that he could indeed write about any type of "learning" events, especially those occurring beyond school spaces, Leo initially proposed a recent experience—a shopping trip to Chicago when his father instructed him to visit several luxury stores and to purchase a jacket for business occasions.

At the time of my research, a weekend trip to Chicago—consisting of a 5-hour bus ride with Michigan Flyer's express shuttle, shopping at department and luxury stores on the bustling Michigan Avenue, staying at the iconic downtown Trump Hotel, and sharing meals in authentic Chinese restaurants in the historic Chinatown—was a staple of Chinese international students' social life. I was nonetheless surprised by Leo's enthusiastic recollection of his recent shopping trip because he never struck me as the consumerist type. Indeed, Leo was visibly different from the stereotypically wealthy Chinese international students on campus, whose BMWs, Valentino Rockstud backpacks, Givenchy rottweiler T-shirts, and Yeezy 350 sneakers gave visible testimony to their affluence. In contrast, Leo's shopping trips were intended as opportunities to expose him to a luxury lifestyle rather than acquiring material goods:

> My dad has a unique way of teaching me things—he never tells me why he wants me to do this or that, nor does he give me any advice beforehand. After I am done making a fool of myself, he will talk to me about his intention and help me see the lesson. I asked him if I should buy formal clothing for job interviews, and he said, "You pick a brand, but it cannot be a brand with shops in malls; it needs to have its own storefront." My friends

and I passed the Burberry's store in Chicago; it met the "having-its-own-building" criterion. I dragged my friend inside, but it was so embarrassing. Six good-looking people were waiting on us and the girls in ridiculously high heels were taller than me. They had a Chinese-speaking client specialist; he communicated with staff members in the back through a wireless earbud so that he didn't leave my side while someone got the merchandise. They helped me accessorize. My friend was so stunned that he refused to go to the second floor. I was terrified, feeling like a peasant visiting the city for the first time. It was such a fancy store, with floors dedicated to shoes, shirts, and suits. Its vaulted ceilings, beautiful decorations, and mirrored walls made the space look so grand. My jacket probably costs more than what many people make in a whole year.

Earlier on the trip, Leo had already visited Hermes' flagship store in Chicago, with instructions from his father to simply browse without buying anything. The experience was equally nerve-wrecking after his friend abandoned him, leaving Leo to persevere through the "tortuous" experience. After the trip, he took these issues to his father and received one lesson that he was to "see the world of luxury for yourself, for if you want to be a businessman, you need to look and behave like one." As he delved into details about his trip, it became clear that shopping was but one of many experiences his father orchestrated to socialize Leo into the worlds of China's political and business elite. As impactful and significant as this "learning" experience was, Leo hesitated and eventually rejected it as a learning event he could explore in his essay, insisting the story would be inappropriate because unnecessary revelation of his privilege might invite antipathy and jealousy.

Reflecting on this experience in connection to prevalent wealth flaunting on campus, Leo revealed that he carefully maintained a "loser" look to mask the various privileges he had always enjoyed, such as having a live-in nanny when he was a child, an abundance of expensive extracurricular activities, and his shopping adventures. For the time I had known Leo, he was habitually dressed in the same pair of slightly oversized Nike sneakers, a pair of loose black jeans, a simplistically styled beige jacket, and a Tigers baseball cap he bought from the campus bookstore. Nothing of his appearance gave the impression that he cared about fashion or came from money. Along with the plain and low-profile look he maintained was his careful choice of wording in describing himself. He was cautious with class labels such as second-generation rich, *tuhao* (vulgar and rich), or 屌丝 (*diaosi*, loser), terms his peers used frivolously and sarcastically to describe themselves and others. It was after months of working with me that he divulged the fact that peers who knew him well would refer to him as a second-generation government official. He suggested that he felt comfortable being called a *diaosi* (loser) because of the careless ways in which he dressed and his refrain from voicing his opinion on serious social issues, arguing that he had inadvertently attracted unwanted attention in middle school, when his classmates expressed jealousy about his talents, intelligence, and his family's political power.

Here we observe concrete evidence of Leo balancing what Gere describes as the seductiveness of the "pleasure of writing revelations" and the felt need to shield private aspects of his life from the glare of the public light (2001, p. 209). Such tensions are especially visible in personal writing assignments aligned with expressivist pedagogy, which encourages students to draw upon, write about, and reflect on their own lives. Pleasure for student writers arises from the invitation to make sense of their own experiences, to claim their own positions in the world, and to become protagonists in their own stories. At the same time, revealing intimate details of an intense emotional experience could evoke pain, embarrassment, and jealousy as Leo noted here. To some extent, Leo was also troubled by the potential (ill) fit between this narrative topic and pedagogical expectations for this assignment, which his teacher worked in collaboration with the students to surface. Leo, noting that most "good" topics that surfaced through an in-class invention activity, during which students volunteered their tentative topics followed by class discussions, were "positive" stories about overcoming an obstacle such as a learning disability, achieving a challenging goal, or healing from a traumatic experience such as the loss of a family pet. As such, Leo's reservation mirrors what Gere describes as a common experience for students from "boring" and privileged backgrounds, who "fall into an inarticulate silence because they feel that their life experiences have not given them access to narratives" (2001, p. 207).

In addition to his concern for the conceptual fit of his topic, Leo's strategic silence was informed by sustained familial teaching that focused on masking the many privileges Leo enjoyed as a second-generation government official, a class label that was distinctly contrasted with second-generation rich, whose ostentatious consumerism and unrestrained flaunt of family wealth made it a very visible social class in China and on the university campus (Higgins, 2013; Louie & Qin, 2019). Leo's incremental reckoning with his class identity as a second-generation government official, which came with privileges and perils, played out against the backdrop of the sociopolitical circumstances of contemporary Chinese society, where widespread social discontent over shifting social structures and intensifying wealth disparity energized increasing government scrutiny of the social elite.

Although Leo did not engage in ostentatious consumerism as many of his peers did, his family nonetheless offered access to class privileges by providing opportunities that exposed him to the luxury lifestyle of the global elite; they also orchestrated induction experiences that educated Leo about the etiquette, opportunities, and risks of the business world. As Leo recalled, he had often received invitations to social gatherings hosted by business owners hoping to curry favors from his father. Leo described a recent incident in which a business associate invited him to a weekend getaway in a nearby metropolitan city. After having rejected numerous invitations in the past, Leo, now a university student, received permission from his father to attend. In addition to using this occasion to practice business etiquette, Leo received detailed instructions on how to reject unwelcome business advances aiming at securing a contract from a lucrative government project his father oversaw:

> He took me to a luxury hotel near the Lake [a historical landmark]. The hotel was modeled after classical Chinese gardens, you know those with arched stone bridges and meandering streams caressing each villa. You can hardly hear the traffic outside; but it was in the middle of a bustling city. After treating me to a soothing spa, he slipped a membership card into the pocket of my robe, saying that it would give me unlimited access to the hotel. I didn't reject him on the spot but asked the hotel's concierge to return the card when I checked out. We were walking back to my room when I saw a blue Lamborghini parked in front of one villa. I decided there and then my goal was to buy my own Lamborghini before I turned 30. He must have seen the spark in my eyes. The next day, he took me to a car dealer and literally pushed me inside a McLaren, saying, "I can tell you have good tastes. Say the word and I will get this car for you." I was shocked by his bluntness, but I turned him down gently by saying that I would rather buy it with my own money. After we came back, my dad praised me for how I handled the situation. I got out of a tricky situation without damaging professional relationships.

Keenly cognizant of the fact that the business associate was using him to gain leverage with his dad, Leo rejected such advances firmly and courteously. According to him, his failure to return the membership card could entrap his dad in sticky graft allegations. As a young man who had been inducted to the world of business dealings, he saw such interactions as grounds to engage in "psychological games" and to outsmart his opponents. He was also well informed of principles of reciprocity that underlined such transactions:

> I would have to take something valuable from him to be indebted to him; my dad would then have to repay my debt with business favors. He could own and leverage my dad for his own interests if I am not careful. I will never put my dad in that vulnerable position.

These experiences uniquely positioned Leo as an important, invisible player in forging business connections. While his father did not encourage him to leverage the business and political influence his family possessed, such "adventures" were important to educate Leo about the codes for acting, behaving, and engaging with others in the business world. It was through such experiences that Leo learned to inhabit his class identity in distinction from other categories of second-generation privilege, specifically second-generation rich, whose family wealth does not translate into class status elevation.

It is important to consider Leo's identity practices against the backdrop of shifting social classifications, which has recently returned to public perception and discourse after a long period of erasure in the Marxist-Leninist-Maoist tradition that created social strata that distinguished the peasants, industrial workers, intellectuals, and the Communist Party cadres (Dong & Blommaert, 2016). As these scholars argue, drastic social and economic transformations since the 1980s have upended social classifications by giving birth to social groups such as the second-generation rich, celebrity, and government official, who experienced difficulties in defining their class status from the lack of historical continuity and the absence of a reliable frame of reference based on indicators such as income, occupation, and education. China's social elites, some occupying positions of power and others accumulating immense wealth, are complexly entangled together but work hard to distinguish themselves from each other.

Second-generation rich are often perceived to have inherited the "vulgar lifestyle" of their parents, whose accumulation of immense wealth often results from opportunistic manipulation of loopholes in a poorly regulated market economy. With no aristocratic models to emulate and no templates for spending immense fortune, second-generation rich are often associated with extravagant spending in luxury goods and unruly behavior, which easily instigated disparagement and antipathy from the public. By contrast, second-generation government officials often enjoy a life of comfort, as pressures to participate in cutthroat competition is lower and entry into stable and comfortable career trajectories is made easier with family connections. Furthermore, in an economy where resources are controlled by state-owned corporations, private enterprises often leverage *guanxi* practices (Wang, 2017; Ling, 2011) to procure contracts for state-funded projects, which provide government officials with opportunities to leverage their political capital in reciprocation of financial and material benefits. In different ways, children of second-generation privileges are reaping the benefits of shifting social structures, which operate with winner-take-all mechanisms and mindsets deplored by social critics in China (Li, 2012).

It is through induction activities such as these that Leo gained valuable insights into the norms and practices of conducting business at the intersection of private and state enterprises, political influence and business interests, and opportunities and perils. Such experiences were also important pathways for him to discover his position in highly hierarchical and simultaneously fluid social structures. For one thing, Leo's family used these opportunities to cultivate soft status markers, such as one's fine taste in cars, wine collecting, and regular international travel to distinguish him from the poorly educated, newly rich business owners. Cultural experiences, such as a weekend luxury shopping trip, vacation in reclusive hotels, and learning about exotic sports cars, progressively inscribed Leo with social structures that helped him develop class-specific dispositions and practices.

Embodied moments of living his multilingual life, manifested through his humble appearance, orchestrated performance of artistic talents, calculated decision to withhold information, and consistent practice to shield aspects of his life from public view, coalesced to make up a repertoire of strategies for performing silence. He contrasted strategic silence, which allowed him to explore complex emotions and aspirations in subtle ways, with the ostensible wealth-flaunting of his classmates, many of whom fell into the category of the second-generation rich. The need to mask class privileges even though his family possessed the cultural knowledge and financial means to support his participation in elite, consumerist lifestyles was justified through the lens of Confucianist philosophies. Along these lines, discursive moves that enacted strategic silence played out against competing social, political, and pedagogical discourses that encourage reflective sharing of authentic experiences, perpetuate social norms for conducting oneself, and hierarchically valuates class-specific ways to access and use privileges. Attending to dispersed moments when Leo made decisions to eliminate topics, omit details, and mask feelings and desires as chronotopically figured performances of strategic silence unraveled a complexity of familial, social, and political discourses that powerfully mediated Leo's approach to occupy his class identity.

This analysis shows how embodied activities across spacetimes are intricately intertwined to give rise to strategic silence, an identity and literacy practice Leo deployed to navigate dynamic social situations and emergent relationships. Multiple historical trajectories coalesced in messy and uneven ways to generate dissonance and resonate meanings and purposes for the practice. Moment-to-moment performance of strategic silence wove together multiple activity spheres, bodies of conceptual and experiential knowledge, and rhetorical and semiotic repertoires. Never a one-time process, chronotopic figuring invites us to consider the messy and exploratory ways in which bits and pieces of ideas, narratives, artifacts, voices, and practices mobilize, energize, and detach from one another across spacetimes to create new and qualitatively different meanings that a single experience could not produce. In this sense, strategic silence is the practice and process of Leo becoming those differently invested and interested in the privileges, resources, and opportunities provided by his class identity. Leo's performances of the practice were contingent, as he attuned the particularities of power dynamics and relationships entailed in each social situation.

Exercising Censorship to Navigate Perilous Class Identity

> Sometimes I couldn't help but feel aggrieved. I can't drive cars that I desire. I can't share details of my vacation; however modest they are. I can't even post about me waiting for a flight; a reprimand phone call would be waiting for me when I arrive at the destination airport. I yelled at my dad, "Are we so poor that I can't even take a flight?" But I get his point. Deleted my post in a second.
> —Leo

During the interview, from which the above excerpt above was taken, Leo shared his grievance over a recent conflict with his father, who reprimanded him for posting about his return trip from a brief vacation. Leo's audience on WeChat, primarily composed of peers and friends he acquired through familial, academic, and professional networks in China and the US, was viewed with suspicion. His family performed routine surveillance of his social media to help him navigate the perils associated with their class identity. Invoking the Chinese idiom 韬光养晦 (*tao guang yang hui*, hide rightness and nourish obscurity), which drew on historical narratives of heroes persevering through humiliation toward eventual triumph to encourage strategic concealment of one's strengths, his family justified the exercise of surveillance by suggesting that modesty was a means of coaxing one's enemies into lowering their guard, which was key to one's effort to realize one's ambition. As I detailed in Chapter 4, Leo practiced self-censorship with rigor, specifically in his frequent deletion of social media content.

Leo's family modeled strategic silence through sustained parental surveillance of his social media, partly in response to prevalent censorship mechanisms implemented by the Chinese government to silence dissenting voices. Leo's practice resonates with the tension motivating Chinese Internet users' performance of evasive practices to find their voice in a tightly regulated Internet ecology, which routinely monitors, censors, and silences voices deemed unharmonious. China studies scholars have documented how Chinese netizens use memes to engage with state discourse, evade censorship, and deliver political commentary (Yang, 2016) and to provide implicit critique of increasing income disparity and hardening of social structures that produce class frictions (Szablewicz, 2014). In these cases, Internet users used memes, such as the self-deprecating class label of "loser" and images of an empty chair, to provide implicit commentary on social issues and to voice dissenting voices in response to Chinese government's detainment of a Nobel Prize winner. Sarcastic commentaries on class issues, humorous jabs at social and political concerns, and ostensible display of wealth sit uncomfortably with the authoritarian state because they disrupt state control. Leo's strategic silence is therefore an effort to remedy what he came to recognize as transgression against state control and social norm.

Strategic silence is part of a repertoire of survival strategies that his family developed to cope with pressures arising from intensified public and government surveillance of those in positions of privilege. Familial efforts to mask privileges started early, as Leo was "tricked into believing his family was barely making ends meet and [he] should not embrace grand goals and aspirations." Leo recounted a "hilarious" event in elementary school, when he was given a financial aid application after he described his father as a truck driver during a school activity. He joked about his own shock when he discovered that his father was the head of a state-owned enterprise, who led projects that drew government investment in the billions.

As much as material luxury desired by Leo emblematized the promise of China's fast economic growth, ostentatious wealth flaunting by those in positions of power has instigated public outrage, especially after a series of social scandals exposing privileged youngsters leveraging parental influence to evade legal and social consequences of criminal wrongdoings (Kan, 2013). The most notable example was a 2012 scandal following a Ferrari crash in Beijing that involved two young women and the son of a top aide to President Hu Jintao, all of whom were partially naked when they were thrown from the car, instigating public outrage, arrest of the government official, and corruption charges. Outrageous wealth-flaunting by children of powerful government officials posed serious risks to social harmony and political stability, two staples of the Communist Party's governing policy. Social scandals such as this imbued the class label "second-generation government official," with sarcastic antipathy, leading to the word now being synonymous with corruption and used to describe the lack of moral compass among those who abuse political influences for personal gains.

In response, the Chinese government has launched comprehensive anti-corruption campaigns and austerity measures to simultaneously appease societal discontent, propel economic transformation, and modify political structure (Fabre, 2017; Xi, 2016). The sweeping anti-corruption campaign has led to intensified surveillance of the political elites by specifically targeting powerful government officials such as Leo's father. Pained to witness his father's efforts to tread perilous grounds, Leo critiqued a debilitating political environment that continuously tightened its grip through a harsh anti-corruption agenda. Moreover, he critiqued mainstream media for fueling an anti-privilege discourse by sensationalizing reports of social scandals involving children of second-generation privilege:

> [As a government official, you need to] combat too many temptations. And the current trend is to place a lot of emphasis on austerity in how government agents conduct personal and official business. It has gone this far—you could be jailed for attending a dinner gathering that has a tiny business purpose. Current circumstances have reached a point where the ancient adage applies, "Water that is too clear has few fish; one who is too critical has few friends." It is incredibly harsh. Also, the Chinese media has no conscience. They capitalize on sensational details when reporting on news to stir up anti-rich rhetoric. It is terrifying how the Chinese public shows their hatred towards the rich. For example, a Chinese international student had a car accident [in the United States], Chinese media does not report on the loss of a life; they focus on the car. If it was a BMW, the headlines are sure to read "Second generation rich crashing in a luxury car," and everyone in China says, "They deserve it [to die] in their luxury cars bought with corruption money." But BMW or Mercedes Benz are not even luxury cars here at all.

Here, Leo developed a nuanced understanding of public attitudes toward rapid change in social hierarchy in contemporary Chinese society. He specifically critiqued the austerity measures to curb official spending, which banned first-class air travel, gifting of luxury items, and extravagant dinners with public funds (Jacobs, 2013), for depriving those in positions of power of agency. The most comprehensive and high-profile anti-corruption campaign in 2013 has led to the investigation of thousands of officials and the prosecution of hundreds of communist party officials on charges of embezzlement, bribery, and graft. These measures have not only gained the government popular support but have been used to purge political rivals and to solidify party legitimacy, leaving officials such as Leo's father particularly vulnerable to the scrutiny of political rivals (The Economist, 2014, Zhu & Zhang, 2017).

Public outrage toward social scandals that exposed the luxury lifestyles of children of government officials was further instigated by reports of the scale of corruption and graft from high-profile investigations revealing government officials laundering corruption money by sending their spouse and children to live overseas (Sevastopulo, 2014). Despite his critique of a toxic media culture, he also recognized public discontent over class calcification and expanding wealth disparity, which resulted from China's economic transformation that has largely benefited the country's social elite, who leveraged partial monopoly of state-controlled assets (land, oil, iron) to gain from a dynamic, fragmented, and under-regulated market economy. Although robust growth has lifted millions out of poverty and has broadly enabled upward social mobility, the accumulation of wealth has unevenly benefited a minority of the population and created flagrant social polarization.

Considered against the backdrop of sweeping anti-corruption campaigns and broad social discontent, strategic silence was key for surviving a perilous political environment. Leo's family grew keenly aware of the scrutiny from business associates, political rivals, and government investigators, who sought opportunities to exploit any vulnerabilities. Leo did not come to fully appreciate his parents' wisdom until news arrived about the flamboyant lifestyle of a childhood friend attracting state investigation, leading to the downfall of their family. The intensity of these investigations was further enhanced by government efforts to mobilize a disgruntled public, whose immediate interests were harmed by corruptive practices, to provide leads that would guide judicial investigation and prosecution of government officials (Xiong, 2011). Particular attention was given to Leo's social media partly because of technological advances such as automated text analysis, machine learning techniques, and high-powered computing that enable systematic mining of online activities (Edmond, 2013; Qin et al., 2017).

The impact of increasing government surveillance and public scrutiny was intimately felt across all aspects of Leo's life. He shunned the second-generation government official label because he was acutely aware of stigmas attached to this class identity, the scathing commentary on expanding disparity of social wealth, and public outrage toward uneven access to and irresponsible abuse of public resources. Leo carefully curated his appearance to embody government-enforced austerity. Strategic silence, linguistically performed through his writing, was part of a broader semiotic reticence, which manifested through choices made about selecting, displaying, and hiding clothing, cars, photos, and housing. Although Leo was critical of his peers, whose revving engines never failed to draw shouts of admiration and mockery from what he characterized as an antipathetic audience, he suppressed intense desires for such material luxury. Despite his extensive knowledge of luxury cars, he did not purchase a personal vehicle. Professionally, Leo was dissuaded from a career in politics despite his father's professional success, fearing that a social structure that fails to disentangle political and economic mechanisms would present more perils than opportunities.

The constant monitoring, warning, and censoring of showy behaviors translated into strategic silence he used to manage his literacy and social life. Strategic silence is the product of an entanglement of rhetorical knowledge, familial teachings, public discourse, and sociopolitical circumstances. Such strategies were carefully modeled, taught, and framed within parental expectations for him to cultivate his character and talents with the same assiduity with which to resist the impulse to shine. Confucianist teaching and practices, cultivated by those in close proximity to state powers and through the long historical trajectory spanning many dynasties, were transformatively repurposed in response to current sociopolitical exigencies. They materialized through the teaching and practice of Tai Chi and calligraphy, which were oriented to inculcate such lessons. Working through these entangled narratives, discourses, and interactions, Leo developed strategies to safely occupy his class identity. Indeed, Leo embodied the many paradoxes of the second-generation government official: His plain outfit contrasted with frequent shopping trips to luxury stores, his grand goal to own a Lamborghini by the time he turned 30 contrasted with frustration over parental reprimand to curb showy behaviors, and his discontent over imposed austerity contrasted with his contempt for second-generation rich's "crude ways of showing wealth" as well as their "stupid reasons for violating rules." Threading together such paradoxical circumstances was his family's efforts to help him navigate the rewards and perils associated with his class identity.

Chronotopic figuring performs what Haraway calls "tentacular" thinking, which recognizes the open and knotted patterning of material and semiotic worlds (2016). Leo related to and stayed in becoming with others through unexpected associations, risky partnerships, relentless contingencies, and improvised solutions. Semiotic fibers from family sayings, newspaper headlines, class labels, social scandals, and political slogans tangled and moved through material and semiotic practices. These semiotic fibers accumulate meaning and become tangled to inform ways of acting, dressing, relating, and speaking in accordance with one's class identity. It points to the simultaneously intentional and improvisational nature of the literacy practices as Leo's family developed surveillance practices in response to government surveillance and censorship mechanisms. These semiotic fibers twist, pass, reciprocate, and extend across activities and spacetimes to help Leo navigate the perils associated with his class identity. Yet well-rehearsed practices could also lose traction as evidenced in Leo's desire to obtain luxury goods, to perform his talents, and to relate through the sharing of personal experiences. In departing from strategic silence, his impromptu writing could lead to knots becoming untied, relationships breaking, and tension arising.

Following strategic silence makes it imperative to examine the mess and complexity of Leo knotting multiple life worlds together. It is important to embrace the willingness to wander and to resist the impulse to follow a single path, such as one act of deleting a post, a single story, or one stream of interactions. A full understanding of Leo's self-censorship is not complete without the attention to how multiple historical trajectories coalesce into a resonating theme (Sheldrake, 2020, p. 55). Following a single path might beguile the fact that Leo constantly weighed multiple connections and leads, assessed the viability and feasibility of writing topics, and made decisions reflective of multiple streams of hearsay advice and learned practices that were often in conflict with inspirations and feelings. Wandering invites me to follow practices that surfaced and silenced ideas, narratives, and identity labels that mobilized Leo to indeterminate ends. Picking up the material traces of these threads and observing how they were dropped allowed me to trace the relentlessly contingent ways in which associations were broken, imaginary possibilities were negated, voices and perspectives were silenced. Such a move invited traversal across temporal scales, such as the momentary decision to delete a post that takes a second, efforts to end a conversation that unfolded in minutes, the breaking of social scandals and prosecutions that took years to materialize, and heeding political campaigns that spanned decades.

Chronotopic Figuring

A chronotopic analysis of strategic silence necessarily positions a writerly strategy within an emergent repertoire of rhetorical, material, and semiotic strategies for survival, illustrating what Prior et al. theorizes as a "robust ontology of moments that illuminate the textures and consequences of experience within and across moments" (2023, p. 6). That is, rather than seeing strategic silence as a writerly move located within the writer, I posit that strategic silence is the outcome of Leo's co-emergence with his historical-material environments and the transnationally mobilized social and political circumstances specific to his class identity. While the analysis offered here does not specifically focus on the multilingual writer or his writing as Chapter 4 did, it provides important insights into the multilingual person, whose dispositions, cultural tastes, lifestyle choices, outfits, aspirations, and trepidations all carried implications for what and how he wrote in reaction to which audiences. It provides a view of Leo as constantly becoming through the dynamic whole of embodied persons and sociomaterial environments in moments of activities. Semiotic and writerly strategies deployed within embodied moments, such as the decision to eliminate a topic, exclude a detail, or silence a voice, needs to be considered as dialogically emerging with rhizomatic assemblages of the multilingual, transnational student's ways of being, doing, knowing, and relating in the world.

The life of the calligraphy story was marked with various forms of silence. A temporal hiatus could be used to describe the years, months, and days that passed when the story fell into the black hole of Leo's memory with little hope of recovery; silence could become affectively charged, sparking new ideas for writing, generating feelings of thrill, humility, and trepidation, and leading to exigencies for producing or erasing traces of literacy work. Silence, as experienced at different scales and across a wide range of social and rhetorical situations, was differently motivated to disengage from hostile perspectives, create ambiguity, pique curiosities, shield Leo's life from public view, process difficult experiences, regulate interactions deviating from an intended route, and survive private scrutiny and public surveillance. Attending to the aesthetic resources of silence, as Gere (2001) argues, provides an understanding of multilingual writing that "acknowledges partial understandings, gaps between lived experience and textual representations, oscillations between set and fleeting, and the continuously unfinished search for meaning" (pp. 211–212).

Moreover, Leo's strategic silences provide compelling illustrations of how each of us participates in silence as both a strategic choice and an enforced imposition (Glenn, 2004, p. 13). Whether consciously or unconsciously, Leo's deployment of rhetorical silence oscillates between the impulse to act in response to powerful exigencies and the desire to shine, which entered into dialogue with learned vigilance toward his audience, familial teaching on restraint, and anxiety over hostile scrutiny. Silence is as communicative, revealing, and informative as utterances, social media posts, and speech as evidence of multilingual writing. Leo's silences surfaced the intense sociality of his writing; they revealed his incredible attentiveness and sophisticated understandings of the expectations and needs of his diverse audience; they denoted the delicate work entailed in navigating the rewards and perils of privilege; and they showed the labor for occupying, deploying, or deferring to power. When an utterance from a peer was perceived to enact the discourse of public discontent, it triggered Leo's deployment of strategic silence, often to the surprise of those participating in the conversation.

Reading silence through a chronotopic lens positions ephemeral, embodied activities within historical trajectories, connects improvised performance with cultivated practices, and observes writerly idiosyncrasies as the outcome of finding one's positioning in the world through multiple activities. Such an analysis invites attention to temporal labor and historical trajectories. Temporal labor is especially evident in Leo's WeChat Time Travel practices. Leo's imaginary traversal across representational and embodied spacetimes echoes Karimzad and Catedral's (2018) analysis of how Uzbek and Iranian migrants assemble social media representation of "imagined homeland" there-and-now and embodied memories of life in homeland there-and-then to construct and revise images of life in the homeland. In these scenarios, transnational, multilingual writers hybridize and reconfigure chronotopic meanings to enable and explore their own physical and imaginary traversals.

Time, as experienced by Leo, is not a "succession of evenly spaced individual moments," nor is it just "there as substance or measure, a background uniformly available to all . . . as a reference or an ontological primitive against which change and stasis can be measured" (Barad, 2007, p. 180). Silences are the products of temporal labor and can be heard through the moments Leo spent on contemplating the inclusion of vivid details and gaps left unfilled, in the minutes when he waited for his peers to react to his story, the seconds to rush toward the deletion of his post, and the permanent gap his erasures left on his social media. Temporality is produced through iterative intra-action among Leo's temporally situated selves, his peers, and the story itself, which acquired materiality, agency, and temporal quality. In particular, the narrative simultaneously became semiotic "matter" with sedimented historicity and discursive mattering—the process where spacetime mattering is iteratively enacted and emergent through the ongoing efforts to represent, mobilize, and juxtapose a meaningful life experience (Barad, 2007). The story energized the multilingual writer and his audience through iterative uptakes, which gave it new purposes and allowed it to acquire its own polyphonic rhythm. The story, as "matter," "carried within itself the sedimented historicity of the practices through which it was produced as part of its ongoing becoming—it is ingrained and enriched in its becoming" (Barad, 2007, p. 180). Time was less useful as exterior parameters that tracked the narrative's movement; rather, the reflective insight and affective meaning emerged and (re)configured through time. Each iteration of the narrative created something like a ring in a tree, which embodied the story within and became part of Leo's worlds. The story's past was never left behind or finished and its future was never determined by what was unfolding in the present. Rather, the calligraphy story, differentiated in past, present, and future tenses, was haphazardly produced in the enmeshing of its emergent forms. Time, as we so conventionally know it, was not a reliable parameter to account for the contingent, improvisational, and happenstance nature of literacy lives unfolding and meanings in becoming. A conception of time as cyclical, evenly paced, and continuous fails to account for how the narrative resided in stasis, gained and accelerated mobility, achieved meaning, or lost visibility in highly accidental and indeterminate ways.

Following chronotopic figuring allows us to explore contingent, idiosyncratic decisions as situated within long personal, familial, and political trajectories. Leo's effort to exercise strategic silence and self-censorship was complexly entangled in interactional histories, public discourses, social scandals, personal encounters, political campaigns, and class strata associated with his identity. The idiosyncratic quirks, manifesting in seemingly impromptu decisions to delete a harmless post, tabbed into the rhythms of his familial teaching, whose prosperity and survival rested on coordinated efforts to evade public scrutiny and government surveillance. His multilingual writing was deeply implicated with cultivated, classed identity practices, social discourses that punitively amplified his class privilege, and repeated past and future efforts to navigate such identity practices and discourses. It was through these embodied moments of encounter that the multilingual writer came to understand and inhabit his identity through utterances and silences. These moments of coordination came in and out of existence through political contingencies such as deepening socioeconomic disparity, rising public outrage, and sweeping anti-corruption campaigns. Class hierarchies, encoded in class labels, were mobilized during everyday conversations and interactions. The strategic silence that haphazardly emerged from harmless and playful banters with peers was the indeterminate outcome of transnational students finding their positions in relation to each other at the university and in society. Leo's encounters with elegant Burberry jackets or a flashy Lamborghini necessarily drew us into stories of living and hiding second-generation privileges as well as the imaginaries, aspirations, and frustration fueled by class attributes and distinctions, similar to what Kate Pahl has documented in her study of transnational families (2004). Understanding Leo's multilingual writing therefore required attention to polyphonic assemblages, the contingent gathering of individual and collective ways of being in the world. In Tsing's words, "To appreciate polyphony one must listen both to the separate melody lines and their coming together in unexpected moments of harmony or dissonance" (2015, p. 158).

Spatially and temporally dispersed encounters produce semiotic artifacts that embody inscribed class norms. Multiple life, imaginary, and representational worlds were spliced into everyday encounters, conversations, and interactions in tentacular ways. They crystallized into powerful memories, feelings, and strategies that continued to travel to inform literacy and social practices across a wide range of academic, professional, and social contexts. Objects, such as an expensive jacket or an exotic sports car, were not valued as symbols of class privilege but used as a means of learning to inhabit one's class identity. They embodied a lifestyle in which the social elite managed privileges that simultaneously satisfied and threatened. These objects were laced with memories and feelings and became semiotic artifacts that constituted imaginaries of the life of global elite with financial resources, expensive cultural tastes, and a savvy business acumen. Furthermore, the calligraphy story materializes through the movement, manipulation, hybridization, and reconfiguration of material things (e.g., bits of dialogue, snippets of written narrative, screenshots). Material joints sustain meaning, enabling chronotopic figuring in what Catherine Kell called "meaning-making trajectories" (2015). Inscriptions and materials bring "the wealth and variety of texts and textualities that inform people's lives' into entanglements across disciplinary, professional, community and personal engagements" (Roozen, 2021, p. 45). Chronotopic analysis of Leo's strategic silence compels attention to the tentacular meshing of a wide array of literacy and learning activities. Threading these embodied moments chronotopically requires that we redraw the maps of literacy activities, listen for resonances when affects, memories, and meanings accumulate and intensify across multiple temporal trajectories, and notice dissonances when meanings fail to connect (Prior, 2019).

6
Working With Multilingual Writers in Entanglement

A deep dive into the literacy practices of Leo and Morgan has surfaced aspects of their multilingual writing processes that often elide research attention: ephemeral encounters that energize and inspire writing, reciprocal relationships that sustain the productive distribution of writing labor, accidents and surprises that steer contours of writing in unpredictable ways, and the chronotopic figuring and thickening of writing and identity practices across multiple historical trajectories. Analysis guided by such theoretical ideas has alerted me to the need to move our gaze beyond the singular moment of writing in one spacetime and for one purpose and to trace the emergence of writing across multiple moments of being, living, and making meaning across lines of differences.

Pedagogically, an entanglement perspective surfaces the interanimating ways in which Leo and Morgan acquire, mobilize, and attune writing-related knowledge and practices across their own literacy spheres and academic units at the university. My own involvements with various departmental and cross-disciplinary research collaborations throughout this research process has given me access to the entanglements of academic units that shaped these students' literacy and writing practices. At the time of the research, I routinely taught sections of the bridge writing class welcoming diverse

https://doi.org/10.7330/9781646427628.c006

students such as Leo and Morgan; in the context of the bridge writing class, I worked with my colleagues to revise the curriculum, goals, and pedagogy while developing and theorizing our pedagogical innovations through a translingual lens. Alongside my own ethnographic research into the students' experiences within and beyond honor designated FYW classes, I was also a member of a research team consisting of colleagues from the writing program, the English Language Center (ELC), and the university's Writing Center as we collaboratively inquired into how multilingual writers accessed and assembled literacy resources and developed their language and literacy skills (De Costa, Li, & Lee, 2022). Throughout my research with Morgan and Leo, these disparate streams of research unfolded simultaneously, providing me with access to explore the (dis)connected ways in which pedagogical practices and student experiences moved across academic units responsible for introducing language practices of the academia to international students at the university.

In this chapter, I explore how student learning entangled in messy and transformative ways with an array of curriculum and pedagogical practices across the bridge and honors FYW classes, with some details given to the students' experiences in the ELC and the university's Writing Center. My purpose here is twofold. First, I draw on interview and observation data to discuss the uneven ways in which multilingual students' writing practices entangled with writing pedagogies within and across academic units operating with monolingual, multilingual, and translingual ideologies. I offer analysis of four snapshots that captured gaps between student writers' experiences and pedagogical practices before proposing recommendations for how pedagogical practices could be revised to usefully engage with multilingual writing in entanglement. Second, I explore the affordances of an asset-based curriculum enacted in the bridge writing class. I argue such assignments, which strategically surface students' own languages and cultures, better support students to navigate the tensions and frictions produced by competing monolingual, multilingual, and translingual ideologies and language representations (Ayash, 2019). I draw on samples of focal students' writing to discuss how an asset-based curriculum provides spaces to discuss, value, and name strategies that facilitate students' ongoing efforts to attune their rhetorical and semiotic repertoires in FYW classes. In contrast to previous chapters, in which I use student writing and accounts to surface aspects of their literacy practices, I use interview, observation, and writing sample data here to illustrate the affordances and limitations of these assignments.

Drawing on these observations, I make broader pedagogical recommendations from an entanglement perspective. Extending asset-based pedagogy, I propose a multilingual writing pedagogy that is sensitive to relationships, multiplicities, unpredictable encounters, and polyphony, arguing that this ecologically reimagined pedagogy entails changes to how we teach and assess the writing of multilingual students. An ecologically reimagined writing classroom should invite reflections on distributed multilingual writing processes across linguistic, cultural, and rhetorical differences; support sustained relationships within FYW and across academic units; encourage translingual and transcultural conversations that center students' language and practices as assets for learning; and attend to unpredictable encounters as opportunities to discover, invent, and make meaning.

Reconsidering Pedagogical Practices in First-Year Writing

In this section, I draw from students' accounts of their own struggles navigating the material, discursive, and pedagogical norms of their honors FYW classes to discuss how such difficulties might arise from pedagogical norms that embody an American-centric frame for imagining student participation, managing material configurations, and creating pathways for learning. I provide four snapshots that encapsulate the struggles students like Leo and Morgan experienced in their efforts to inhabit, claim, and own the institutional spaces where the learning of writing happened. I then unpack pedagogical practices that contributed to students' felt dissonances before offering pedagogical recommendations.

SUPPORTING PRECARIOUS RELATIONSHIPS

Snapshot

Morgan came back from her hour-long consultation at the writing center, looking satisfied. Her draft, in its present state, bears the handwriting of two reviewers, Nicole and Morgan's favorite writing center consultant, Brenda (pseudonym). Morgan scheduled her appointment based on Brenda's availability, suggesting that she especially valued Brenda's approach to writing center consultation:

> She listens to me and works on things I need the most help with. I have met other writing center tutors following their own practices. They always ask you to read your essays aloud and they say reading it aloud helps me hear

my own problems. I am like, what is this?! If I can hear my own problems, why would I come to you?

This snapshot reveals ways in which writing center practices grounded in American-centric frames of reference often fail to support multilingual writers. To Morgan, reading her essays aloud was inefficient, stressful, and poorly matched with her needs as a writer. When she followed such guidance during her first writing center consultations, she felt self-conscious about her accents, had trouble pronouncing unfamiliar vocabulary she painstakingly translated into English, and struggled to finish reading the essay in time. She often left such consultations with main issues identified by her peers and writing teacher largely unaddressed. As she learned later that she could determine the purpose of the meeting, she found most consultants unwilling and inadequately equipped to help her with a wide range of grammar issues for which she needed the most help. Writing center consultants—mostly upper-class undergraduate students—often lacked the linguistic knowledge required to address issues that were variously lexical (e.g., a desire to use archaic vocabulary that might carry subtle connotations unclear to the writer and readers alike), syntactic (e.g., faulty parallelism due to misuse of words with shared meaning but different parts of speech), and rhetorical (e.g., efforts to adapt rhetorical devices from other language and rhetorical traditions).

However, it was from one such random writing center consultation that a robust relationship emerged. Brenda, a consultant who demonstrated good humor and patience, became Morgan's "special" writing center consultant, whose appointments Morgan sought to monopolize whenever she could for 3 years of Morgan's undergraduate career until Brenda's graduation from the university. Their relationship, originating in Morgan's first year, when Morgan took the bridge writing class, had allowed the two to develop mutual trust, rituals for how to organize a productive meeting, an inventory of issues they continuously worked to address, and a repertoire of strategies for navigating new challenges. Instead of "wasting" 30 minutes on reading, Morgan and Brenda often dedicated the first few minutes of their meeting discussing Morgan's progress and needs, followed by them working through two pages of the five-page essay and scheduling a follow-up meeting to complete the review process. During the hour-long consultation, Brenda worked with Morgan to clarify meanings, rework sentences, and discuss strategies and alternatives for revision. Brenda was willing to listen to

Morgan's rather lengthy description of her experiences with different reviewers, thereby allowing them to set priorities in accord with the needs emerging from Morgan's dynamic, multilingual writing process. Brenda's patience and willingness to listen allowed Morgan to surface the multiple streams of review, including her in-class review that identified insight and rhetorical devices as areas of her strengths, multiple in-class and self-sponsored reviews pointing to grammar as a focal area of attention, and her multilingual reviewers' requests that she seek language help from the "Americans." Morgan and Brenda strategically focused the limited time and energy on these issues, with Brenda joining Nicole's efforts to use American idiomatic expressions in place of "awkward" translations and enhancing the flow of the essay at the sentence level.

Like Morgan, Leo also developed sustaining relationships with trusted reviewers, who also turned into good friends and joined him for meals, attended his graduation ceremony, and supported his graduate school applications, most notably with his instructor from the university's ELC. When he took reading and writing classes from the ELC, Leo made the point to visit his instructor during office hours, shared aspects of his literacy history, and joked about cultural oddities he encountered on campus. The teacher, who had lived and taught abroad and accumulated extensive experiences working with multilingual writers, developed a nuanced understanding of Leo's style. Their shared history gave the teacher access to Leo's strengths and areas of struggle over the course of 2 years through revisions of multiple drafts of multiple assignments, allowing the two to approach a new writing assignment from a shared frame of reference and a position of familiarity. Leo's attempt to schedule a last-minute appointment with his teacher was met with special attention—his teacher postponed a later appointment to extend Leo's 30-minute meeting to an hour, allowing them to adequately dive into the essay. His teacher frequently invited Leo to elucidate his ideas, explain the rhetorical strategies that appeared opaque to a Western audience, and identify rhetorical strategies to be kept intact or to be substantially revised.

As I have discussed throughout the book, fungi provide concrete examples for understanding entanglements through the lens of reciprocal partnerships and open assemblages. Like mycorrhizal fungi, whose existence is sustained through reciprocal relationships they share with trees, humans, and animals, Morgan and Leo entangled with the important literacy others in their multilingual worlds, communicating their ideas, intentions, and struggles in a language that was intelligible to those best positioned to help them. They reciprocated with material tokens of appreciation, thought-provoking conversations, intellectual curiosities, and opportunities for learning. Multiplicity of relationships were drawn into open assemblages to drive effective reviews and consultations. Each student's multilingual writing was made possible through material practices and embodied activities (e.g., conversing, annotating, commenting, questioning) that drew rhetorical, language, and academic resources into dynamic relationships. In this view, all the players, encompassing teachers, classmates, friends, roommates and a host of other friendly or suspicious readers operating with distinct ideological orientations toward language differences, enter open-ended assemblages and participate in the ongoing becoming-with-each-other, through diverse kinds of relationalities, and with varying degrees of openness to opportunistic assemblages. Entanglement, made possible through relationships across cultural and rhetorical differences, highlights the role played by an expansive repertoire of languages, experiences, and practices as affording certain kinds of collaboration and communication.

As evidenced here, self-sponsored reviews with trusted mentors were paced to allow slow, recursive, and deep engagement with rhetorical and linguistic differences. The relationships underlying these productive reviews bring their own historical trajectories and provide unique resources to move the multilingual process forward. These relationships were the chosen few, taking hold from numerous efforts to seek coordination and reciprocation, and they lasted through active efforts to cultivate and deepen the collaboration. Morgan compares her efforts to build relationships to planting seeds, as one never knows if a classmate or a neighbor might turn into an important connection in the future. Drawing on Steve Jobs's 2005 commencement address, when the innovator discussed how a calligraphy class he took at Reed College surfaced in unexpected ways to inform the design of the first Macintosh computer, Morgan suggested that she "paid attention to random relationships" as dots that may someday connect to help her in unexpected ways. For students like Leo and Morgan, relationships, randomly encountered and carefully cultivated, are instrumental in helping them connect multiple spheres of their multilingual lives. The writers' histories are in the making through such relationships, as writers and reviewers continue to develop a shared repertoire of diagnosis, terminology, rituals, and strategies that are recursively enacted and continuously attuned to cope with new needs. Multilingual writers leverage such relationships not only to access literacy resources but to find their positioning in peer circles and to pool learning, professional, and social resources at the university (Fraiberg et al., 2017). These relationships, some fleeting and others lasting, weave together the shifting ecologies these multilingual writers inhabit and traverse.

In my experience working with international students, productive relationships have often transformed into genuine friendships. I attended one student's wedding, at which her writing center consultant served as her maid of honor and gave a beautiful toast; a writing center consultant reached out to me on behalf of a student with questions about a project idea they were working to integrate into an application letter; a lone American student in a Chinese-majority bridge writing class made a month-long trip in China visiting multiple friends he made in the class; international students who trusted me as an advocate and friend brought their disputes with leasing offices and the university's disciplinary board for help, made surprise appearances at my daughter's birthday parties, and asked to park their luxury cars in my garage during the summer. Such relationships defy institutional boundaries that actively separate professional and personal connections and continue to crisscross in messy ways.

Recommendations

Writing centers might do well by recruiting and training advanced multilingual writers as writing center consultants. As Zhaozhe Wang has detailed in one of his case studies, Manna, a Chinese international student who trained and worked as a writing center consultant, was able to leverage her cultural differences, such as her upbringing in a different cultural context and her experiences of learning, to perform writing tutorial effectively. Specifically, her own experiences of crossing borders equipped her with a cultural sensibility to listen and learn from her clients, view and interact with the world from a unique perspective, and develop her own literacy and language skills as a writer (2024). Yu-Kyung Kang has similarly argued that the presence of multilingual writing consultants at the writing center sent powerful messages to students and faculty by positioning L2 writers as legitimate and skilled users of English (2018). Specifically, Kang (2016) observes how undergraduate writing groups oriented toward students with the shared first language background and facilitated by a consultant in that language provides a space for multilingual writers to confront internalized deficit perspectives toward their own languages and to restore their confidence by understanding their literacy histories and ideologies (2016). Populating writing centers with multilingual tutors helps create a space where language, cultural, and rhetorical differences become an area of inquiry. Relatedly, successful multilingual writing tutors might leverage their own experiences of navigating competing expectations, norms, and practices to model, surface, and strategize best practices in translingual negotiation. Second, it might be worthwhile for writing center tutors to learn about rhetorical and cultural differences that shape multilingual writers' approaches to writing center consultation. For one thing, students like Morgan and Leo might be hesitant to assume agency despite their clear understanding of their revision needs. For students from educational contexts where deference to authority figures is the norm, it might be useful to provide explicit guidance to help student writers co-direct consultations to their benefit, develop pedagogical language to name writing-related issues, and provide modeling strategies for collaboratively determining the purposes of consultations. Lastly, for students less skilled in forging and developing relationships with literacy brokers within and beyond the writing center, it might be worthwhile to discuss strategies for identifying reviewers and consultants operating from a translingual disposition and discussing strategies for sustaining and developing productive relationships.

LISTENING TO THE POLYPHONY OF ACADEMIA

Snapshot

> I met Jill, Leo's teacher, in the hallway and we chatted over coffee (for her) and tea (for me). Jill said she was pleased that Leo was speaking to me about his experiences in the honors writing class. Leo had mentioned to Jill that he was speaking to me, Jeff, his ELC teacher, and a writing tutor about his essay. Jill was impressed by Leo's ability to understand and use the writing techniques they discussed in class. In my reading of his draft, I could see that he was indeed skilled in using a variety of writing techniques that Jill mentioned, such as personification, metaphor, flashback, and imagery. I thought of my conversation with Leo, when he mentioned his worry about using sophisticated Chinese rhetorical strategies, such as "contrast between environmental ambience and inner feelings." I communicated similar concerns that his American readers would not be able to appreciate such subtle strategies. He had taken a few paragraphs to Jeff, who insisted that Leo keep these rhetorical strategies and educate his American peers about different rhetorical traditions. When I mentioned that Leo was concerned about grammatical errors, Jill smiled and said that a few grammatical errors make the writing of international students more authentic and personal.

This snapshot provides an illustration of the pervasiveness of language ideologies in everyday language usage that are inextricably localized and imbued with sociohistorical meanings. As Nancy Bou Ayash (2019) argues, such language ideologies make their way into postsecondary writing classrooms through monolingual, multilingual, and translingual language representations, which directly impact strategies for meaning making for instructors and students alike. Indeed, the writing processes of Morgan and Leo have revealed the multiplicity of voices that enact nuanced ideologies about language irregularity and rhetorical differences through their comments and feedback. These beliefs about and representations of multilingual writing carried weight but were at odds at times. Jill's perspective adopted a monolingual language representation, which asserts static, universal attributes of academic writing, which left little room for strategic departures from the monolingual norm. This language ideology, complicated by expressivist pedagogy's emphasis on authenticity, shaped Jill's pedagogical decision to "tolerate" sporadic instances of linguistic irregularities as evidence of Leo's voice. Language differences were still to be eradicated, not treated as sites of inquiry or considered in dynamic relationship to English.

Jeff's experiences as a Spanish and English bilingual and an ESL teacher in the US and abroad made him a curious reader who was intrigued by Leo's creative choices reflective of his knowledge of Chinese rhetorical strategies. Jeff's approach embodied a multilingual language representation, which recognized the breadth and depth of multilingual language repertoires and conceptualized different language varieties as isolatable, distinct, and self-contained systems. In fact, Jeff often elevated rhetorical traditions of other cultures, contrasting them, with a grain of sarcasm and self-deprecation, to monolingual writers' efforts to deploy "boring" and "shallow" writing strategies. Leo often returned from his conversations with Jeff feeling elated and confident, ready to take on challenges his writing class had to offer.

I, as a Chinese and English bilingual trained in rhetoric and composition and recently introduced to translingual theory, tended to be more cautious toward Leo's bold suggestion to import rhetorical flourishes drafted in Chinese wholesale. I worked to enact a translingual language representation by encouraging him to not only embrace language and rhetorical differences but also contemplate his choices against the backdrop of our shared struggles to balance authorial intention and audience expectations. Admittedly, these voices communicated such beliefs explicitly and subtly, swaying Leo in one direction or another. However, a key question emerged with regard to how the multiple voices, each resonating with competing perspectives, ideologies, and representations of multilingual writing, entered polyphony in a way that still made sense to Leo.

The world of mushrooms calls our attention to the dynamic interplay of disciplinary norms and pedagogical traditions that make up the university in entanglement. Our reading of these "life worlds" of the university, materializing through the curriculum, pedagogy, and goals of academic departments that were framed within discipline-specific epistemologies, modes of reasoning, knowledge-making practices, and philosophical orientations, could benefit from polyphony as a useful metaphor. As Leo and Morgan traversed these disciplinary worlds, they wove the autonomous epistemological, pedagogical, and curricular lines in dissonant ways. As multilingual writers meandered along these lines, they encountered distinct ways of conceiving, teaching, and practicing writing, which "intertwine without ceasing to be many" (Sheldrake, 2020, p. 54). While they could be loosely unified by overarching themes for theorizing, teaching, and assessing writing, they do not always present a shared, unified perspective, leaving it to the students to weigh, reconcile, and negotiate disciplinary differences. What was missing here was intentional effort to cultivate interdisciplinary polyphony, when teachers listen for, respond to, and improvise in reaction to the values, pedagogies, and curriculums of the other.

We could consider ways to draw distinct voices and perspectives students encounter across multiple spheres of their literacy lives into polyphony, through which writing-related knowledge, strategies, and dispositions can be continuously assessed and attuned. In a writing classroom where multilingual students were both the linguistic and cultural minority, they often found themselves in positions of vulnerability, deprived of voice and agency. Their ability to succeed depended on their ability to draw disparate streams of reviews and revisions into polyphony. In-class peer reviews were incredibly useful because students operated with a shared frame of reference, which was collaboratively produced through shared reading, discussion, modeling, and practice. As I have discussed, however, Leo and Morgan tended to benefit less from teacher conferences and instructor-facilitated peer review because such interactions around writing quickly dissipated beyond classroom activities and rarely entered polyphony with other voices and perspectives.

Self-sponsored conversations with trusted mentors, tutors, and friends outside the classroom are often premised on shared, genuine curiosity and appreciation for linguistic and cultural differences, a disposition of open inquiry into and discovery of new possibilities from multiplicities, the willingness to challenge and revise one's own cultural assumptions and practices, and the patience and expertise to engage with language irregularities as logical choices with expressive potentials. These literacy brokers—often trained consultants, multilingual language users, experienced writers, invested advocates, and dedicated teachers—are significantly more effective in supporting and participating in ongoing inquiries into language differences. In this spirit, such practices are more likely to achieve tentacular figuring with the multilingual writing process. When these disparate streams of activities coalesced, they help writers address a wider range of global and local issues, as different literacy brokers bring valuable knowledge in writing, rhetoric, and linguistics to help writers develop metalinguistic knowledge and metacognitive awareness that are key to their ongoing efforts to negotiate across differences. From a temporal perspective, teacher-facilitated and self-sponsored peer reviews afford multilingual writers with learning opportunities that are distinct in terms of their pace, duration, frequency, and purpose.

Polyphonic listening entails the willingness and ability to hear the multiplicity of voices and perspectives. For this multiplicity to grow into a productive dialogue in polyphony, however, shared melodic lines need to emerge. One shared melodic line might manifest in more strategic ways to scaffold discussions of language irregularities as patterned performance of linguistic structures and rhetorical traditions that are different from those encoded in the monolingual norm. Efforts could be made to surface, name, and strategize toward such language irregularities, such as discussion of parts of speech; inflection based on tenses, plurality, and gender; or idiomatic phrases as differently conceived and practiced across languages. Such discussions are not only helpful in surfacing students' metalinguistic knowledge but facilitate the ongoing attuning of such knowledge across conversations with different literacy brokers. A repertoire of shared vocabulary and strategies for naming, diagnosing, and managing language and rhetorical differences will not only help multilingual writers recognize patterns of language irregularities manifesting in their writing, but will help them better articulate their needs, formulate requests for support, and set priorities in collaboration with reviewers with different capacities. This shared and nuanced vocabulary is critical in moving the conversation beyond the vague umbrella terms such as "bad grammar." Along with students, teachers might benefit from interdisciplinary efforts to unpack entrenched orientations, to learn about the curriculum, pedagogy, and assignments offered at other academic units, and to imagine ways to coordinate, build on, and extend learning goals in the sequence of courses that student migrate through. In making such a move, teachers and writers alike engage in the back-and-forth shuttling between languages, genres, and texts, learning to develop the disposition to approach language irregularities with dexterity, inviting monolingual readers and multilingual writers to engage in mutual negotiation rather than dictating change from a monolingual stance.

Additionally, I found my informal conversation with Jill to be thought-provoking as we traded stories about how we each responded to Leo's questions, clarified the reasoning underlying our reactions, and attuned our strategies as writing teachers. Admittedly, these connections did not present themselves readily. I was never able to speak with Jeff about his experiences working with Leo due to various scheduling conflicts. At the programmatic and institutional level, however, pedagogical conversations across key academic units should and could happen. Such connections could unfold through cross-agency research collaborations, pedagogical workshops facing practitioners from across units and levels, and faculty interest groups that enable conversations with a shared pedagogical focus.

Recommendations

Cross-unit collaboration could create opportunities to communicate across academic units regarding learning objectives, pedagogical practices, and curriculum and assignments. Teachers could find ways to communicate discipline-specific expectations for what we value in student writing. Disciplinary jargon like invention, insight, and evidence should be unpacked, clarified, and embedded in writing instruction provided across academic units to facilitate student learning. Also, writing instructors could dedicate class discussions to generate pedagogical vocabulary for naming, diagnosing, and managing language irregularities. Rather than instruction of prescriptive grammar, instructors could invite students to share their own vocabulary for naming instances of language irregularity surfacing in their own writing. Instructors could offer mini lessons targeting patterns of issues and support the use of such vocabulary to guide teacher-, peer-, and self-initiated review and revision. Writing instructors and writing center consultants could collaborate on developing pedagogical training to help monolingual writing instructors and writing center consultants explore linguistic features of other languages, identify pedagogical practices informed by monolingual, multilingual, and translingual orientations, and consider ways to shift pedagogical practices in accordance with the unique needs of multilingual writers.

ENCOUNTERS WITH NEW CULTURES AND DISCIPLINES

Snapshot

> Leo visited me after the delivery of a presentation on business etiquette in his honors writing class. Although he was feeling elated about how well his audience received his well-rehearsed jokes, he was caught off guard by a fellow student's comment during the Q&A session. In his account, the student responded to a previous comment made by a peer and framed his own comment with what I suspect to be the floor-claiming device of "piggybacking." The term was so unfamiliar that Leo completely missed the comment that ensued; he smiled and asked for clarification several times. He threw his arms in the air and exclaimed, "He said something about a pig, pig something, and he was nodding to the other student. The other student was smiling back at him, and I thought it was not something bad. But I said 'pardon?' He repeated his comment without the pig thing, but I kept obsessing about what it was."

As my colleagues and I have explored elsewhere, multilingual students struggle with the language that disciplinary and academic insiders routinely use to organize classroom activities and to articulate expectations for academic learning (Meier et al., 2023). As an anthropology professor uses "transcript" to describe a written record of an interview, an international student, who had just gone through the rigorous college admission process, might mistake the word to mean a holistic report of his coursework and grades. An economics professor who uses "Hershey's chocolate" or "Twizzlers" as examples of candy during a lecture on the principles of supply and demand might create additional barriers for international students, who are not familiar with American household names for candy. In Leo's case, his difficulty to respond to an audience member's comment arises from his lack of familiarity with democratic frames of participation in classroom conversations that aim to cultivate students' ability to affirm, extend, and challenge each other's opinions. While his American peers have learned to use floor-claiming devices such as dovetailing and piggybacking to claim the floor, his educational experiences had not equipped him with comparable strategies for navigating the classroom dynamic. Elsewhere, I have observed how students like Morgan and Leo came from educational environments with minimal expectations for student participation and discourage voluntary student participation, therefore inadequately preparing them for seminar discussions (Wang, 2019a).

Here we observe a compelling example of unpredictable encounters as the outcome of forging relationships across cultural and disciplinary boundaries. For multilingual writers like Leo and Morgan, surprises, accidents, and transformative encounters were the norm. Although they are as skilled as fungi in navigating spatial and discursive labyrinths of classroom learning, exploratory paths for navigating democratic frames of participation, and tentative solutions for working through problems, they face significant challenges in reading and navigating the new material and discursive landscape of the academia in the United States. The obstruction, manifesting in the difficulty to recognize or perform a discursive move for claiming or giving the floor, prevented Leo's ongoing efforts to find his way through the classroom organized through distinct, unfamiliar spatial features. To overcome the obstacle, Leo needed to improvise and adjust the pace of his presentation, retool familiar material and discursive practices, draw on social and spatial cues to make inferences about the unfolding event, and prepare for the social and academic consequences of not repairing the interaction. Such work takes great ingenuity, and it is this ingenuity that allows multilingual writers to develop linguistic and cultural dexterities that are critical for mobilizing practices, resources, and knowledge.

Instructors could become important "brokers of entanglement" who introduce strategies to participate in complex and dynamic classroom activities. Teachers need to recognize that practices assumed to be normal and predictable for most might become sites of unpredictable encounters for linguistically and culturally minoritized students. Moreover, classroom practices and expectations are presented in instructional language unfamiliar to multilingual students. To help these students reorganize new forms and adapt behaviors in response to changing circumstances, teachers could incorporate explicit explanation and modeling of discursive tools such as piggybacking on or dovetailing on someone's idea into classroom practices. Such pedagogical efforts begin with the understanding that words along with the cultures they reflect may be inscrutable to some students. To "piggyback on" may suggest how one's idea builds on another's. Yet both "piggybacking" and "dovetailing" reflect teaching strategies that are often unfamiliar to students with limited experience with strategies for navigating seminar-style classroom discussions that are framed in said linguistic knowledge. For Leo, this unfamiliar phrase presented an unnecessary challenge because the idiomatic expression did not contribute to the core of his peer's comment in substantial ways but instead confused and distracted him. This snapshot points to the need to examine the role of instructional language that embodies the norms and language of academia, which are grounded in Western cultural contexts that are too often out of reach to nontraditional students, monolingual and multilingual alike. Consequently, instructors who use these strategies might encounter confusion and inaction on the students' part due to a profound gap between understanding of discursive and material conventions students and instructors bring to the table.

Although these unpredictable encounters are more visible for multilingual writers socialized into different culturally inflected educational practices in their home countries, they are equally present for novice learners navigating discipline-specific discursive conventions and modes of reasoning. Indeed, monolingual students from the US may struggle equally to engage with the type of intellectual moves embodied by task directives and terminologies used by instructors, such as directional verbs (analyze, synthesize, argue) commonly used in project descriptions, course goals, and instructional announcements because these verbs embody discipline-specific modes of reasoning and knowledge making, thereby dictating different intellectual tasks across disciplines. To analyze data in a biology class is different from the kind of analysis expected in a literature class. For multilingual students in particular, translations of directional words like "synthesize," "summarize," and "annotate" might share the same signifier, have opaque meanings, or carry meanings in students' home languages that diverge from instructor expectations, making it even more difficult to follow such directions and materialize learning outcomes.

At the center of this coordination are historical contingencies and unpredictable, sporadic, yet consequential encounters. The joining of the historical trajectories of disciplinary and pedagogical norms and individual students' literacy and educational experiences play out against the contingencies of the classroom. Collaboration among students, teachers, and academic programs, which entails working across uncertainties and differences, is a precondition for the success of all. From this perspective, a classroom in entanglement encourages each player to provide and receive help from another. While multilingual students develop strategies to acquire and perform new material and discursive practices, teachers should be intentional in attuning pedagogical practices, shifting cultural frames of reference, and learning from students about their cultures and languages. Each is transformed by their encounter with the other in intended and unpredictable ways. This perspective encourages our attention to the full range of the classroom phenomenon, complete with mess, mismatched expectations, and unintended outcomes, as sites of collaborative inquiry and translingual/transcultural negotiation.

Recommendations

Instructors could unpack norms of participation through explicit instruction and modeling. This can be achieved through time spent unpacking the meanings of frequently used floor-claiming words, modeling and creating opportunities for practicing such strategies, and explaining behaviors, modes of thinking, and textual practices expected therein. Instructors could create opportunities for students to share their interpretations of pedagogical language through multimodal activities such as a sketch, where teams of students perform short scenarios based on concrete tasks (e.g., analyze data in biology, dovetail on someone's idea, give evidence for a political argument). Such tasks could surface students' understanding, help to identify cultural gaps, provide opportunities for peer-led modeling, and create a shared repertoire of strategies and vocabulary that enable transfer across disciplinary contexts. Instructors could position students' own spatial knowledge of the classroom as sites of inquiry. I have worked with students to construct visual maps of the classroom, which might surface students' lived experiences with the material geography of the classroom and perceived spatial hierarchies. Coupled with class sharing, these visual maps might invite discussion of seating arrangements, information flow, and ways of participating as rhetorical choices.

DESTABILIZING DEFICIT PERSPECTIVES

Snapshot

> For Leo's second assignment, which invited students to research and analyze the meaning of a cultural artifact, Jill, his instructor, used one-on-one conferences during the inventive stage to help students navigate the assignment and explore different topics. Leo wanted to write about business etiquette, relaying anecdotes of formal business banquets he attended with his father. During his meeting with me, he talked at length about the importance of cultural dexterity and the ability to maintain one's ethical bottom line without damaging business relationships. His conference with Jill, however, turned out to be unsettling. I juxtapose the accounts from Leo and Jill to show significant gaps that prevented the instructor and student

from communicating across cultural differences about how they interpreted the purpose and function of such a pedagogical event.

Evidenced here are gaps in how Leo and Jill differently imagined the pedagogical purpose of the conference. While Leo used the conference to seek approval for an idea he had already committed to, Jill was invested in using the meeting to surface, explore, and develop possibilities. Although Jill genuinely positioned herself as a facilitator during the inventive stage of student writing, operating with the assumption that students have the freedom and agency to pursue any topic they deemed appropriate, Leo enacted a different framework that positioned the teacher as the authority figure, whose approval was critical to his decision to pursue a given topic. Therefore, Jill's effort to expand the problem space through the generous sharing of comparable examples was read by Leo as a polite rejection of his proposal. Indeed, Leo left the conference with the belief that Jill was pressing him to write about an American sport, which would not allow him to write from a position of knowledge and expertise. Leo's anxiety was further compounded by the pedagogical language used in the project description, which perpetuated deficit perspective on student learning. Leo was especially concerned with one stipulation from the assignment description, which outlined unacceptable topics:

> **Unacceptable Topics:** Cultural Artifacts/Practices from other countries (such as chop sticks, tea ceremonies, abacus); Religious artifacts (such as the Bible, menorahs, rosaries, or baptism); obvious patriotic symbols, such as flags and military uniforms. Brand-name products, such as Disney, Barbie Dolls; Coca-cola; Starbucks; Nike; Victoria's Secret and PINK; Overdone topics such as social media, such as Facebook and Twitter; and mainstream sports (such as baseball, basketball, or football).

Leo made two observations in response to this clause, which encompassed his topic under the "ban." First, he noted a significant dissonance between the deficit position this clause embodied and a guiding principle that was introduced throughout the class—writing about what you know. Whereas his personal experience was celebrated for the Memoir assignment, his culture, caricatured through artifacts such as chopsticks, tea ceremonies, and abacus, became unacceptable for the second assignment. Second, he questioned the clause for taking away student agency, especially in response to Jill's explanation that it was intended to encourage students to move away from easy topics that tended to get recycled in FYW classes across sections and semesters.

TABLE 6.1. Contrasting Perspectives on the Purpose of Teacher Conference

Interview Transcript with Leo	Interview Transcript with Jill
I proposed business etiquette. She started talking about golf and talked about how her financial advisor would invite his clients to stay at his cabin or play golf. I said I had never played golf because it was not popular in China. She said I should try it. It is a casual event, but people make business decisions playing golf. I then proposed a business banquet because my dad has taken me to many business banquets. And I have watched quite a few American movies with scenes of people at formal banquets. There was a scene in one of the Batman movies where he gave a banquet to officially introduce the white knight. I can connect that to how my dad introduced me to important business associates. That way, I can keep the Chinese part and connect it to international business etiquette. She then gave me an example of how President Bush stuck out his leg during a meeting in the middle east without knowing it was offensive. I know nothing about golf. I wanted to talk about how your body language, clothing, smile, how you propose a toast, are all parts of your business etiquette because that's what I learned from attending these events with my dad.	I was so worried I might have confused him during our conference. When he came in, he talked about business etiquette, with a nice little story about an uncle taking him shopping for a nice car. Retrospectively, I should have helped him with what it [etiquette] is and how [to write about it] questions. In an American style, in the short fifteen minutes we get, I would hope to get all the possibilities. We would usually just talk, going in every direction and the American student would go home and choose one idea. But for him, I felt like he felt I was bombarding him with stuff.

He argues, "I really do think the teacher should trust us more. We are honors students after all. Given more freedom, we might surprise her."

This dissonance between the writer's multilingual, transnational repertoire of semiotic and experiential knowledge and the monolingual pedagogy of the classroom was a dynamic process of writing as becoming. Leo and Jill held different assumptions and beliefs about the purpose of the teacher conference, which emerged in messy, uneven, and haphazard ways as heterogeneous activities were knotted across disparate life trajectories of the person, the student, and the teacher. The pedagogical event was an ongoing, open-ended, and multi-actor process that spanned materialities, activities, cultural and rhetorical traditions, and spacetimes. Leo's trepidation was honed through past educational experiences. His efforts to challenge teacher authorities, to depart from pedagogical expectations, and to take creative risks were consistently discouraged through bad grades, repeated reminders, and public shaming (as noted in Chapter 4, Leo had vivid memories of an incident of his essay and creative ideas being torn apart). For many students from educational cultures that discourage strategic departures, pedagogical language that encourages novelty of topics and multiple perspectives for examining a theme is often interpreted as masqueraded gestures of dissuasion. Leo, whose status as a linguistic and cultural minority in the class felt further accentuated through the placement of his culture at the top of the list, interpreted the pedagogical "ban" as a sweeping rejection of his culture, not as a pedagogical move to sway students away from platitudes. On the other hand, the language of the pedagogical ban also emerged as an unintended outcome of the FYW program, which historically adopted a shared curriculum across many sections of the bridge, regular, and honors writing classes. In my experiences teaching the bridge and regular FYW classes, students resorted to familiar, well-researched cultural tropes that were perceived to be more representative of their home cultures, producing multiple essays on Starbucks, chopsticks, and tea each semester. There were also instances when well-written essays were recycled across semesters. The frequent recurrences of such topics did create a compelling exigency for pedagogical intervention. More broadly, however, such pedagogical practices perpetuate a deficit perspective that positions students as inadequately inquisitive; such language also embodies a monolingual ideology that dismisses students' cultures and languages as misaligned with expectations of academia. In doing so, this pedagogical language worked to lay down the rules rather than to surface the problems, its root cause in connection to issues with curricular design, and their consequences.

Elsewhere, my colleagues and I have grappled with the problem of pedagogical practices rooted in deficit orientation, such as the use of reading materials that assumed student knowledge of American history and culture (Wang, 2019a) and use of examples informed by "familiar" cultural tropes, sports, and assumptions (Meier et al., 2023). For instance, a business professor using baseball metaphors artfully sprinkled throughout his lectures could be successful with an audience composed of American students because these allusions build on students' prior knowledge and therefore introduce unfamiliar disciplinary concepts through the frame of familiar cultural knowledge. Jill's use of golfing, a familiar recreational sport in the US, might strike a chord with a student familiar with the expectations for the sport as a site for discussing and sealing business transactions, making it a compelling parallel example to Leo's proposal for business dining in China. However, this example posed a significant challenge for Leo because of his lack of familiarity with the sport. These pedagogical practices could create double barriers for multilingual writers, who need to learn about the myriad practices, tactics, and narratives associated with the sport before arriving at a good understanding of the disciplinary concepts.

The need for pedagogical change is most tellingly felt when familiar cultural references, examples, and allusions stop working. In such moments, students must not only unpack disciplinary jargon and terminology that are referenced in textbooks and recursively visited during lectures and assignments but also draw on experiential knowledge acquired through other embodied, multimodal ways of learning to facilitate learning. For most international students, who were already under tremendous stress for completing classroom-related learning tasks, their venue and motivation to study cultural allusions and knowledge are significantly limited. The problem, however, is not that these cultural references are made but that they go unexplained, because instructors ironically see them as the very means by which disciplinary concepts are accessed, clarified, and unpacked. The well-intentioned act, which seeks to aid student understanding by putting new information in dialectical relationships with old schemas, in fact impedes student learning for those from positions of cultural unfamiliarity. Furthermore, concepts such as novelty and invention in composition classrooms embody disciplinary history of the field, enact modes of reasoning unique to studies in the humanities broadly, and do not easily translate into other languages. Loose translations that students routinely access could be differentially colored by cultural and ethnic frames of reference. For students raised in contemporary Chinese culture, where entrepreneurial advancement is often equated with invention and novelty is tied to technological innovation, these ideas might be especially difficult to comprehend in relation to writing. Cultural differences such as these are subsumed under a deficit, monolingual frame of reference whereas they could become resources.

Chronotopic figuring encourages open-ended inquiry into temporaneous and uncertain knotting between the life world of the students and the teacher, the willingness to work with the contingency, and the curiosity to inquire into the conflicting ideas and practices resulting from entangling multiplicities. Well-rehearsed examples grounded in one culture stop working when they fail to string figure with embodied activities and experiential learning developed in another culture. One way to surface and leverage the chronotopic figuring and thickening of writing practices across multilingual students' historical trajectories might reside in assignments that specifically invite students' inquiry into the dissonances they experience crossing cultural and disciplinary borders. Instructors of FYW classes are well positioned to engage multilingual writers with the wide array of "cultural shocks" that could be broadly construed to include unfamiliar pedagogical practices, disciplinary jargon, instructional language, and cultural norms they encounter at the university. Through a Culture Shock assignment, I have worked with my students to identify and discuss various social and academic scenarios where they felt compelled to examine unfamiliar cultural assumptions and practices. Students write about their shock when witnessing a roommate jump into bed without taking off their shoes; they express frustration with quiz questions that ask them to identify pricing strategies for hard and chocolate candies when multiple-choice answers do not clearly connect brand names to candy types; they name good pedagogical practices when a biology professor brings a rose plant into the classroom and has the students smell and touch the plant before introducing mechanisms of plant propagation and protection. We then develop strategies for responding to these challenges, asking questions about when and how it is appropriate to request clarification, challenge a professor's interpretation, or supply a parallel example. Through exercises like these, writing instructors could help students develop strategies to string figure historical trajectories.

Recommendations

Instructors could work in collaboration with students to gather and (re)invent pedagogical examples and unpack pedagogical language. Instructors could make cultural allusions more accessible through verbal explanations, examples, and multimodal demonstration. More importantly, writing instructors could consider ways of shifting their frames of reference in consultation with students. Teachers could invite students' contribution of examples of cultural narratives, symbols, and metaphors in their culture. A Korean student might bring a lullaby and discuss its use of an oyster as a symbol of good fortune; a Ghanaian student talks about the importance of colors, referencing green as the color of fertility and chuckling at an American peer's sarcastic response that green is the color of capitalist greed; a Chinese student describes the symbolic meaning of the full moon as invoking feelings of nostalgia for one's family as a Twilight fan or Harry Potter fan provides a counter example of how the full moon triggers the transformation of werewolves. In making these moves, instructors invite students to name similar and different strategies for activating the reader's knowledge and expectation in subtle and nuanced ways and to explore the challenges of communicating across lines of difference. Such a move also surfaces the complex, sophisticated, and historical traditions of Asian, African, and Arabic cultures and encourages students to place the concept at hand in relation to their prior knowledge of their cultural and rhetorical traditions. Moreover, instructors should carefully consider their use of exclusionary language in pedagogical documents shared with students, such as syllabus, project description, and assessment tools. This language often positions students in deficit positions despite good intentions on the part of teachers who work hard to help students go beyond platitude and safe topics. Lastly, instructors could benefit from pedagogical training that communicates key principles of professional writing for a global audience, such as simplicity, clarity, and translation readiness. Instructors could develop strategies for surfacing the social, cultural, and historical circumstances that give meaning to examples, allusions, and idiomatic expressions that are especially challenging for diverse learners.

Asset-Based Assignments in Bridge Writing

As illustrated above, FYW programs are an important academic unit key to introducing multilingual, transnational students to the language, material, and disciplinary practices for academic writing specifically and for learning at the university broadly. The bridge writing class, as one of the first courses multilingual students take at the university, is an ideal space for students to reflect on, name, and inquire into their own transition to the linguistic, cultural, and disciplinary norms of the university. Pedagogically, the bridge writing class also provides a space for teachers to develop curriculum, assignments, and activities to better support such students' literacy learning through strategic leverage of their rhetorical repertoire. During my ethnographic research, a team of teacher scholars housed in the FYW program worked collaboratively to revise the curriculum, pedagogy, and learning goals for the bridge writing class, which welcomed more than 900 multilingual, heritage, and first-generation students annually. Through monthly reading of translingual scholarship, collaborative design and refinement of assignments, and ongoing efforts to disseminate the findings from such teacher inquiry, I worked with my colleagues to revise the curriculum and pedagogy of the course, which now enacts a translingual orientation by centering students' semiotic repertoires, cultural knowledge, and reflective practices. The reinvented curriculum foregrounds students' linguistic, rhetorical, and cultural resources as assets through a series of assignments that could be flexibly assembled based on the needs of the instructor and the class, such as Translation Narrative (Kiernan et al., 2016), Writing Theory Cartoon (Wang, 2021), I Am From Poetry (Wang, 2022), Border Crossing Comics (Fraiberg, Wang, & Wen, 2017), and Service Learning (Meier, 2018).

Below, I offer two examples of writing assignments that create a space for students to analyze their struggles and triumphs in navigating linguistic and cultural border crossing. Specifically, these assignments encourage students to forge connections across differences, explore all language acts as emergent processes of negotiation, and attune old knowledge in response to new exigencies and contingencies. Drawing on examples of student writing and reflection, I discuss how such assignments encourage an attitude of openness toward language differences by inviting students' exploration of their semiotic and rhetorical repertoire as resources and supporting continuous theorization and attunement of such repertoires across multiple languages and modes of inquiry and representation. For each assignment, I provide a brief description of the procedure and offer examples of student writing, followed by discussion of the pedagogical facility in enabling translingual negotiation. Doing so allows me to illustrate how these assignments support students' effort to develop an open disposition toward multiplicity and surprise and to develop strategies to access and attune an evolving repertoire of languages, resources, and relationships.

TRANSLATION NARRATIVE

The Translation Narrative, the very first assignment in a series of pedagogical innovations, reflects the goal of our research-informed teaching practices, which surfaces students' home languages and cultures as well as reflective practice. Despite the diverse linguistic backgrounds, pedagogical orientations, and teaching approaches among the core faculty involved, there are several commonalities in each iteration of this writing task.

Procedure

The assignment can be divided into three stages: a group translation, a comparative reflection, and a translation narrative. Stage one is a collaborative translation: Students work in groups of three and four based on their home language and choose a text that is written in this language. Excerpts of texts are identified, distributed and translated into English. Members in the group then translate the excerpts individually before sharing their individual translation with the group. Stage two of this assignment, the comparative reflection, is a collaborative process in which students share their translated texts, compare differences and similarities in translation, and reflect on personal experiences, feelings, and choices during the translation process. The third stage of this assignment is the translation narrative, which incorporates all previous steps and encourages students to create a final personal narrative, where they consider their translation process, strategies, and practices. In what follows, I offer examples from one student's translation narrative to discuss the pedagogical affordances of the assignment, including understanding language as cultural and linguistic structures, language differences as resources for learning, and writing as mobile literacy practice.

Affordance

When students translated an idiom, song, or cultural tale, they often worked to achieve balance between representing the intention of the original text and adjusting textual and linguistic features in anticipation of audience expectations. Multilingual writers learned to negotiate meaning to make it accessible to their readers even if perfect semantic equivalents were out of reach. Morgan chose to entitle her translation reflection paper "The Difficulty of Explaining Chinese Feelings to Foreign People" and theorize translation as a profoundly rhetorical practice:

> When Chinese writers describe how sad they are when we lose something valuable, we write about standing in front of a loquat tree, staring at it, and immersed in your memories. This was a successful [strategy] to catch the reader's attention in Chinese, but it would never work here.

This reflection took insights from Morgan's translation of an excerpt from an essay written in classical Chinese, 有枇杷树，吾妻死之年所手植也，今已亭亭如盖矣, which captured a moment when Su Shi, a renowned Chinese classical essayist, stood in solitude in front of a luscious loquat tree planted in his backyard, which reminded him of his beloved, deceased wife. Morgan translated the sentence into English: *[There] was [this] loquat tree, [which I] planted by hand [when] my wife died. [It is] now flourishing as an umbrella.* Individual translation and comparison of translations with members in her group invited her to consider productive means to negotiate syntactic, semantic, and rhetorical structures when moving meaning across languages.

Evidenced here is the affordance of the assignment to not only provide a space to develop metalinguistic understanding of languages as complexly tangled in histories with emergent but flexible patterning, which are often reduced to grammatic rules. Such metalinguistic awareness manifested in Morgan's understanding of the need to adjust syntax structure and her ability to recognize the grammatical properties of words, for which equivalents might or might not exist in other languages. These translation activities not only encourage students to "draw on their cultural and linguistic knowledge to derive meaning" (Jiménez et al., 2015, p. 249) but also position translation as a metalinguistic activity involving systematic comparison of, reflection on, and manipulation of multiple languages (Kiernan et al., 2016). Foregrounding translation as a resource for learning, the assignment also leads to discussions of how semantic choices are determined by social and cultural meanings. Morgan discusses her translation of 蓋 (*gai*, cover of pot or ceremonial umbrella) into "umbrella." She suggests:

> 蓋 (*gai*, umbrella, cap) in classical Chinese has different meanings. It could be the cover of the tea pot or the beautiful decorative umbrellas used by emperors. To make my story more attractive and readable, I used more familiar words. Umbrella lets the reader feel more familiar.

These semantic choices reflect Morgan's effort to shift her own familiar frame of cultural reference for her American audience, who is perceived to be unfamiliar with the Chinese cultural rituals of tea drinking or imperial ceremonial events. The need to adapt to her American audience was explained in her reflections, where she complicated, named, and elucidated her efforts to unpack cultural ways of being, acting, and relating. Additionally, she theorizes language practice as informed by rhetorical traditions and strategies. Morgan recognizes the inadequacy of literal translation, which fails to capture the subtle expression of the poet's feelings of sorrow now embodied by the loquat tree he planted with his wife. She reflects:

> To make my readers understand, I can't say he was staring at a loquat tree. I added a sentence to explain that he was thinking of his wife and how long she has died. The tree represented his sadness.

This reflection focuses on unpacking culturally specific aesthetics, rhetorical styles, and ideological features of languages as operative within community, disciplinary, and cultural contexts. Morgan's use of the loquat tree embodies a sophisticated use of the rhetorical strategy to "combine emotion with scenery" (see Chapter 2), which is often used by classical authors to articulate their emotions and aspirations. The tree embodies affectionate memories of a loved one, which contrasts with the feeling of loss to accentuate the gravity of sorrow. Inferring that her American audience might not be aware of cultural motifs and tropes familiar to a Chinese reader, Morgan approached the affective meaning of the text by surfacing it in a straightforward manner. This move partially resulted from ongoing conversations with a diverse audience, which brought into convergence multiple interpretive possibilities afforded by different rhetorical traditions. Through sustained individual and collective exploration, Morgan recognizes the importance of decoding the "hidden meanings" of examples, canonical texts, and cultural tropes in consideration of her audience's needs and expectations. Loquat trees, the moon, or bamboo plants emerge as tropes through intertextual histories of poets and essayists referencing, critiquing, and conversing with each other, anthologies and textbooks being compiled for teaching and testing, and students reciting, interpreting, and emulating such texts. Enfolded in Morgan's literary sensitivities are these historical trajectories, which become intertextually linked and incrementally coalesced into strong, centripetal forces that help to define the core values and practices of cultural and language education in China.

This assignment theorizes multilingual writers' ability to draw on holistic semiotic repertoires to negotiate meaning across linguistic, cultural, and disciplinary differences, placing emphasis on the disposition of open inquiry into and the ability to negotiate such differences at the core of such language work (Canagarajah, 2006; Lorimer Leonard, 2013; Lu & Horner, 2013; Wang, 2020). It mirrors translingual scholars' focus on the practice-based, adaptive, emergent, and mutually constitutive nature of languages (Canagarajah, 2013; Guerra, 2016; Lu & Horner, 2013) and disrupts a monolingual view of languages as "discrete, preexisting, and enumerable entities" bound to geographical territories, nation states, or speech communities (Lu & Horner, 2013). By incorporating students' own examples and positioning their linguistic, rhetorical, and cultural resources as objects of inquiry, this assignment provides opportunities for students to unpack specific aesthetics, rhetorical styles, and ideological features of languages that guide their own writing practices. Student-generated cultural idioms, stories, and lyrics as well as disciplinary texts written in other languages become sites of inquiry as multilingual students explore and theorize their entangled literacy landscape that buzzed with multiple perspectives, interpretative frames, rhetorical traditions, and linguistic forms. Such acts of linguistic, cultural, and disciplinary border crossing involve the ongoing attunement of students' semiotic repertoires, cultivation of disposition of open inquiry into language differences, and translingual practices toward language negotiation.

In the bridge writing class I taught, Morgan completed the translation reflection assignment; her essay demonstrated how the assignment allowed focused analysis of the exigencies and consequences of linguistic and cultural crossing. In her honors FYW class, Morgan continued to juggle language, cultural, and rhetorical differences—she relied on Chinese to explore the insight and global structure of her essay, engaged in extensive translation of familiar idioms and cultural examples from Chinese to English, and recruited multiple readers to help her identify areas in her essay that required the strategic unpacking of nuanced meanings, constantly attuning her strategies for shifting frames of reference. Doing so invited her to temporarily suspend established, familiar assumptions about her language and culture, while learning to consider her language/culture in the context of another, thereby developing transcultural awareness. Recognizing the complexity of translation labor, she became more intentional in her effort to build relationships with and seek help from literacy brokers, focus reviewers' energy on grammatical irregularity, and embrace a labor-intensive, iterative multilingual writing process—strategies proven effective in her honors FYW course.

I AM FROM POETRY

I Am From Poetry is an assignment I offered to facilitate students' understanding of linguistic, cultural, and disciplinary border crossing as unfolding at the intersection of overlapping historical trajectories and contingencies. The assignment was designed in response to calls to position translingual practices as a means for "students to construct and constantly modify their sociocultural identities and values, as they respond to their historical and present conditions critically and creatively" (García & Wei, 2014, p. 62). Undergirding the assignment was an interest in understanding transnational students' language practices and literacy identities as negotiated across time-space relationships through the mediation of assemblages of artifacts, persons, practices, and texts (Wang, 2020). With attention to literacy as simultaneously fluid, frictive, and fixed mobile practices that are differently valuated (Lorimer Leonard, 2017), instructors could use I Am From Poetry to engage students in reflections on their literacy and identities as negotiated across social, cultural, and rhetorical circumstances operating with different value systems. According to Stewart and Hansen-Thomas (2016), I Am From

Poetry writing sanctions a space for students to perform purposeful examination of transnational experiences, engage in translingual practice by integrating phrases from multiple languages into the poem, and access a range of cultural and linguistic resources to express creativity and criticality. It is in this spirit that I adapted the assignment, which encourages multilingual writers to understand their literacy repertoire and identity as shaped by and shaping their social world.

Procedure

This poetry assignment consists of class reading of multicultural texts, journal writing around cultural themes, class construction of artifactual literacies, and the creation of a multimodal poetry writing project. Each element is chosen purposefully to connect to students' transnational lives and allows multiple opportunities for translingual performance. At the outset, the class read biographical poetry about the (transnational) life of Supreme Court Justice Sonia Sotomayor, and autobiographical accounts by multicultural authors ("Mother Tongue" by Amy Tan, "The Myth of Latin Woman" by Judith Ortiz Cofer), with the conversation focused on understanding culture as a fluid composite of components and experiences. Using photos from their personal albums, students explore visceral experiences with their home communities and select artifacts representative of their literacy and cultural practices, which give rise to growing theorization of their movements across languages and cultures as sites for inquiry into differences. Working from the original I Am From Poem template (Lyon, 1993), students then interpret such artifactual and visual information into a multimodal poem, with key concepts illustrated with photos. In what follows, I draw on Leo's poem to discuss the assignment as an opportunity to help students surface meaningful literacy experiences and tacit cultural assumptions.

Affordance

> I am from Slam Dunk,
> from street dancing and my first deck of magic cards.
> I am from stage lights,
> (blinding, deafening, my heart pounding).
>
> I am from reading beautiful Chinese poetry and practicing Kung Fu,
> From surgeon and business manager.

> I am from late night emergency calls and long business trips,
> from You are too naughty! and Don't brag!
>
> I am from a walk under the moon and watch the shadows of bamboo trees,
> The silence of the moment teaches me the importance of knowing your friends from your enemies.
>
> *(Excerpt from Leo's Where I Am From Poem)*

In his poem, Leo surfaced a wide range of extracurricular activities that are intricately entangled with his literacy experiences as a writer, including *Slam Dunk*, a Japanese anime series aired from 1993 to 1996 worldwide, and his stage performance experiences as an amateur street dancer and magician. I invited every student to read their poem in class, which was followed by questions and comments. During his sharing, Leo unpacked some themes in his poem, generating knowing smiles and inviting curious inquiry into his "talents," for which he readily and gladly provided improvised performances. In particular, he described how his stage performance experiences helped him engage with his audience. For one thing, taking insights from the perspective of a stage performer, Leo educated his classmates about how he strategically picked his seat in the classroom. He tried to sit in the center of the second row in the classroom, which he argued to be the most "visible" position in the classroom, which would help ensure that his teacher noticed him during lectures. Noting the importance of rehearsal, humor, and confidence in engaging with his audience, he made multiple visits during my office hours to rehearse for major presentations in front of a "live audience." Especially poignant here was his renewed appreciation of such talents as imparting important skills that figured into dialogical connection with writing practices to perform his identity as a talented, intelligent, and successful student. Leo also used the poem as an opportunity to explore the complex relationship between familial teaching and his class identity, which manifested through the tension between his parents, who were preoccupied with work, and Leo, who spent much of his childhood in extracurricular classes orchestrated to cultivate his mind and body (as I detailed in Chapter 4).

Leo's rhetorical knowledge surfaced through his mentioning of a walk he took in the quietude of the evening. When I further probed into his selection of this detail, Leo named an important rhetorical strategy that he acquired as a writer in Chinese. The rhetorical strategy of articulating values through objects was an advanced writing technique used by classical and popular authors he liked, such as Murakami Haruki and Guo Jingming. He referenced a quote from the Japanese novelist Murakami Haruki, who wrote about "wondering if his soap has become slimmer or larger" during his absence to describe his longing to return to his home. By contrast, the Chinese popular-author-turned-movie-producer Guo Jingming would use the opportunity for brand name-dropping as he described his "2015, [Hermes'] Birkin's limited-edition bar of soap, not knowing if the **H**-shaped logo has faded." Celebrating Haruki's elegance and simplicity in conveying genuine emotions, Leo critiqued Guo's deployment of the same strategy as gaudy, "unflustered, naked wealth flaunting for which [he] doesn't have the stomach." This theme, the privileges and perils young people with different class identifications navigate, surfaced again in his writing in honors FYW (as I was noted in Chapters 4 and 5).

Leo's poem also referenced a lesson imparted by his middle school Chinese teacher, who provided stimulating discussion of classical literature and made conscious effort to introduce reading materials outside the state-sanctioned standard curriculum to cultivate students' literary taste. His mentioning of the walk echoed a classical essay, "In Memory a Night Visit to Chengtian Temple," by Su Shi, a renowned classical essayist. The essay speaks of the essayist being inspired by the beautiful moonlight and making an unplanned visit to a friend in Chengtian Temple. As the two friends stroll in the courtyard, they appreciate the beauty of the moonlight, which creates intricate patterns with bamboo and pine trees. The essayist ends with a short reflection with an implicit critique of the emperor's decision to demote him, which forces unwanted leisure and deprives him of the possibility to pursue his political ambitions. Personifying the moon as an uninvited friend, the author laments the fickleness of human relationships as his friends abandon him in humiliation. Leo exclaims, "You think he was talking about the moon pouring its silvery light? You think he was talking about bamboo and pine trees? No! He was being cynical. In a very insidious way, he was attacking a vacuous emperor and the political buffoons showering him with flattery. He was also celebrating his own good taste and noble character."

Enfolded in Leo's literacy and rhetorical practice was China's long history of disseminating and studying classical texts, which was institutionalized through the implementation of high-stakes civil examination used to certify the literati for service to the rulers. As Prior & Lunsford (2008) have argued, classical Confucian texts powerfully informed civic rhetoric and were deployed with high expectation for erudition in intertextual allusions and references by both authors and readers (p. 107). Knowledge of and practice with such rhetorical strategies manifested in Leo's reflection above and resurfaced in his honors FYW class, as he contrasted such strategies with a skit activity, when Jill invited a team of students to depict the "stubbornness" of an office worker through showing rather than telling. Leo provided a polite critique of his classmates' portrayal of a salesperson refusing to recognize a mistake after encountering a series of complaints from co-workers, customers, and a supervisor, suggesting the "American way" presents, according to Leo, "an obvious, one-dimensional representation of the person, lacking in layers and complexity." When one of the students asked how he would approach the assignment, Leo said he would portray a pencil breaking as the worker squeezed it with increasing intensity. To him, Chinese rhetorical strategies provided subtle ways to wrestle with complex human emotions.

As suggested here, low-stakes writing assignments provide a space for students to surface, name, and strategize writing-related knowledge and practices accumulated across moments of reading, writing, and conversing in multiple language and rhetorical traditions. An understanding of literacy practices as chronotopically figured prepares students to assemble and retool writing and rhetorical knowledge; name difficulties in working through differences; and assess creative, improvised choices. Informal sharing of and conversations around such writing products gives students the opportunity to further clarify, unpack, and articulate their theories, practices, and strategies for navigating multiple rhetorical and language traditions.

These low-stakes assignments could complement more formalized assignments such as the Memoir to help students incrementally discover, interpret, and compose meaningful life stories. Offering multiple entries into reflective practices, such as drafting, reading, sharing, and responding to teacher and student inquiries, allows students like Leo to explore ways other than strategic silence to engage with issues of class privilege, aspirations, and perils. Embodied performance, which portrays a stubborn worker through raised voice or a broken pencil, provides multimodal means for engaging with rhetorical practices that often remain tethered to the written words. Students could discuss and examine the affordances and constraints of rhetorical strategies across modalities, thereby allowing the class to explore the aesthetic, intellectual, and political affordances of dynamic semiotic and rhetorical repertoires and disparate cultural frames of reference.

Informed by entanglement, this assignment provides a useful lens for examining the transformative and dynamic ways in which students inquire into and strategize the subtle and invisible acts of composing their multilingual lives into meaning, which involves the ongoing efforts to access and assess semiotic resources across multiple lines of difference. As I have illustrated throughout this book, these efforts involve strategies to mobilize, attune, and reconfigure tested practices as well as improvised acts to hybridize, reimagine, and develop old and new strategies in response to new exigencies and contingencies. Entanglement encourages me to notice semiotic fibers (e.g., stories, jokes, rhetorical practices) that are picked up across activities, assignments, and courses, alerting me to the surprising, improvised, and negotiated ways in which they transform through the writer's encounters. These moments of literacy work materialize through language innovation, which often evades our attention not only because they unfold through fleeting decisions that fold into seemingly routine parts of language practices and thereby becomes invisible, but also because they are rarely captured, surfaced, and theorized. Assignments such as these tap into the rich cultural and language knowledge of students, thereby making it possible for the transfer of meta-knowledge of writing (DePalma & Ringer, 2011; Lorimer Leonard & Nowacek, 2016). Enacting chronotopic figuring, this assignment gives writing teachers an opportunity to trace the affective, emergent, and surprising aspects of language negotiation, thereby providing a way to avoid flattening the nuanced ways in which writers from distinct backgrounds engage with language differences (Gilyard, 2016; Matsuda, 2014). As such, this assignment draws our attention to moment-to-moment, embodied practices, providing evidence of inquiry-driven discussion and negotiation, surfacing cultural and rhetorical knowledge that guides strategic choices, highlighting exigencies for innovation and improvisation, and unraveling multi-voiced, collaborative negotiation through layers of translation across languages, modes, genres, cultures, and spacetimes.

Enacting Asset-Based Pedagogy

As discussed above, pedagogical attention to entanglement in the writing classroom begins with efforts to center students' languages and cultures as objects of inquiry and to invite students to mobilize and attune semiotic and rhetorical repertoires developed across multiple literacy and activity spheres of students' lives. An asset-based pedagogy can provide the opportunity for multilingual writers to configure and reconfigure rhetorical resources and strategies and to explore their social and cultural experiences along with diverse audiences across linguistic, cultural, and disciplinary boundaries. Placing multiple languages in juxtaposition to each other, these assignments invite students to examine and challenge binaries that separate languages as sealed and isolated entities, while developing metalinguistic understandings of language as linguistic, cultural, and ideological structures that can be negotiated and retooled. In so doing, students might begin to see language differences as the norm, meaning as fulfilled through negotiated marshaling of linguistic and semiotic resources, and themselves as agents who make adaptive and creative uses of rhetorical repertoires that embody shifting social, cultural, and historical meanings.

These assignments worked to open the conceptual space of teaching and learning that encourage linguistic and cultural border crossing, helping to prepare students for the rather daunting challenges of succeeding in honors-designated FYW. However, they have not begun to address the vast range of challenges of transnational students learning to navigate the discursive, material, and disciplinary conventions of the FYW classroom, which often operated with monolingual ideologies and embodies an American-centric frame of reference for understanding and assessing student learning, participation, and writing. As hinted in Leo's reflection, how students are emplaced in the classroom in relation to the teacher, the projection board, and fellow students matters for how writing and the learning of writing unfolds. Indeed, a writer's embodied presence, including all its sensations, affects, and memories, is entangled in the material geography of writing, such as the material-spatial configuration of the classroom or the shines and hues of wall decor, and unfolds through a dynamic choreography between the writer's moving body in partnership with things, all bearing the marks of lingering memories and steady habits (Pigg, 2014; Reynolds, 2007). As Hannah Rule argues, to move with writers through composing is to "uncover the small, embodied, material actions that give shape differently to all writing acts," to "see writing processes as located, differentiated, and contingent," and to grapple with "the inconsistencies, failures, and material partnerships and disruptions in their everyday writing attempts" (Rule, 2019, p. 70).

These assignments and pedagogical practices build on and extend current efforts to foreground students' languages and cultures, encourage meaning negotiation across multiple lines of difference, and support students' development of an attitude of openness toward such differences (De Costa et al., 2017; Kiernan et al., 2021; Sun & Lan, 2020). In a way, such moves shift our emphasis from the polished final drafts toward students' theorization and practice of complex language negotiation that happens in all communicative acts, even those that seemingly adhere to and replicate standard conventions. They position multilingual writers' linguistic, cultural, and rhetorical knowledge as resources for learning and their linguistic performance as a site of inquiry, negotiation, and improvisation. Centering students' experiences and languages not only facilitates the development of rhetorical awareness and understanding of how local contingencies constantly influence linguistic performance but also positions such inquiry as emergent with students' linguistic, cultural, and disciplinary border crossing with all its thrills, struggles, and surprises.

From an entanglement perspective, such pedagogical moves are especially useful in unraveling the rich, distributed, and negotiated labor performed by multilingual writers. They seek to build connections across academic units, enable the mobility of emerging drafts across languages, modes, writers, and readers, support relationships students forge with each other, teachers, and mentors, encourage continuous efforts to recognize, name, and retool strategies, and help students recognize the value of attunement and improvisation. Indeed, it was from Morgan's Translation Narrative assignment that I gained renewed appreciation for the complexity of translation labor that she continued to perform in FYW. Such recognition, coupled with Morgan's enthusiasm to explain and theorize her own practices, provided the framing for the ethnographic research revolving around her. Similarly, Leo's poem provided a window into the dynamic social life he was leading and the perils and privileges of his class identity. As these lines of inquiry entangled, they also continued to inform pedagogical innovations, ethnographic research questions, efforts to attune methodological choices, and disciplinary traversal that made theorization of these students' literacy and writing practices from an entanglement perspective possible. In comparison to the intense class aspirations and anxieties he experienced with his peers, writing assignments offered in the bridge writing class became a low-stakes opportunity to consider his class identity. The co-emergence of two distinct strands of my research interests, pedagogical inquiry and ethnographic research, continued to shape what I was able to see, capture, and theorize as a researcher. They also continued to draw the students, their teachers and friends, and the multiple trajectories of personal, disciplinary, and institutional histories into the entanglement of my inquiry.

By positioning the discursive, material, and institutional norms of the classroom as sites of inquiry, we begin to move further away from the humanist presupposition that undergirds Western assumptions of writing: ideas for writing lie within the writer, thinking belongs to the individual writer, and writing is the process of uncovering, recording, and representing personal truth and thinking. An entanglement perspective calls for efforts to reconceptualize the writer at work with the material geography of their environ, in partnership with natural, cultural, and literate beings, and through the fluidity of ideas and thoughts that stay emergent through multiple acts of translation across languages, modes, persons, and spacetimes. Vulnerability lies at the heart of the productive reimagination of the writing classroom as transformative entanglements are driven by contingent and sustained relationships, mediated by expansive semiotic repertoires, and amenable to surprises and unpredictable encounters. The vulnerability of the individual writer, who brings their theories, eccentricities, and idiosyncrasies for managing the writing space and process; the vulnerability of the teacher, who is willing to suspend established assumptions about how the teaching of writing is to work or how students' writing processes look; the vulnerability of the institutional structure that is capable of recognizing the need to support and sponsor cross-unit dialogue and collaboration, to acknowledge the limitations and harm of monolingual and monocultural orientations, and to allocate the resources that reward pedagogical innovation and scholarly inquiry initiated by a large population of contingent faculty whose work with multilingual writers are inadequately compensated or supported.

Conclusion

Entanglement invites scrutiny of the intentional and strategic singular author marshaling a dynamic repertoire of semiotic and rhetorical resources to write *about* the world. During presentations and talks I gave on my research, variations of this question often surfaced: If multilingual writing is as entangled as suggested here, what do we do with the singular author? Writing teachers and researchers have often suspected backstage scenes of student collaboration. We have all noticed international students using sidebar conversations in their home language to seek clarifications about classroom tasks instead of asking the teacher; we know that students work together to gauge and rearticulate their interpretations of instructor expectations; they share personal notes, images of PowerPoint slides, and resources gathered from independent research; they help each other navigate the overwhelming number of platforms, practices, and structures of the indecipherable institutional and bureaucratic maze of the university; they rely on digital dictionaries, each other, trusted teachers, friends, tutors, and paid services across academic units and transnational networks for language support and help. For some international students, their reliance on their peers' suggestions creates barriers, limits access to campus resources and support, and generates uncertainties (Fraiberg et al., 2017).

We are not quite certain if and how we should recalibrate writing instruction in consideration of the promises and challenges of multilingual writing in entanglement. As illustrated throughout this book, scenes of multilingual writing seem too distributed, uncertain, and dispersed across spacetimes to adequately sustain the notion of the single author working to invent, articulate, and craft meaning. But then how do we know if ideas, sentences, and techniques we are reading and assessing belong to the one student author whose name happens to appear on the top of the grading draft? If we recognize the surprising, improvisational, and unexpected ways of writing, how do we offer interventions and instructions, which likely would not anticipate the full range of idiosyncratic whims of writers and their circumstances? To what extent do we trust that we are hearing the voice of this individual author, with all its quirks, truths, and idiosyncrasies that make writing a beautiful and worthwhile enterprise? Where do we draw the line between productive peer support and plagiarism if the notion of the single author does not hold as fast?

I do not have good answers to these questions, but I kept thinking about my own writing process as a biliterate scholar and a multilingual writer. I have worked hard to develop opportunities at professional conferences to share aspects of my research at various stages of its development. I attended "meet the editor" sessions at conferences to learn about editorial values and practices that would usefully guide my own drafting and revision efforts. I have embraced low-stakes professional development opportunities, such as departmental "lightning round" talks, where each faculty gave a three-minute presentation on a project. Snacks were provided; poetic finger snaps erupted at the end of each presentation; ideas and thoughts carried forward into the hallways, mixing into conversations over coffee or committee meetings. I have learned to enjoy professional collaboration, which helped me find opportunities for publication, develop ideas, strategize revision, and learn about others' writing practices. I found such exchanges incredibly useful in orienting me to the myriad literacy and social practices of the profession.

I routinely brought my working drafts to trusted friends and colleagues for language support in specific areas, such as article placement and tense inflections, just like the multilingual students I taught and researched with. I still struggle to properly place the articles "the" or "a," a part of speech that is absent in my home language, without any feelings of certainty if I am using them correctly or if an article is even necessary in the first place. Although such peer mentorship, motivated by the need for mutual support and rooted in reciprocal generosity in sharing our time and expertise, almost never resulted in well-articulated and reliable rules, I benefited from the corrections, enjoyed the jokes we told about our own writing quirks and rituals, and incrementally developed an intuition to gauge my own usage based on what "sounds right" or "sounds better." I had asked trusted friends to read reviews on manuscripts that were too daunting in size and rigor for me to process. I have organized study groups to provide a structured environment to develop and receive feedback on my project. Having recognized my own lack of capacity to leverage small talk, humor, and social charisma to forge connections, I resorted to an established blind peer-review system to get insightful feedback from experts in my field. In reciprocation, I always responded to invitations for review with positivity and assiduity.

Here is the question then. How are my writing-in-entanglements—affectively moved, driving and driven by relationships, and mobilizing and mobilized by my semiotic repertoire—any different from the multilingual students' writing processes I document and analyze in this book? If I am rewarded, through publication and job and promotion opportunities, for my ability to forge productive connections and manage collaborative survival in the "publish-or-perish" environ of academia, why shouldn't student writers' extraordinary efforts to assemble thickets of relationships and streams of writing-related resources, knowledge, and practices be acknowledged and valued positively?

I offer entanglement as a useful framework for theorizing and following connected, transformative, and dynamic writing phenomena at work and on the move. Throughout the book, I have worked to explore various propositions for attending to the intentional and improvised ways of stitching together multiplicities of relationships, ways of being in the world, and voices, theories, and idiosyncrasies of writing across spacetimes. Entanglement encourages me to follow Hannah Rule's call to examine writing as emplaced and embodied in conditions of many kinds,

> not just as differences in broad contexts or rhetorical situations or an unfamiliar library versus a home study, but also in the tiniest, most immediate of conditions (like bodily movement, hesitations, interruptions, or interactions with tools, glasses of water, dogs, books, and others) and in the most distant and abstract macro-constraints (including genre, audience, historical moment, community discourse, and so on). (2019, p. 153)

Entanglement propositions, with their attention to the ephemeral, contingent, and mobile ways of relationships, not only allow me to observe how inspirations and ideas for writing emerge through contingent weaving together of rhetorical exigencies, embodied experiences, and bodies of knowledge and meanings, but also unearth ways in which writing continues to emerge, grow, transform, or disappear as it moves and relates across bodies, spheres, languages, modes, and spacetimes in determinate and indeterminate ways. Although I approach each proposition from one stream of ethnographic data from one case study, these themes surface across cases in compelling ways. In this conclusion, I work to further articulate the implications of these themes for writing research broadly.

Writers In-Becoming With Others

Attention to becoming-with biological, cultural, and literacy others dismantles the Western conception of the singular, solitary author who scribbles thoughts, transcribes observations, invents meanings, and orchestrates grammatical and rhetorical structures to write about the world. I echo what Hannah Rule critiques as the "disembodied, transcendent" conception of writers that takes them out of the materiality that moves, inspires, and limits them, for imagining writing processes as somehow sealed off from contexts immediate and distant, and for preventing us from recognizing the social and cultural situatedness as well as the lived experience that we must reckon with (2019, p. 71). As I have illustrated throughout this book, the rushing noise of the river, the birds and squirrels who share the riverbank with human pedestrians, the vibrant colors of maple leaves swaying in the crisp fall breeze, the warmth of the setting sun, the bustle of a campus dining hall and its offering of comfort food, the chuckle mixed with incredulity over a humorous comment from a friend, or the encouraging or critical voices of reviewers, constitute the material, semiotic, affective, and physical conditions for writing for dynamic and diverse purposes. Writing unfolds through and with living, perceiving, and being in the world with others. Multilingual writers are not just writing about the world; they write themselves and the material worlds into being.

As in the cases of Morgan and Leo, they act in reaction to the affective energies and bodily sensations emerging from their chance encounters with the natural, cultural, and literacy others. These others could be the material and embodied ones such as a river, a supportive or critical reader, or vestiges of old memories and new anecdotes. These encounters could move the writer so intensely that they spill over into their writing, impregnating the writing with sensations, affects, and memories stretching out further into innumerable scenes of reminiscing, talking, joking, and thinking about specific experiences from multilingual living. In the case of Morgan, the river gains momentum through its mobile journey to inform creative ways of relating to and reflecting on it; the river stays in becoming through the recursive and dialogical juxtaposition of multiple voices and perspectives that indeterminately interprets and constructs its meaning. For Leo, his ongoing effort to find a good writing topic emerges through the constant temporal traversal that brought the past and present selves and others into action with and reaction to each other, stirring up intense class aspirations and anxieties. The story could be differently backgrounded and foregrounded, celebrated or censored according to decorum that are differently enacted and expected by those involved in such encounters. These instances of writing emerge through actions, interactions, and reactions that are predictably and haphazardly connected across spacetimes. From this perspective, writing stays alive in entanglement with the beings and doings of others. Stories are not representations of the world waiting to be discovered. Rather, they become with the writer, acquiring nuanced, emergent, and transformative meanings in open articulation of the material world.

Thickets of Relationships

Entanglement happens through the stitching together of relationships mediated by a dynamic, expansive semiotic repertoire. In the world of multilingual writers, relationships propel the movements of meanings across persons, documents, languages, and modes. These relationships, old and new, carefully cultivated and continuously improvised, are motivated by the desire to be heard and seen, to respond and share, and to participate in a network of literacy, cultural, and professional knowledge, expertise, and experiences. Relationships could grow from old friendships, but they also emerge through chance encounters with a friendly neighbor, a patient consultant, or a great conversationalist. As in the world of fungi, these relationships are forged and maintained across lines of linguistic, cultural, rhetorical, and ontological differences; they are reciprocal, collaborative, and competitive; they have the capacity to fuse with, fork from, and absorb other relationships depending on changing circumstances and exigencies; they yoke the literacy others into dialogues through the mediation of mobile artifacts and mobilizing technologies.

As in the case of Morgan, her dynamic relating with the natural, cultural, and literacy others across ontological categories moved and transformed the writer. Morgan was imaginatively moved by visceral and affective experiences with the river; ideas generated in one spacetime become encoded and mobilized through digitally managed comments, highlights, edits, and chat; documents intersected across spacetimes and engendered resonance and dissonance. Textual meaning gained mobility through the working of relationships, which further mobilized and wove writing-related practices, strategies, and theories into improvised assemblages. In the case of Leo, knowledge of and strategies for forging and maintaining relationships were honed across familial, professional, and writing contexts to produce idiosyncrasies, narratives, and audience awareness that could cause tension, make trouble, and interrupt the writer's efforts to relate to others in his transnational network. Thickets of relationships provide a way to consider how circuits are made through coordination and encounters or how connections might thicken or dissipate. It provides a window into how writers continue to enact and align with diverse ideological orientations, referential frameworks, and rhetorical traditions when meaning moves from one person, document, or spacetime to another. Life worlds are formed through efforts to move, connect, and transform through relationships.

The Surprising Ways of Encounters

The lesson I take from living, thinking, researching, and writing with multilingual writers is the need to embrace and move with the adventures entailed in multilingual living. Multilingual writing co-emerges with multilingual living, which entails unpredictable encounters with life forms wittingly and unwittingly woven into writers' literacy landscapes. The contingent weaving together of these components creates opportunities to discover, contemplate, and engage, generating feelings of awe, thrill, fear, anger, and humiliation. An entanglement perspective shifts our attention away from the writer as the center of analysis; it reveals how dynamic, temporaneous, and improvised acts of relating to natural, cultural, and literacy others could powerfully direct the contours of multilingual writing. Placing shifting possibilities of the writer becoming with the world at the center of analysis invites attention to unintended coordination, unpredictable encounters, and indeterminate meanings as core features of such an enterprise. As much as indeterminacy manifests in fungal hyphal tips that fork and fuse in their search for a friendly tree root, I see bountiful examples of multilingual writers drawing and being drawn into precarious, surprising, and productive associations.

Dwelling on surprises requires patience, curiosity, and fortitude. It calls for us to wander with writers, as they readily move in dialogue with many voices, perspectives, and expectations for using, theorizing, and valuing writing. It invites the willingness to abandon some of my assumptions of what the writing process should look like as I follow the unpredictable journeys of writers and texts. Leo's calligraphy story, for example, became unpredictably foregrounded and backgrounded in the writer's literacy landscape at different moments of his life, assuming intellectual and emotional significance at times and falling off the page at other times. To dive into its meaning requires that one partake in the constant temporal traversal that brings multiple selves and others into dialogue. To dwell on surprises, I learned not to rush the writer toward what I thought should be the next stage of the writing process and to shut my mouth as I personally felt the anxiety of witnessing a writer's struggle to meet an impending deadline. I learned to swallow questions such as, "What is wrong with the Kung Fu story again?" or "Did you find the translation for that word after all?" because these moments of the writer seemingly idling in distraction or "recklessly" departing from *the* plan are equally important sites for inquiry, negotiation, and learning. I learned to slow my pace and venture into unexpected corners of Morgan's material and literacy environs, where stories of how we learned to love writing surfaced when we talked about rocks, benches, trees, and books that were important to us as readers and writers.

Chronotopic Figuring

If surprises are manifestations of the fickle and precarious world we are in open articulation with, chronotopic figuring offers a way to engage with the messy entanglement woven together by unpredictable encounters. It asks us to extend our gaze beyond one writer acting in the moment through one relationship or encounter and invites into question stabilized parameters and boundaries with which we consider space and time. In the process of writing this book, I was constantly reminded of the radical mobility of all things. Ideas with the potential for writing never seem to settle in time. In Leo and Morgan's multilingual writing processes we see evidence of ideas, drafts, and persons forging open and knotted patterning of material and semiotic worlds. For these students, each effort to write the story into partial articulation needs to be considered in dialogue with and connection to other instances of the writer remembering, processing, discussing, and sharing the story across languages and modes. For example, a teasing joke that engenders thrills, embarrassment, and discomfort is to be analyzed against the backdrop of many historical trajectories—popular and youth culture where the joke originated, the friendship between the writer and their commenter, and the writer's ongoing efforts to theorize and strategize their own identities. It is in these moments of tangling and knotting that we observe how individual writers develop agility and attune skills for navigating the uncertainties and precarities of relating to and flourishing with others with, through, and against the overwhelming waves of historical contingencies. In moments when coordination forges or breaks, it is never about one writer making a singular decision that affects one draft. Instead, it is the result of separate melodic lines of multilingual living coalescing, changing, and dissolving in sporadic but consequential ways.

Chronotopic figuring allows us to explore seemingly contingent, idiosyncratic decisions as situated within long personal, familial, literacy, educational, and political trajectories. Leo's effort to exercise strategic silence and Morgan's rhetorical translation strategies were complexly entangled in discourses, experiences, and practices that crystalized and stabilized across multiple temporal trajectories of them learning to inhabit their literacy and class identities. They surface in familial teaching that initiated Leo into the privileges and perils of his class identity and helped him develop strategies for leveraging them for his academic and professional endeavors. They were articulated in Morgan's personal encounters, fueling her aspirations for cosmopolitan living. They resonated with the ebb and flow of cultural trends, social discourse, and political campaigns, which were transnationally mobilized to shape students' capacity and willingness to profess such class aspirations through literacy activities. Makeshift relationships are made when multiple life, imaginary, and representational worlds are spliced into everyday encounters, conversations, and interactions. They crystallize into powerful memories, feelings, and strategies that continue to inform literacy and social practices. They work in messy ways as they cut across class, cultural, and rhetorical differences, economic disparities, and competing interests.

Chronotopic figuring also encourages us to listen to the multiple, competing rhythms of students' literacy lives. While it is important to examine course syllabi, project descriptions, and classroom activities as we explore the temporal flow of writing-related activities, it is also important to recognize that such flow is but one of many competing temporal rhythms that shape students' multilingual lives. For students like Leo and Morgan, writing rings with polyphonic rhythms. For one thing, their social media activities were intimately entangled with writing for FYW and drew many other histories in and out of coordination. To tell the adventures of multilingual writers, we are not to limit our analysis to one creature, one relationship, or one unpredictable encounter at a time.

The notion of chronotopic figuring, which places emphasis on the emergent layering, back-and-forth trading, and improvised designs of the other, provides a way to conceptualize the recursive, cyclical, and uneven ways in which textual meaning gains foothold or lose traction. It articulates a disposition toward open-ended inquiry into temporaneous and uncertain knotting, the energy and skill to examine multi-actor flourishing, the willingness to work with contingency, and the readiness to move with mess and multiplicities. Chronotopic figuring entails what Haraway (2016) calls tentacular thinking, one that recognizes that myriad tentacular feelers' ability to feel, try, attach, and weave historical trajectories into open and knotted patterning of material semiotic worlds. It is a way to think with writers as wayfarers living along with nets and networks of lines and becoming through unexpected associations and collaborations, risky partners, relentless contingencies, interlaced trails, improvised solutions, and emergent spacetimes.

Asset-Based Multilingual Writing Pedagogy

Entanglement disrupts ontological categories and erodes boundaries of many kinds. It raises questions about where, when, and how to look for acts of writing. It offers ways to examine what happens in the naturally, culturally, and digitally embedded writing extracurriculars in dialogical connection to what happens inside FYW classrooms, where rather singularly imagined temporal rhythm still exerts its power through curricular documents and pedagogical practices that move a monocrop of students in advancements toward institutionally and programmatically inscribed learning goals through the enforcement of deadlines, assignments, and attendance policies. This resembles the plantationocene that Donna Haraway and Anna Tsing critique to have disturbed landscapes and caused dispossession and inequality (Mitman, 2019). As the global Covid-19 pandemic has shown us, however, the spatial and temporal boundaries we maintain about students' academic lives, tethered to institutional and ancillary instructional times and bounded by spatial boundaries of classrooms, dining halls, dorms, and campuses, crumble easily. Many of us have spoken into the black hole of the Zoom screen knowing our students are juxtaposing the competing needs of sleeping, learning, and working; my students have tried to tune in for a class while riding the bus to and from work; I have had the pleasure of meeting the many siblings, children, and parents of students, for whom the spatial boundaries between school and home were forced open. As these multiple contours and trajectories of academic, social, and professional lives were jolted out of their conventional lanes, we all developed the agility to navigate the sudden congestion of the multiplicities. It is not that these boundaries should not be maintained but that we need to reconsider the theoretical metaphors with which we imagine how, where, and when student learning happens.

These case studies present a nuanced picture of multilingual students' self- and school-sponsored literacies as deeply interwoven in an assemblage of languages, texts, technologies, practices, and spaces. It complicates previous accounts that focus on the productive ways in which self-sponsored literacies strengthen and extend academic literacy by pointing to deeply felt fissures that make traversal across such literacy landscapes challenging and difficult. The way in which texts, languages, practices, and strategies are woven and rewoven across spaces is filled with tensions that are difficult to reconcile and cannot be fully understood unless positioned against the backdrop of a far-flung network of literacy activities feeding into local, situated literacy activities. Such a perspective positions multilinguals' extended reading and writing practices as a site of translingual negotiation involving ongoing, improvisational reconfiguration of a repertoire of multilingual resources and translingual practices. For both Morgan and Leo, informal writing, driven by inspirations and arising from chance encounters, provides spaces for preparing and rehearsing for writing in FYW. However, such crossing is never smooth, as self-sponsored writing never translates into an assignment, but takes shape through "repeated movements across social, semiotic, and geographic borders [that foster] a sense of rhetorical attunement to translingual and transmodal practices" (Fraiberg, 2017, p. 111).

Throughout the book, I have also shown constant negotiation along lines of differences as a core feature of multilingual writing. Both Leo and Morgan mobilize rhetorical strategies and translation practices to meet the expectations and needs of their past and present audience. Understanding translation as rhetorical acts of language negotiation invites literacy educators to develop nuanced and responsive pedagogies that make translation a central part of the work of teachers and students alike. Such a pedagogical shift is critical especially considering a long history of shunning translation practice and cross-language negotiation in the academy at large and in writing instruction more particularly. In FYW class and writing center consultations, there are multiple missed opportunities for leveraging such perceived linguistic irregularities to enable productive conversations of language difference—in the instructors circling an "odd" word without explanation or simply brushing it off as indication of the student writer's authentic voice, peer reviewers noting a wide range of issues as bad grammar, and writing consultant's efforts to smooth over such differences without attending to the beautiful nuances they embody. In contrast to the rushed classroom space that emphasizes clarity and demonstration of creative writing techniques in student writing, self-sponsored reviews were managed slowly and recursively to allow extensive explanation and negotiation and thus provided many opportunities to distribute translation labor, negotiate slippages and perceptions, and enact writing knowledge and strategies.

In naming these gaps in students' multilingual reality and writing pedagogy, this book further challenges a deficit view that treats languages and rhetorical traditions as statically separated and hierarchically ordered. Textual meanings do travel when multilingual writers fuse and retool writing-related knowledge and strategies to write their experiences into meaning. The focus on such language work not only points to the labor involved in doing so but also highlights the inherent dynamism and innovation of multilingual composing—authorial intentions materialize through coordinated work of many readers and writers who seek clarity, raise questions, and provide suggestions. Such conversations take shape through multiple personal, institutional, and cultural trajectories of language and literacy experiences; they stay mobile and transform through distributed labor by writers situated across multiple physical, virtual, and imaginary locales. When writing teachers attend to the static, finished products that seem to operate in accordance with monolingual norms and conventions, we should never forget the mobile, multilingual trajectories they have traveled.

To mirror the intensely translingual, self-sponsored language negotiation observed here, writing instructors could develop curricular and pedagogical activities that not only position students' linguistic repertoires and cultural expertise as sites of inquiry and subject of analysis (Kiernan et al., 2016) but offer scaffolded instruction on translation (Gonzales, 2018; Jiménez et al., 2015) and paraphrasing skills (Donahue, 2021; Orellana, 2009) to help students recognize that writing, translation, and paraphrase involve different degrees of "telling" through modification in light of historical and contingent meanings. Finally, readers and writers alike need to develop interactional strategies for co-constructing meaning by achieving imaginative alignment and adopting a multisensory orientation toward texts (Canagarajah, 2013). Such alignments and orientations could be explicitly addressed during peer-review and conference, when readers and writers explore the exigencies and consequences of negotiating across cultural and linguistic differences. Such discussions might require slowly and recursively organized inquiry into textual features and discursive conventions that inform authors' linguistic choices, readers' attempts to offer alternatives, and discussion of meanings gained and lost through translation and paraphrase.

When instructors across the disciplines open their classrooms to include and appreciate the multiple temporalities, spatialities, and trajectories that are embodied by the students' own knowledge, they also make more transparent classroom and learning expectations. Concrete strategies that introduce explicit modeling, collaborative unpacking, and multimodal demonstration of pedagogical language, disciplinary jargon, and material and discursive norms of the classroom would give students the opportunities to bring their histories, to leverage their cultural repertoire, and to teach each other the value of difference. In Vivian Zamel's words (1995), adopting such practices in the express interest of better teaching of multilingual students translates as "good pedagogy for everyone" (p. 519).

Epilogue

The final revision of this book was completed during my research travel in Yunnan, China in the summer of 2024. The ethnographic field work on the literacy practices of migrant women brought me to a village near Dali, a touristy town in the northeast of the province, which sat at the foothills of the Himalayas. The high altitude, cool temperature, and historical absence of industrial development contribute to the impressive biodiversity of these mountainous terrains and make them home to matsutake, which make brief appearances during the warm summer months. During a research break, I found a local guide who agreed to take me and my children along for one of her expeditions in search of termite mushrooms, another rare mountain delicacy enjoyed by Chinese epicures.

We departed at 5:00 a.m. A quick car ride brought us to the foot of the Cang Mountain, where we began our ascension into the daunting, towering peaks. The rising sun silhouetted the mountain in a hazy glow, illuminating the ominous rock trenches that hikers clambered over to find their way into the forest. The town we left at dawn slowly receded into messy shades of lush green. The tranquility of the forest was only disrupted by the rustling of pine needles shifting with the curious pokes of the inexperienced mushroom hunters and our guide's soft chuckle, "If you listen closely, you might hear the mushrooms pop."

Following our guide, who is a true connoisseur of the forest, my daughters and I came to the thrilling discovery of a one-pound "grandpa's head," the pearlescent white of its sizable caps dotted with specks of dirt. We followed the meandering parade of perfectly round red button mushrooms into the deep crevices of mossy rocks. My children shrieked with joy as missteps propelled them on a downhill slide on a thick cushion of leaves and landed them right in front of a cluster of vibrant pink "corals," the minuscule wells lining their walls teeming with insect activities. Beaming with joy, we filled our basket with fungal gifts from nature and learned about ways to stir fry, grill, boil, sauté, and dry them.

At the end of a strenuous 4-hour hike, however, our hearts were heavy with chagrin from not finding a single termite mushroom, whose brief appearance in July motivated our morning expedition. Celebrated for their alluring fragrance, exquisite crisp, and notable rarity, these mushrooms were known to satisfy the most critical epicures. At a small clearing on a slope, we set down our baskets to rest. To an inexperienced eye, the mosaic of dull browns and sandy grays would be unworthy of further inspection, but Liping, our guide, scanned the vicinity with the intuition of a veteran mushroom hunter. She detected a small heap of broken mushroom stems discarded by a careless explorer and felt the forest floor for bumps or cracks. Letting out a small yelp, Liping cautioned us to tread lightly in small steps. Along a fallen tree, a scattering of pearly white umbrellas peered through dry grass. The closer we were to the cluster, the more distinct their woody aroma became.

Termites, known as trusted symbiotic partners of the mushroom, dispersed in panic, providing further evidence of the fungi's elusive proximity. With the help of a small wooden spatula, we pried around each slender mushroom, adequately loosening the soil and gently elevating the stem in preparation for excavation. The final act of plucking required extreme caution. A hasty pull might break the stem; a lousy move would fail to dislodge it. With a succession of crisp pops, we quickly accumulated a small pile of termite mushrooms while learning to help with the spread of spores with a gentle pat on the mushroom caps. In the forest, I found another way to entangle with the mushroom.

We could not stop our chatter around the forest adventure after our return to the rental apartment. Our host, a young woman who received her graduate degree in the United States and "retired" into her current life as an Airbnb host, burst into boisterous laughter when she heard our complaints about not finding a single matsutake mushroom. They grow in the nearby Shangri La region, which intimidates the regular tourists with its daunting landscape and even higher altitudes. She proudly promoted her online store, which specializes in seasonable mountain delicacies, including matsutake! Within the 2 hours when my children and I took showers and did laundry, she managed to have a pound of the prized mushroom delivered to our door. She showed me how to use a wet paper towel to clean the mushroom without damaging the delicate filaments. We debated about the usage of metal knives to cut mushrooms. As I pan fried the sliced mushrooms with butter, its fragrance commanded the attention of everyone relaxing in the courtyard. In the setting sun, we enjoyed a luxurious meal featuring pan-fried matsutake, steamed termite mushrooms with sausage, lamb skewers, vegetable stir fries, and milk tea.

My encounters with mushrooms during that day felt like a perfect conclusion of a research project that spanned a decade of time, two institutions of higher education, multiple linguistic and rhetorical traditions, and many conversations across disciplinary contexts. I cannot help but notice the uncanny ways in which my research process resembles my mushroom encounters. Foraging for mushrooms required all my senses. I learned to discern their woody aromas; I learned to scan the forest floor for promising cracks and bumps; I listened for words of wisdom from my local guides along with the bustling activities of all living things in the forest; as I cleaned and prepared the mushrooms for cooking, I relied on my touch to distinguish graininess of earth from the delicacy of slimy filaments; I savored the richness and softness of butter-saturated matsutakes and the delicate crisp of termite mushrooms. Visceral reactions, bodily sensations, affective exchanges, and surprising discoveries were complexly tangled with social connections, acquired knowledge and practices, and scholarly inquiry to make entanglement with mushrooms visible. In many ways, the same curiosities about how others live and exist in the world drove my inquiries into the mess of multilingual writing. My efforts to follow and theorize multilingual writing, with all its ephemerality, mess, and uncertainty, co-emerged with my intellectual and physical labors of wandering and dwelling in my garden, with books, and in the mountain. Termite and matsutake mushrooms, along with guides, hosts, vegetable vendors, and fellow travelers, showed me the need and ways to look beyond what is immediately visible and available, to follow sustained partnerships and connections, and to listen to the polyphony of living, voicing, and becoming with others through collaboration, negotiation, and improvisation.

At the end of an incredible day of looking for, learning about, and cooking with mushrooms, I returned to my manuscript with a renewed understanding of multilingual writing and living in entanglement.

Appendix

Data Collected

Data Strand	Count		Purpose
	Morgan	Leo	
Semi-structured interview	3 (Total: 225 min.)	3 (Total, 200 min.)	Students' literacy experiences in connection to identity, broader challenges in transitioning to the university, literacy history with particular emphasis on writing and reading expertise, interests, and hobbies
Field notes and audio recordings of informal writing sessions	13 (Total: 620 min.)	11 (Total: 520 min.)	Observation of student literacy activities in various stages of their writing process (brainstorming, outlining, drafting, revising) across informal locales
Prompted think-aloud	1 (Total: 45 min.)	None	Morgan was prompted to provide a think-aloud as she used digital tools to engage in complex translation from Chinese into English

continued on next page

Data Collected

Data Strand	Count		Purpose
	Morgan	Leo	
Writing artifacts	2 outlines (Chinese & English) 4 drafts (English, with the exception of draft 1, which has a few notes in Chinese) 6 drafts with reviewer comments (Ryan, Jessie, Nicole, 2 writing center consultations, 1 teacher conference) 1 project reflection	1 outline (Chinese & English) 3 drafts (1 in Chinese, 2 in English) 3 drafts with teacher, writing center tutor, and reviewer comments 1 project reflection	Documentation of the multilingual writing process, with a specific focus on entanglement of literacy brokers, digital tools, writing technologies, semiotic repertoire; exploration of multilingual writing
WeChat Moments posts	81	79	Self-reflection on different aspects of FYW class (e.g., venting about peer review, meeting with a friend, review or course reading, tribute to helpful friends), performance of various talents (e.g., humor, piano, street dance, magic tricks), everyday events (e.g., moving, vacation, campus events), cultural content (e.g., literary quotes, cultural jokes, Japanese anime)
WeChat post-review interactions and transcripts	7 (Total: 35 min.)	None	Morgan's interactions with literacy brokers to negotiate language and cultural differences arising from revision of the essay
Teacher interview	None	1 (23 min.)	Instructor's perspective on Leo's performance in class and comments on his writing

References

"About the FYW curriculum." (N.d.). Department of Writing, Rhetoric, and Cultures. Michigan State University. Retrieved April 9, 2025, from https://wrac.msu.edu/wra-101-195h/

Alexander, J., Lunsford, K., & Whithaus, C. (2020). Toward wayfinding: A metaphor for understanding writing experiences. *Written Communication, 37*(1), 104–131.

Alvarez, S. (2018). *Brokering tareas: Mexican immigrant families translanguaging homework literacies*. State University of New York Press.

Anson, C. M. (2016). The Pop Warner chronicles: A case study in contextual adaptation and the transfer of writing ability. *College Composition and Communication, 67*(4), 518–549.

Atkinson, D., & Tardy, C. M. (2018). SLW at the crossroads: Finding a way in the field. *Journal of Second Language Writing, 42*, 86–92. https://doi.org/10.1016/j.jslw.2018.10.011

Ayash, N. B. (2019). *Toward translingual realities in composition: (Re)working local language representation and practices*. University Press of Colorado.

Bakhtin, M. M. (1981). Forms of time and of the chronotope in the novel: Notes toward a historical poetics (C. Emerson & M. Holquist, Trans.). In M. Holquist (Ed.), *The dialogic imagination: Four essays* (pp. 84–258). University of Texas Press.

Bang, M. (2017). Towards an ethic of decolonial trans-ontologies in sociocultural theories of learning and development. In I. Esmonde & A. Booker (Eds.), *Power and privilege in the learning sciences: Critical and sociocultural theories of learning* (pp. 115–138). Taylor and Francis. https://doi.org/10.4324/9781315685762

Barad, K. (2007). *Meeting the universe halfway: Quantum physics and the entanglement of matter and meaning*. Duke University Press.

Bawarshi, A. S. (2001). The ecology of genre. In C. R. Weisser & S. I. Dobrin (Eds.), *Ecocomposition: Theoretical and pedagogical approaches* (pp. 1–9). State University of New York Press.

Belanoff, P. (2003). Silence: Reflection, literacy, learning, and teaching. *College Composition and Communication, 52*(3), 399–428.

Black, R. W. (2005). Access and affiliation: The literacy and composition practices of English-language learners in an online fanfiction community. *Journal of Adolescent and Adult Literacy, 49*(2), 118–128.

Blommaert, J., Collins, J., & Slembrouch, S. (2005). Spaces of multilingualism. *Language and Communication, 25*, 197–216.

Canagarajah, S. A. (2006). Toward a writing pedagogy of shuttling between languages: Learning from multilingual writers. *College English, 68*(5), 589–604. https://ncte.org/resources/journals/college-english/

Canagarajah, S. A. (2011). Codemeshing in academic writing: Identifying teachable strategies of translanguaging. *Modern Language Journal. 95*(3), 401–417.

Canagarajah, S. A. (2012). *Translingual practice: Global Englishes and cosmopolitan relations*. Routledge.

Canagarajah, S. A. (2013). Negotiating translingual literacy: An enactment. *Research in the Teaching of English, 48*(1), 40–67.

Casanave, C. P. (2005). Uses of narrative in L2 writing research. In P. Matsuda & T. Silva (Eds.), *Second language writing research: Perspectives on the process of knowledge construction* (pp. 17–32). Lawrence Erlbaum.

Christiansen, S. M. (2017). Creating a unique transnational place: Reterritorialized discourse and the blending of time and space in online social media. *Written Communication, 34*(2), 1–30. https://doi.org/10.1177/0741088317693996

Christiansen, S. M. (2019). "Listisimo para los #XVdeRubi:" Constructing a chronotope as a shared imagined experience in Twitter to enact Mexicanness outside of Mexico. *Lingua, 225*, 1–15. https://doi.org/10.1016/j.lingua.2019.05.002

Coe, R. M. (1975). Eco-logic for the composition classroom. *College Composition and Communication, 26*(3), 232–237.

Cohen, A. D., & Brooks-Carson, A. (2002). Research on direct versus translated writing: Students' strategies and their results. *Modern Language Journal, 8*(2), 169–18. https://doi.org/10.1111/0026-7902.00103

Cooper, M. M. (1986). The ecology of writing. *College English, 48*(4), 364–375.

Creese, A., & Blackledge, A. (2010). Translanguaging in the bilingual classroom: A pedagogy for learning and teaching. *Modern Language Journal, 94*(1), 103–115.

Cumming, A. (1990). Metalinguistic and ideational thinking in second language composing. *Written Communication, 7*(4), 482–511. https://doi.org/10.1177/0741088390007004003

De Costa, P., Canagarajah, S., Singh, J., Wang, X., Fraiberg, S., & Milu, E. (2017). Pedagogizing translingual practice: Prospects and possibilities. *Research in the Teaching of English, 51*(4), 464–472.

De Costa, P., Li, W., & Lee, J. (2022). *International students' multilingual literacy practices: An asset-based approach to understanding academic discourse socialization*. Multilingual Matters.

De Fina, A., Paternostro, G., & Amoruso, M. (2020). Odysseus the traveler: Appropriation of a chronotope in a community of practice. *Language and Communication, 70*, 71–81. https://doi.org/10.1016/j.langcom.2019.01.001

DeJoy, N., Craig, C., Lessner, S., & Williams, B. (2011). *Reading and Writing Literacies*. Pearson/Longman.

DePalma, M., & Ringer, J. M. (2011). Toward a theory of adaptive transfer: Expanding disciplinary discussions of "transfer" in second-language writing and composition studies. *Journal of Second Language Writing, 20*(2), 134–147. https://doi.org/10.1016/j.jslw.2011.02.003

Department of Writing, Rhetoric, and American Cultures. (n.d.). *Program learning goals for first-year writing*. Michigan State University. Retrieved August 1, 2022, from https://wrac.msu.edu/learning-outcomes/

Dobrin, S. I. (2001). Writing takes place. In C. P. Weisser & S. I. Dobrin (Eds.), *Ecocomposition: Theoretical and pedagogical approaches* (pp. 12–25). State University of New York Press.

Donahue, C. (2021). Mobile knowledge for a mobile era: Studying linguistic and rhetorical flexibility in composition. In B. Horner, M. Faver, H. A. Kumari & L. S. Matravers (Eds.), *Mobility work in composition* (pp. 17–36). Utah State University Press.

Dong, J., & Blommaert, J. (2016). Global informal learning environments and the making of Chinese middle class. *Linguistics and Education, 34*, 33–26.

The Economist. (2014, June 28). Unnatural deaths: Xi Jinping's anti-corruption campaign may have led to a spate of official suicides. *The Economist*, 3–5.

Edmond, C. (2013). Information manipulation, coordination, and regime change. *Review of Economic Studies, 80*(4), 1422–1458.

Ehret, C., & Hollett T. (2014). Embodied composition in real virtualities: Adolescents' literacy practices and felt experiences moving with digital, mobile devices in school. *Research in the Teaching of English, 46*(4), 428–452.

Emig, J. A. (1964). The use of the unconscious in composing. *College Composition and Communication, 15*(1), 6–11.

English Language Center. (2022, March 1). *March's kind of from the horse's mouth-2022*. Michigan State University. https://elc.msu.edu/wp-content/uploads/sites/44/2022/01/The-IEP-Curriculum-1.docx.pdf

Fabre, G. (2017). Xi Jinping's challenge: What is behind China's anti-corruption campaign. *Journal of Self-Governance and Management Economics, 2*(7), 7–28.

Fleckenstein, K. S., Spinuzzi, C., Rickly, R. J., & Papper, C. C. (2008). The importance of harmony: An ecological metaphor for writing research. *College Composition and Communication, 50*(2), 388–419.

Fraiberg, S. (2010). Composition 2.0: Toward a multilingual and multimodal framework. *College Composition and Communication, 62*(1), 100–126.

Fraiberg, S. (2017). Pretty bullets: Tracing transmedia/translingual literacies of an Israeli soldier across regimes of practice. *College Composition and Communication,* 69(1), 87–117.

Fraiberg, S., & Cui, X. (2016). Weaving relationship webs: Tracing how Iming practices mediate the trajectories of Chinese international student. *Computers and Composition, 39,* 83–103.

Fraiberg, S., Wang, X., & Wen, K. (2017). "Shock You Chocolate": Mobilizing translocal networks in a first-year writing course. In N. DeJoy & B. Smith (Eds.), *Collaborations and innovations: Supporting multilingual writers across campus units* (pp. 136–167). University of Michigan Press.

Fraiberg, S., Wang, X., & You, X. (2017). *Inventing the world grant university: Chinese international students' mobilities, literacies, and identities.* Utah State University Press.

García, O., & Wei, L. (2014). *Translanguaging: Language, bilingualism, and education.* Palgrave Macmillan.

Genoz, J., & Gorter, D. (2011). Focus on multilingualism: A study of trilingual writing. *Modern Language Journal, 95*(3), 356–369. https://doi.org/10.1111/j.15404781.2011.01206.x

Gentil, G. (2011). A Biliteracy agenda for genre research. *Journal of Second Language Writing,* 20(1), 6–23.

Gere, A. R. (1994). Kitchen tables and rented rooms: The extracurriculum of composition. *College Composition and Communication,* 45(1), 75–91.

Gere, A. R. (2001). Revealing silence: Rethinking personal writing. *College Composition and Communication,* 53(2), 203–223.

Gilyard, K. (2016) The rhetoric of translingualism. *College English,* 78(3), 284–289. https://ncte.org/resources/journals/college-english/

Glenn, C. (2004). *Unspoken: A rhetoric of silence.* Southern Illinois University Press.

Gonzales, L. (2018). *Sites of translation: What multilinguals can teach us about digital writing and rhetoric.* University of Michigan Press.

Guerra, J. C. (1998). *Close to home: Oral and literate practices in a transnational Mexicano community.* Teachers College Press.

Guerra, J. C. (2016). Cultivating a rhetorical sensibility in the translingual writing classroom. *College English,* 78(3), 228–33. https://ncte.org/resources/journals/college-english/

Haraway, D. 2016. *Staying with the trouble: Making kin in the Chthulucene.* Duke University Press.

Hass, C., & Witte, S. P. (2001). Writing as an embodied practice: The case of engineering standards. *Journal of Business and Technical Communication,* 15(4), 412–457. https://doi.org/10.1177/105065190101500402

Hathaway, M. J. (2022). *What a mushroom lives for: Matsutake and the worlds they make.* Princeton University Press.

Higgins, T. (2013, December 20). *Chinese students major in luxury cars: Auto dealers in U.S. college towns are hawking pricey rides to mainland kids on education visas.* Bloomberg. https://www.bloomberg.com/news/articles/2013-12-19/chinese-students-in-u-dot-s-dot-boost-luxury-car-sales

Holland, D., & Leander, K. M. (2004). Ethnographic studies of positioning and subjectivity: An introduction. *Ethos*, 32(2), 127–139.

Hornberger, N., & Link, H. (2012). Translanguaging in today's classrooms: A biliteracy lens. *Theory into Practice*, 51(4), 239–247. https://doi.org/10.1080/00405841.2012.726051

Horner, B., Lu, M.-Z., Royster, J. J., & Trimbur, J. (2011). Language difference in writing: Toward a translingual approach. *College English*, 73(3), 303–321.

Horner, B., & Tetreault, L. (2016). Translation as (global) writing. *Composition Studies*, 44(1), 13–30. https://compstudiesjournal.com/

Hutchins, E. (1995). *Cognition in the wild*. MIT Press.

Inghilleri, M. (2017). *Translation and migration*. Routledge.

Inoue, A. B. (2015). *Antiracist writing assessment ecologies: Teaching and assessing writing for a socially just future*. Parlor Press/WAC Clearinghouse.

Jacobs, A. (2013, March 28). Elite in China face austerity under Xi's rule. *The New York Times*. https://www.nytimes.com/2013/03/28/

Jordan, J. (2015). Material translingual ecologies. *College English*, 77(4), 364–382.

Jiang, Y. (2013), *Cyber-nationalism in China: Challenging western media portrayals of internet censorship in China*. University of Adelaide Press.

Jiménez, R. T., David, S., Fagan, K., Risko, V. J., Pacheco, M., Pray, L., & Gonzales, M. (2015). Using translation to drive conceptual development for students becoming literate in English as an additional language. *Research in the Teaching of English*, 49(3), 248–272.

Kan, K. (2013). The new "lost generation": Inequality and discontent among Chinese youth. *China Perspectives*, 2(94), 67–73.

Karimzad, F., & Catedral, L. (2018). Mobile (dis)connection: New technology and rechronotopized images of the homeland. *Journal of Linguistic Anthropology*, 28(3), 293–312.

Karimzad, F., & Catedral, L. (2021). *Chronotopes and migration: Language, social imagination, and behavior*. Routledge.

Kang, Y. (2016). *English—only when necessary: Literacy practices of Korean undergraduate students at a 'global' university* [Doctoral dissertation, University of Illinois at Urbana-Champaign]. ProQuest Dissertation Publishing. Publication no. 10301856. https://pitt.idm.oclc.org/login?url=https://www.proquest.com/dissertations-theses/english-only-when-necessary-literacy-practices/docview/1857874683/se-2?accountid=14709

Kang, Y. (2018). Expanding the role of the writing center at a global university. In S. Rose & I. Weiser (Eds.), *The internationalization of US writing programs* (pp. 132–151). Utah State University Press.

Kell, C. (2015). "Making people happen": Materiality and movement in meaning-making trajectories. *Social Semiotics*, 45(2), 423–445.

Kiernan, J., Frost, A., & Malley, S. B. (2021). *Translingual pedagogical perspectives: Engaging domestic and international students in the composition classroom*. Utah State University Press.

Kiernan, J., Meier, J., & Wang, X. (2016). Negotiating languages and cultures: Enacting translingualism through a translation assignment. *Composition Studies*, 44(1), 89–107.

Kobayashi, H., & Rinnert, C. (2013). L1/L2/L3 writing development: Longitudinal case study of a Japanese multicompetent writer. *Journal of Second Language Writing*, 22, 4–33. https://doi.org/10.1016/j.jslw.2012.11.001

Lam, W. S. E. (2009). Multiliteracies on instant messaging in negotiating local, translocal, and transnational affiliations: A case of an adolescent immigrant. *Reading Research Quarterly*, 44(4), 377–397.

Lam, W. S. E., & Christiansen, M. S. (2022). Transnational Mexican youth negotiating languages, identities, and cultures online: A chronotopic lens. *TESOL Quarterly*, 56(3), 907–933.

Lam, W. S. E., & Warriner, D. S. (2012). Transnationalism and literacy: Investigating the mobility of people, languages, texts, and practices in contexts of migration. *Reading Research Quarterly*, 47(2), 191–215.

Latour, B. (1999). *Pandora's hope: Essays on the reality of science studies*. Harvard University Press.

Law, J. (2004). *After method: Mess in social science research*. Routledge.

Leander, K. M. (2001). "This is our freedom bus going home right now": Producing and hybridizing space-time contexts in pedagogical discourse. *Journal of Literacy Research*, 33(4), 637–679.

Leander, K. M. (2002). Locating Latanya: The situated production of identity artifacts in classroom interaction. *Research in the Teaching of English*, 37(2), 198–250.

Leander, K. M., & Sheehy, M. (2004). *Spatializing literacy research and practice*. Peter Lang Publishing.

Lemke, J. (2000). Across the scales of time: Artifacts, activities, and meanings in ecosocial systems. *Mind & Culture*, 4, 273–290.

Li, B. (2012). Class strata-calcification and breakthrough阶层结构——僵化与突破. *South Reviews*.

Li, W. (2018). Translanguaging as a practical theory of language. *Applied Linguistics*, 39(1), 9–30.

Lillis, T., & Curry, M. J. (2010). *Academic writing in a global context: The politics and practices of publishing in English*. Routledge.

Ling L. (2011). Performing bribery in China: Guanxi-practice, corruption with a human face. *Journal of Contemporary China*, 20(68), 1–20. https://doi.org/10.1080/10670564.2011.520841

Lorimer Leonard, R. (2013). Traveling literacies: Multilingual writing on the move. *Research in the Teaching of English*, 48, 13–39.

Lorimer Leonard, R. (2015). Writing through bureaucracy: Migrant correspondence and managed mobility. *Written Communication*, 32(1), 87–113.

Lorimer Leonard, R. (2017). *Writing on the move: Migrant women and the value of literacy*. University of Pittsburgh Press.

Lorimer Leonard, R., & Nowacek, R. (2016) Transfer and translingualism. *College English*, 78(3), 258–264. https://ncte.org/resources/journals/college-english/

Louie, A., & Qin, D. B. (2019). "Car talk": Automobility and Chinese international students in Michigan. *Identities, 26*(2), 146–164. https://doi.org/10.1080/1070289X.2017.1380941

Lowe, C., & Zemliansky, P. (Eds.). (2011). *Writing space: Readings on writing, volume 2.* The WAC Clearinghouse. https://wac.colostate.edu/books/writingspaces/writingspaces2/

Lu, M.-Z. (2006). Living-English work. *College English, 68*(6), 605–618.

Lu, M.-Z., & Horner, B. (2013). Translingual literacy, language difference and matters of agency. *College English, 75*(6), 582–601.

Lyon, G. E. (1993). *Where I'm from.* George Ella Lyon. http://www.georgeellalyon.com/where.html

Martínez, R. A., Orellana, M. F., & Pacheco, M. (2008). Found in translation: Connecting translation experiences to academic writing. *Language Arts, 85*(6), 421–431. https://library.ncte.org/journals/la/issues

Matsuda, P. (2006). The myth of linguistic homogeneity in U.S. college composition. *College English, 68*(6), 637–651.

Matsuda, P. K. (2014). The lure of translingual writing. *PMLA, 129*(3), 478–483. https://www.jstor.org/stable/24769484

Mays, C. (2017). Writing complexity, one stability at a time: Teaching writing as a complex system. *College Composition and Communication, 68*(3), 559–585.

Medina, G. (2010). "Reading across communities" in biliteracy practices: Examining translocal discourses and cultural flows in literature discussions. *Reading Research Quarterly, 45*(1), 40–60.

Medway, Peter. (2002). Fuzzy genres and community identities: The case of architecture students' sketchbooks. In R. Coe, L. Lingard, & T. Teslenko (Eds.), *The rhetoric and ideology of genre: Strategies for stability and change* (pp. 123–153). Hampton Press.

Meier, J. (2018). Multimodal, embodied learning and listening: ELLs and intercultural dialogue in two community projects. *The Reading Matrix: An International Online Journal, 18*(2), 147–164.

Meier, J., Wang, X., & Kiernan, J. (2023). Centering our students' languages and cultures: WAC and cross-disciplinary collaboration. In J. Hall & B. Horner (Eds.), *Toward a transnational university: WAC/WID across borders of language, nation, and discipline* (pp. 123–142). WAC Clearinghouse. https://doi.org/10.37514/ATD-B.2023.1527.2.06

Mitman, G. (Moderator). (2019, June 18). *Reflections on the plantationocene: A conversation with Donna Haraway & Anna Tsing* Edge Effects. Retrieved March 18, 2023, from https://edgeeffects.net/wp-content/uploads/2019/06/PlantationoceneReflections_Haraway_Tsing.pdf

Murphy, L., & de Larios, J. R. (2010). Searching for words: One strategic use of the mother tongue by advanced Spanish EFL writers. *Journal of Second Language Writing, 19*, 6181. https://doi.org/10.1016/j.jslw.2010.02.001

Nordquist, B. (2017). *Literacy and mobility: Complexity, uncertainty, and agency at the nexus of high school and college.* Routledge.

Nordquist, B. (2018, October 19). Literacy, mobility, and nonscalability [Symposium]. Circulating and Mobility Symposium, Urbana, IL, United States. https://cws.illinois.edu/circulation-and-mobility-symposium

Orellana, M. F. (2009). *Translating childhoods: Immigrant youth, language, and culture.* Rutgers University Press. http://www.jstor.org/stable/j.ctt5hj1hn

Orellana, M. F., & Reynolds, J. F. (2008). Cultural modeling: Leveraging bilingual skills for school paraphrasing tasks. *Reading Research Quarterly, 43*(1) 48–65.

Pahl, K. (2004). Narratives, artifacts, and cultural identities: An ethnographic study of communicative practices in homes. *Linguistics and Education, 15,* 339–358.

Pennycook, A. (2008) English as a language always in translation. *European Journal of English Studies, 12*(1), 33–47. https://doi.org/10.1080/13825570801900521

Perl, S. (1979). The composing processes of unskilled college writers. *Research in the Teaching of English, 13*(4), 317–336.

Pigg, S. (2014). Emplacing mobile composing habits: A study of academic writing in networked social spaces. *College Composition and Communication, 66*(2), 250–275.

Prior, P. (1999). *Writing/Disciplinarity: A sociohistoric account of literate activity in the academy.* Routledge.

Prior, P. A. (2018). How do moments add up to lives? Trajectories of semiotic becoming vs. Tales of school learning in four modes. In R. Wysocki & M. P. Sheridan (Eds.), *Making future matters.* Computers and Composition Digital Press. http://ccdigitalpress.org/book/makingfuturematters/prior-intro.html

Prior, P. (2019). *How moments add up to lives: Flat CHAT assemblage, embodiment, and lifespan becoming* [Paper presentation]. SIG 10 Invited Symposium: Learning as Material Formation at EARLI, Location.

Prior, P. A., Hengst, J. A., Kovanen, B., Mazuchelli, L., Turnipseed, N., & Ware, R. (2023). Rearticulating theory and methodology for perezhivanie and becoming: Tracing flat CHAT assemblages and embodied intensities. *Outlines-Critical Practice Studies, 24*(1), 4–44.

Prior, P., & Lunsford, K. (2008). History of reflection, theory, and research on writing. In C. Bazerman (Ed.), *Handbook of research on writing: history, society, school, individual, text* (pp. 97–117). L. Erlbaum Associates.

Prior, P., & Shipka, J. (2003). Chronotopic lamination: Tracing the contours of literate activity. In C. Bazerman & D. R. Russell (Eds.), *Writing selves/writing societies: Research from activity perspectives.* WAC Clearinghouse.

Qi, D. S. (1998). An inquiry into language-switching in second language composing processes. *The Canadian Modern Language Review, 54*(3), 414–436. https://doi.org/10.3138/cmlr.54.3.413

Qin, B., Strömberg, D., & Wu, Y. (2017). Why does China allow freer social media? Protests versus surveillance and propaganda. *Journal of Economic Perspectives, 31*(1), 117–140.

Reynolds, N. (2007). *Geographies of writing: Inhabiting please and encountering difference.* Southern Illinois University Press. Carbondale.

Roozen, K. (2009a). Fan fic-ing' English studies: A case study exploring the interplay of vernacular literacies and disciplinary engagement. *Research in the Teach-*

ing of English, 44(2), 136–169. https://ncte.org/resources/journals/research-in-the-teaching-of-english/

Roozen, K. (2009b). From journals to journalism: Tracing trajectories of literate development. *College Composition and Communication*, 60(3), 541–57.

Roozen, K. (2012). Comedy stages, poets projects, sports columns, and kinesiology 341: illuminating the importance of basic writers' self-sponsored literacies. *Journal of Basic Writing*, 31(1), 99–132.

Roozen, K. (2020, March). Coming to act with tables: Tracing the laminated trajectories of an engineer-in-the-making. *Learning, Culture and Social Interaction*, 24, Article 1000284.

Roozen, K. (2021). Acting with inscriptions: Expanding perspectives of writing, learning, and becoming. *JAEPL*, 26, 23–48.

Roozen, K., & Erickson, J. (2017). *Expanding literate landscapes: Persons, practices, and sociohistoric perspectives of disciplinary development.* Computers and Composition Digital Press/Utah State University Press. http://ccdigitalpress.org/expanding/

Rounsaville, A. (2014). Situating transnational genre knowledge: A genre trajectory analysis of one student's personal and academic writing. *Written Communication*, 31(3), 332–364. https://doi.org/10.1177/0741088314537599

Rubinstein-Avila, E. (2007). From the Dominican Republic to Drew High: What counts as literacy for Yanira Lara? *Reading Research Quarterly*, 42(4), 568–589.

Rule, H. J. (2018). Writing's rooms. *College Composition and Communication*, 69(3), 402–432.

Rule, H. J. (2019). *Situating writing processes*. WAC Clearinghouse.

Sanchez, P. (2007). Cultural authenticity and transnational Latina youth: Constructing a meta-narrative across borders. *Linguistics and Education*, 18(3/4), 258–282.

Sarroub, L. K. (2002). In-betweenness: Religion and conflicting visions of literacy. *Reading Research Quarterly*, 37(2), 130–148.

Schor, S. (1986). Composition strategy as translation. *College English*, 48, 187–194.

Sevastopulo, D. (2014, June 8). Guangdong "naked officials" punished. *The Financial Times*.

Sheehy, M. (2004). Between a thick and thin place: Changing literacy practices. In K. M. Leander & M. Sheehy (Eds.), *Spatializing literacy research and practice* (pp. 91–115). Peter Lang Publishing.

Sheldrake, M. (2020). *Entangled life: How fungi make our worlds, change our minds, and shape our futures*. Penguin Random House.

Shimabukuro, M. (2011). "Me inwardly, before I dared": Japanese Americans writing-to-Gaman. *College English*, 73(6), 648–671.

Shipka, J. (2011). *Toward a composition made whole*. University of Pittsburgh Press.

Shipka, J. (2016). *Toward a composition made whole*. University of Pittsburgh Press.

Skerrett, A. (2012). Languages and literacies in translocation: Experiences and perspectives of a transactional youth. *Journal of Literacy Research*, 44, 364–395.

Smith, B. E., Pacheco, M. B., & de Almeida, C. R. (2017). Multimodal codemeshing: Bilingual adolescents processes composing across modes and languages. *Journal of Second Language Writing*, 36, 6–22.

Soja, E. (1996). *Thirdspace: Journey to Los Angeles and other real-and-imagined places*. Blackwell.

"Statistical report." (2016). Michigan State University Office for International Students and Scholars. Retrieved September 24, 2022, from http://oiss.isp.msu.edu/about/statistics.htm

Stewart, M., & Hansen-Thomas, H. (2016). Sanctioning a space for translanguaging in the secondary English classroom: A case of a transnational youth. *Research in the Teaching of English*, 50(4), 450–472. https://ncte.org/resources/journals/research-inthe-teaching-of-english

Stornaiuolo, A., Smith, A., & Phillips, N. C. (2017). Developing a transliteracies framework for a connected world. *Journal of Literacy Research*, 49(1), 68–91.

Suárez-Orozco, C., & Suárez-Orozco, M. M. (2001). *Children of immigration*. Harvard University Press.

Sun, Y., & Lan, G. (2020). Enactment of a translingual approach to writing. *TESOL Quarterly*, 55(2), 398–426. https://doi.org/10.1002/tesq.609

Syverson, M. A. (1999). *The wealth of reality: An ecology of composition*. Southern Illinois University Press.

Szablewicz, M. (2014). The "losers" of China's Internet: Meme as "structures of feeling" for disillusioned young netizens. *China Information*, 28(2), 259–275.

Takayoshi, P. (2015). Short-form writing: Studying process in the context of contemporary composing technologies. *Computers and Composition*, 37, 1–13.

Takayoshi, P. (2018). Writing in social worlds: An argument for researching composing processes. *College Composition and Communication*, 69(4), 550–580.

Tencent Technology (Shenzhen) Company Ltd. (2020). *WeChat statistics report*. https://wechatwiki.com/wp-content/uploads/wechat-report-data-qr-code-economy.pdf

Tsing, A. L. (2005). *Friction: An ethnography of global connection*. Princeton University Press.

Tsing, A. (2012). On scalability: The living world is not amenable to precision-nested scales. *Common Knowledge*, 18(3), 505–524. https://doi.org/10.1215/0961754X-1630424

Tsing, A. L. (2015). *The mushroom at the end of the world: On the possibility of life in capitalist ruins*. Princeton University Press.

Tsing, A. (2012). On scalability: The living world is not amenable to precision-nested scales. *Common Knowledge*, 18(3), 505-524. https://doi.org/10.1215/0961754X-1630424

Vieira, K. (2016). Writing remittances: Migration-driven literacy learning in a Brazilian homeland. *Research in the Teaching of English*, 50(4), 422–449.

Vieira, K. (2019). *Writing for love and money: How migration drives literacy learning in transnational families*. Oxford University Press.

Vision statement. (n.d.). The Writing Center, Michigan State University. Retrieved August 15, 2023, from https://writing.msu.edu/about/vision-statement/

Wang, X. (2017). Spatial and literacy practices of Chinese international students across a college bridge writing classroom and WeChat. *Language and Education*, 31(6), 561–579. http://dx.doi.org/10.1080/09500782.2017.1337128

Wang, X. (2019a). Negotiating disconnects: Reading across personal, academic, and disciplinary contexts in and out of FYW. *College Composition and Communication*, 70(4), 560–589.

Wang, X. (2019b). Observing literacy learning across WeChat and first-year writing: A scalar analysis of one transnational student's multilingualism. *Computers and Composition*, 52, 253–271. https://doi.org/10.1016/j.compcom.2019.02.002

Wang, X. (2020). Becoming multilingual writers through translation. *Research in the Teaching of English*, 54(3), 206–230. https://ncte.org/resources/journals/research-inthe-teaching-of-english

Wang, X. (2021). Writing theory cartoon: Toward a translingual and multimodal pedagogy. In J. Kiernan, S. Blumm, & A. Frost (Eds.), *Translingual pedagogical perspectives* (pp. 159–174). Utah State University Press.

Wang, X. (2022). Writing about where we are from—Writing across languages, genres, and spaces. In P. De Costa, W. Li & J. Lee (Eds.), *International students' multilingual literacy practices: An asset-based approach to using semiotic resources* (pp. 148–167). Multilingual Matters.

Wang, Z. (2024). *Doing difference differently: Four generation-z students' literacy worlds*. Utah State University Press.

Wargo J. (2015). Spatial stories with nomadic narrators: Affect, Snapchat, and "feeling" embodiment in youth mobile composing. *Journal of Language and Literacy Education*, 11(1), 47–51.

Wertsch, J. V. (1998). *Mind as action*. Oxford University Press.

Weisser, C. R. (2001). Ecocomposition and the greening of identity. In C. R. Weisser & S. I. Dobrin (Eds.), *Ecocomposition: Theoretical and pedagogical approaches* (pp. 81–95). State University of New York Press.

Weisser, C. R., & Dobrin, S. I. (2001). Breaking new grounds in ecocomposition: An introduction. In C. R. Weisser & S. I. Dobrin (Eds.), *Ecocomposition: Theoretical and pedagogical approaches* (pp. 1–9). State University of New York Press.

WRA 1004/0102: Preparation for college writing curriculum. (n.d.). Department of Writing, Rhetoric, and American Culture. Retrieved September 5, 2024, from https://wrac.msu.edu/wra-1004-0102-preparation-for-college-writing-curriculum/

Xi, J. (2016, March 4). *Xi Jinping offers advice for entrepreneurs: As public figures of social influence, you should maintain your image*. Sina Finance. https://finance.sina.cn/2016-03-09/detail-

Xiong, Q. (2011). China's anti-corruption strategies from the viewpoint of criminal justice. *Social Sciences in China*, 32(4), 176–191.

Yancey, K. B. (2004). Made not only in words: Composition in a new key. *College Composition and Communication*, 56(2), 297–328.

Yang, F. (2016). Rethinking China's Internet censorship: The practice of recoding and the politics of visibility. *New Media & Society*, 18(7), 1364–1381.

Yi, Y. (2010). Adolescent multilingual writers' transitions across in- and out-of-school writing contexts. *Journal of Second Language Writing*, 19(1), 17–32.

Yi, Y., & Hirvela, A. (2010). Technology and "self-sponsored" writing: A case study of a Korean-American adolescent. *Computers and Composition*, 27, 94–111.

Young, V. A. (2009). "Nah, we straight": An argument against code-switching. *JAC (Journal of Composition)*, 29(1), 49–76.

Zamel, V. (1995). Strangers in academia: The experiences of faculty and ESL students across the curriculum. *College Composition and Communication*, 46(4), 506–521. https://doi.org/10.2307/358325

Zhang-Wu, Q. (2021). *Languaging myths and realities: Journeys of Chinese international students*. Multilingual Matters.

Zhu, J., & Zhang, D. (2017). Weapons of the powerful: Authoritarian elite competition and politicized anticorruption in China. *Comparative Political Studies*, 50(9), 1186–1220.

Index

Page numbers followed by f indicate figures.

academia, 15, 167, 173–78, 180, 184
academic units, 15, 18, 31, 166, 167, 168, 176–77, 187, 199, 201
academic writing. *See* multilingual writing; writing process
aesthetic norms, 45, 65, 67, 6, 144
affective meaning, 4, 6, 67, 99, 100, 109, 117, 163, 191
agential becoming: anthropocentric view, 43; authority, 173, 182; boundaries, 77, 90, 92; collaboration, 177; identity, 5, 7; indeterminacy, 34; intra-action, 40; language differences, 4, 6; linguistic innovations, 81; meaning making, 67, 129–30; mushrooms, 36; peer reviews, 175; temporality, 163; transformative encounters, 68–69; unpredictable encounters, 46; writing process, 59
Aka women, 47–48, 124, 141
Alexander, Jonathan, 112
alternative discourse, 6, 85, 87, 94, 102, 108, 121, 138
American frame of reference: audience, 74, 95, 96, 99, 104, 173; cultural references, 16, 183, 190, 191; curriculum, 19–20; first-year writing (FYW) class, 168, 169, 198; idioms, 71, 73, 74, 94, 103, 104, 170; reading materials, 64, 184; rhetorical strategies, 178, 196; sports, 100
Angelou, Maya, 24, 64
annotation: digital tools, 139; peer reviews, 93f, 97, 103f; screenshots, 24, 122f, 127f, 128, 129, 131f; writing process, 25, 97
Anson, Chris, 112
anthropocentric view: boundary redrawing, 39, 59; entanglement, 11, 35, 36, 41–43, 68, 90–91, 200; human-nature relations, 109–10
anti-corruption campaigns in China, 157, 158, 164
argumentative writing, 21, 72
articulation/open articulation: becoming-with, 76–79; chronotopic lamination, 50; classroom geography, 58; entanglement, 53, 91; indeterminacy, 92; meaning, 7, 8, 13, 54, 87, 88; natural, cultural, and literacy others, 27, 42, 43, 55, 67, 69, 91; reciprocity, 38–39; spacetime, 60; string figuring, 52; translation labor, 106–10, 135; unpredictable encounters, 30, 207–8; world-in-becoming, 10, 12, 40, 65, 77, 93
artifacts, 12, 16, 24–25, 51, 59, 60, 120, 128–29, 140, 155, 164, 181–82, 192–94

assemblages: becoming with, 36, 42, 59; contours of writing, 112; data analysis, 26–27; eco-composition, 9; meaning making, 91, 113; memory, 129–31; negotiation, 6, 7, 84, 192; peer review, 93; polyphony, 34, 138, 164; reciprocity, 10, 35, 38, 55, 170–71; spacetime, 107, 137; strategic silence, 149, 161; transformative encounters, 45–46, 120, 125; translation labor, 108; unpredictable encounters, 139, 205–6
asset-based pedagogy: bridge writing class, 16–17, 22, 115, 167; entanglement, 31; ethnographic research, 24, 48, 61, 199; practices, 209–12; rhetorical resources, 187–88, 197–98
assumptions about the writing process, 11, 207
audience expectation: cultural differences, 173, 190–91; entanglement, 12–13, 95; feedback, 22, 126–27, 178; genre conventions, 88; idioms, 71, 73, 74, 93–94, 189; multilingual writing, 72, 98–99, 140, 161–62; rhetorical strategies, 73, 115, 174; shifting voice, 83; social media, 121, 124–25, 148–49; translation process, 108, 189, 210; unpredictable encounters, 47, 117, 118f, 119–20, 123–24, 137
audio recordings, 24, 216f
auditory details, 65–68, 70–72, 85–86, 88–89
authorial intention: entanglement, 95, 96; idioms, 71, 73, 74, 93, 94; intertextual allusions, 195–96; language differences, 174; multilingual writers, 98–99, 140; rhetorical differences, 174; textual meaning, 136; unpredictable encounters, 47, 67, 117, 118f, 119–20, 123–24, 137; Western perspective, 204

back-and-forth trading, 95, 177, 209
back-translation, 85, 86, 89, 90, 93, 94
Baidu translation, 85–86
Baker, Russel, 72, 73
Bakhtin, Mikhail Mikhailovich, 49
Bang, Megan, 37
Barad, Karen, 11, 12, 40, 77, 90
Bawarshi, Anis, 9
becoming/becoming-with: assemblages, 171; boundaries, 39–40, 76–79; chronotopic figuring, 146–47, 155, 160, 161–65; collective/individual, 163–64, 171; disruption, 11, 28, 33–34, 42; dissonance, 183; emergent process, 45–46, 52, 53, 91; entanglement, 68, 76–79; lived spatiality, 69; multilingual writers, 23, 29, 46–47, 70–75, 79, 83, 204–6; mushrooms, 36; narrative iteration, 163; natural, cultural, and literacy others, 63; negotiation, 74, 79, 108, 204–5; open articulation, 38, 53, 55; pet companions, 59; reciprocity, 10; string figuring, 51–52; sympoiesis, 36; tentacular thinking, 52–53; unpredictable encounters, 11–12, 29, 47, 63–69, 79, 117, 118f, 119–20, 123–25, 140, 206; world-in-becoming, 40, 76, 77, 93; writing process, 60, 183
Belanoff, Pat, 142
Bou Ayash, Nancy, 174
boundaries: cultural identity, 33; embodied experiences, 39, 41–42, 83; entanglement, 44, 58, 76, 77, 209; semiotic practices, 68, 90; translation labor, 81–82
brainstorming, 25, 125, 216f
bridge writing class: curriculum development, 16–17, 187; diversity, 166–67; multilingual students, 22, 72, 115, 169–70

Cang Mountain, 213
canonical texts, 88, 191
China: anti-corruption campaign, 156–57, 159; class identity, 20, 23, 142, 145, 153; education, 19; literacy civil examination, 195–96; WeChat, 18
Chinese rhetorical strategies, 87, 173, 196
Chinglish, 99, 110
Christiansen, Sidury, 113, 130
chronotopic figuring: meaning making, 13, 34, 41, 155; semiotic fibers, 53, 117; sites of inquiry, 23, 52, 113–14, 185; strategic silence, 30, 123, 161, 163–65; temporal polyphony, 48–50, 65; tentacular thinking, 8, 52–53, 160; transnational students, 207–9; writer/person-in-becoming, 29, 52, 146
chronotopic lamination, 13, 34, 49–52
civic rhetoric, 195–96
class identity: entanglement, 20, 159; familial trajectories, 155–56, 160; government surveillance, 155–58; idiosyncratic decision-making, 163–64; Memoir assignments, 24, 149–50; multilingual students, 154, 163–64, 195, 199, 208; public scrutiny, 134, 150–54; second-generation rich, 20, 145, 150, 153, 157, 159; strategic silence, 123, 150–52, 156–59, 161
classical texts, 195–96
classroom learning: collaboration, 180; first-year writing (FYW) class, 198; lived experiences, 70, 181; norms, 212; pedagogical language, 178; sites of inquiry, 52, 113–14, 181; spatial boundaries, 58, 208–10; unpredictable encounters, 178–79
co-becoming, 108–9

co-emergence, 12, 29
Cofer, Judith Ortiz, 193
collaboration/collaboration across differences: authority, 173; classroom environment, 180–81; cross-language, 30, 55, 81; cross-species, 34, 35; cross-unit, 177, 200; digital spaces, 5–6, 112–13; fungi, 10, 33, 42, 49; entanglement, 76–77, 97, 201; home languages, 188–89, 201; knotting, 53; language, cultural, and rhetorical differences, 7, 14, 75, 109, 171, 197, 205; meaning making, 92–93, 97, 106, 123, 124, 140; memory, 117, 121; negotiation, 59, 74, 197; open-ended inquiry, 52, 109; pedagogical instruction, 16–17, 166–67, 176–77, 186, 187; polyphony, 52, 141, 215; spatial-temporal contour, 98; strategic silence, 151; transformative encounters, 38–39; translation process, 82, 94, 100, 188–89; unpredictable encounters, 114, 120, 209
collaborative survival, 35, 40, 45, 46, 55, 97, 203
collective being in the world, 163, 164
colloquialisms, 73, 74
community engagement, 165, 190–91
comparative reflective writing, 24, 188–89
conceptual trespassing, 55
Confucian text, 195–96
connections. *See* interconnectedness
connotations, 85, 86
constructs, 28, 42, 56
contingencies/contingency: entanglement, 40, 49, 79, 109, 163–64, 197, 200, 203–4; memory, 90; multilingual contours of writing, 31; natural, cultural, and literacy others, 11, 63, 188, 192, 198; open-ended inquiry, 68–69, 77, 185, 199; reciprocity, 38–39; strategic silence, 149, 155; string figuring, 52; temporal polyphony, 49; tentacular thinking, 52–53, 160; translation labor, 108; unpredictable encounters, 44–46, 76, 98, 113, 120, 139, 180–81; wandering, 53–54; writing tools, 97
contours of writing: chronotopic figuring, 53; entanglement, 9–10, 31, 99; natural, cultural, and literacy others, 27, 79; spatiality, 59, 60, 65, 68; unintended consequences, 7; unpredictable encounters, 111–12, 166, 206–7; wandering, 38–39, 53
conventional tropes, 88
Cory, Lorene, 73
creative writing, 21–22, 70, 115–16
critical reading, 21, 64
cross-cultural writing assignments, 185–86

cross-disciplinary writing, 166, 176–77
cross-language writing: cultural references, 185–86; grammar, 85; language collaboration, 75, 81; negotiation, 135, 211; problem solving, 80; textual meaning, 4, 136; writing process, 30
cross-unit collaboration, 177–78, 200
Cultural Artifact assignment, 16, 70, 181–82
cultural differences: audience, 72, 115; becoming-with, 29, 46–47, 52; boundaries, 33–34, 44; collaboration, 75; cross-language, 185–86; culture shock, 19–20, 186; embodied experiences, 64, 185; entanglement, 41–43, 97; language irregularities, 18, 103–4; literacy brokers, 217f; meaning making, 34, 129, 171; multilingual writing, 31, 111, 204–8; negotiation, 4–5, 34, 47, 55; otherness, 108; reflective writing, 24, 190–91; rhetorical styles, 88; sites of inquiry, 23, 52, 109–10, 113–14, 185–86, 191–94, 211–12; social media, 137; student participation, 178–79; teacher conferences, 182, 183f; transnational students, 192–93; writing center consultants, 168, 172–73; writing-related knowledge, 196
cultural structure, 83, 198
cultural tropes, 121–22, 184, 191
cultural worlds, 33, 61
curriculum: American, 19–20; bridge writing class, 16–17; development, 187; disciplinary norms, 175; language differences, 62, 211–12; student learning, 167

Dali, China, 213
data collection and analysis: audio recordings, 24, 216f; engagement, 29; entanglement, 26, 61; ethnographic research, 24, 48, 61, 199, 213; field notes, 24, 27, 216f; interviews, 25, 27, 167, 216f, 217f; language skills development, 167; observation, 24, 25, 167; prompted think-aloud, 216f; research participants, 19–23, 62–69, 114–16; researcher positionality, 22–23; social media, 7; WeChat Moments, 18, 217f; writing artifacts, 7, 217f; writing assignments, 24, 167
decision-making, 30, 42, 58, 72, 77, 86–88, 97–98, 115, 136, 161, 163, 208
deficit perspective: exclusionary language, 187; grammatical errors, 173; home languages, 134–35; multilingual writers, 99, 106, 110; pedagogical practices, 182–85; textual meaning, 211
De Fina, Anna, 50–51
determinate meaning, 40, 68, 92

234 : INDEX

digital tools: annotation, 24, 139; collaborative writing, 5–6; dictionaries, 134; drafting, 130, 206; entanglement, 217f; feedback, 22, 104–5; literacy activities, 57; mobilization, 139; multilingual writing, 5, 217f; peer reviews, 103f, 104–5; revisions, 206; social media, 121, 124–25, 128–29; translation labor, 6, 22, 82–84, 107–8, 130–31; unpredictable encounters, 116–17, 118f, 119, 123–24, 139–40; voice memo, 98; writing process, 5, 95–97, 112–13, 139–40, 217f

disciplinary differences: engagement, 165; norms, 175, 177, 212; reflective writing, 190–91; sites of inquiry, 113–14, 185–86, 191–92; terminology, 180

Disciplinary Literacy writing assignment, 16, 70

discursive conventions: academic writing, 110; classroom environment, 212; first-year writing class, 168, 198; meaning making, 77, 129; textual meaning, 108; writing instructors, 179

dispositions/open dispositions: assemblage, 97–98; chronotopic figuring, 209; identity, 154; language differences, 191–92; mobility, 4; multiplicity, 188; peer reviews, 175–76; string figuring, 23, 52; translation labor, 134–35; strategic silence, 149, 161

disruption: becoming, 11, 33–34; diversity, 28; human exceptionalism, 41–42; migrants' social relations, 82; monolingual ideology, 191; ontological categories, 209; writing norms, 4

distributed translation, 94, 166

diversity, 16–17, 22, 28, 115, 166–67, 206

Dobrin, Sidney, 8, 9

dominant narrative, 100–102; meaning making, 106; multilingual writers, 109–110; pedagogical language, 178; singular author, 55; strategic silence, 30, 123; transnational migrants, 4; tropes, 109–10

dovetailing, 178, 179

drafting process: annotations, 24, 93f; audience expectation, 72, 126, 127; digital tools, 206; home languages, 89, 134–35; Memoir assignments, 24, 63, 70, 84, 116–17; peer reviews, 21, 24, 25, 83, 91, 93f, 94, 99–101; reflective practices, 196; spatial-temporal contours, 65, 98, 130–31; teacher conferences, 99, 102–3; timestamps, 130; translation labor, 85–86, 105–6; Western-centric perspective, 99–100; writing process, 17, 54, 91, 112–13, 144–45

Du, Fu, 87

eco-composition, 8–10, 61, 68–69

eco-social arrangements, 54

ecologies: boundary redrawing, 68, 77, 78; entanglement, 68, 78; multilingual writing pedagogy, 168; natural, cultural, and literacy others, 63; relationships, 171–72; unpredictable encounters, 67

edits. *See* drafting process; writing process

Ehret, Christian, 112

embodied experiences: auditory details, 65–68, 70–72, 88–89; boundaries, 44, 68, 83, 90; cultural differences, 185; literacy practices, 55; Memoir assignments, 24, 63, 70, 89, 90; multilingual writers, 4, 96, 100, 109, 154, 171, 183, 212; personal narratives, 151; reflective sharing, 154; semiotic configuring, 50, 90, 117; spatiality, 29, 57–58, 60, 65; strategic silence, 123, 155; translation process, 90; unpredictable encounters, 24, 44–45, 67; writing process, 198, 203–4

emergence/emergent: affects, 117, 131; becoming, 29, 33–34, 45–47, 52, 91, 124, 125; chronotopic lamination, 50–51; co-emergence, 12, 129, 138, 161, 199, 206; contours of writing, 59; digital spaces, 5; entanglement, 9, 54, 55, 72; innovation, 31; lived experiences, 70, 93, 163; meaning, 106, 108–9, 125, 135, 163, 167, 205; memory, 30, 117; multilingual writing processes, 28; natural, cultural, and literacy others, 14, 27, 42, 43, 61, 78, 100, 139, 200, 204; negotiation, 26, 47, 188, 197; otherness, 209; social media, 113, 140; spatiality, 60, 79, 155, 204; tentacular thinking, 52–53; transformative encounters, 13, 31, 38–39, 69, 74–75, 120, 123–24, 131, 138; translation labor, 82, 84, 90, 104; unintentional design, 45; writing across differences, 7, 38

Emig, Janet, 58–59

emotion, combining with scenery, 87, 190–91

emotional labor, 81, 82, 83, 96, 107

engagement, audience, 7, 72, 115, 121, 124–28, 132, 133f, 134–36, 194

English language, 73–75, 86, 99

English Learning Center (ELC), 15–18, 117, 167, 170–71

entanglement perspective: asset-based pedagogy, 16–17, 31; audience expectation, 72, 115, 126; becoming-with, 29, 47, 124–25; boundaries, 44, 58, 68–69, 209; collaboration, 75–77, 201; digital tools, 112–13, 217f; eco-composition, 8–10; embodied experiences, 24, 96; emergent patterns, 52, 55; indeterminate outcomes, 39–40; language

differences, 171, 197; literacy landscape, 57; making meaning, 196–97; material experiences, 70, 107; natural world, 42, 43, 61; negotiation, 94, 95, 97; polyphony, 48–50; research data, 27; reviews, 19, 21, 25, 70, 91, 93f; screenshots, 122f, 127f, 128–29; semiotic fibers, 50, 111, 117; sites of inquiry, 23, 113–14, 137, 185; strategic silence, 123, 159, 160–61; temporal polyphony, 48–50, 65; transformative encounters, 38–39, 45–46, 74–75, 123–24, 131; translation labor, 108, 199; writing process, 200, 203–4
ephemeral happenings, 112–13, 139–40
ethnographic research, 24, 48, 61, 199, 213
exclusionary language, 187
explicit modeling, 212
extracurricular activities, 5, 119

familial influences: class identity, 20, 155–56, 160; decision-making, 162–64; extracurricular activities, 5, 119; literacy practices, 155–61; multilingual students, 146–47, 206, 208; self-censorship, 117; social media, 159; strategic silence, 123, 146, 149–52; writing process, 139
feedback: audience expectation, 72, 126–27; digital tools, 104–5, 112–13; dovetailing, 178–79; follow-up, 169; Memoir assignment, 117; peer mentorship, 202–3; relationship-building, 171–72; reviews, 21, 99, 101f, 102, 103f, 104–5, 171, 211; revisions, 169–70; rhetorical strategies, 109; social media, 22; unpredictable encounters, 120, 123–24, 178–79; voice memos, 98
field notes, 24, 27, 216f
Final Reflection writing assignment, 16, 70
first-year writing (FYW) class: classroom environment, 198; discursive conventions, 168, 198; honors section, 16, 17, 115; language differences, 20–21, 62, 211; material norms, 47, 168; multilingual students, 7, 63, 167; pedagogical norms, 168; peer review, 21, 25, 217f; social media activities, 7, 124–25, 128, 209; translation labor, 187, 199, 198; transnational students, 115, 134; WeChat Moments posts, 64, 217f; writing assignments, 70
flashback, 71, 173
floor-claiming device, 178, 179, 181
fluidity, literary spaces, 6, 9
follow-up feedback practice, 169
frame of reference, 100–2, 180–81, 186
frameshifting, translation process, 107
friction, 96, 98, 108, 109, 124, 127

friendship, 91–92, 97, 172
fungi: boundary redrawing, 42–43; chronotopic figuring, 13; collaboration, 49; entanglement, 29, 35, 36, 37, 40, 205; indeterminacy, 31, 79, 206; multi-species relationships, 33–35; mycelial networks, 38–39, 44; natural, cultural, and literacy others, 63; symbiotic relationships, 10, 97, 136, 170; tentacular thinking, 52; unpredictable encounters, 45, 111, 113, 116, 179, 214

gaman, 142
gaps, lived experiences, 19–20, 161–63, 167
genre conventions: argumentative writing, 72; audience expectation, 72, 88, 115, 126, 127; idioms, 71, 73, 74, 89; linguistic differences, 75, 85; personal narrative, 70, 74–75
geography, writing process, 200
geopolitical circumstances, 6
Gere, Anne Ruggles, 144, 151, 161–62
Glenn, Cheryl, 143
Gonzales, Laura, 82, 107
Google Translate, 85
government surveillance, 155–59
grammar: deficit perspective, 18, 173; multilingual writing, 103–4; translation labor, 85
Growing Up, 73
Guinier, Lani, 143
Gu, Cheng, 64, 65f
Guo, Jingming, 22, 195

Hass, Christina, 90
Han, Han, 22
Hansen-Thomas, Holly, 192–93
Haraway, Donna, 8, 11, 36, 51, 52, 160, 209
Hathway, Michael, 36
Hill, Anita, 143
Himalayas, 213
historical trajectories: language differences, 62, 191; multilingual students, 185; poetry assignments, 192; rhetorical silence, 142; strategic silence, 151–55, 159; translation process, 108; unintentional design, 45, 46; Western ideology, 110; writing assignments, 147–48
Hollett, Ty, 112
home language: collaborative translation, 75, 188–89; cultural tropes, 184; deficit perspective, 134–35; literacy practices, 21–22; multilingual writing, 130; verb inflections, 86; writing process, 17, 89
honors-designated first-year writing class. *See* first-year writing (FYW) class

Horner, Bruce, 74
human exceptionalism, 41–42
human-centric agency, 59–60
humanist perspective, 68
hyphae/hyphal tip: entanglement, 13, 39–40; indeterminacy, 31, 79; reciprocity, 37, 38, 51; tentacular thinking, 52; unpredictable encounters, 43–44, 138–40, 206–7; wandering, 124

I Know Why the Caged Bird Sings, 64
identity practices: indeterminacy, 30, 46, 112; interconnectedness, 46–47, 78; meaning making, 41, 129, 147; spaces, 5–9, 147; strategic silence, 123, 132; student literacy, 216f; writing process, 78
ideological orientations, 171, 198, 206
idioms, 71, 73, 74, 85, 89, 93, 94, 132, 134, 189, 199
idiosyncratic decision-making, 161–64
IEP (Intensive English Program), 16
imagery, 70, 71f, 173
improvise/improvisation: becoming-with, 79; boundaries, 40, 42, 107; collaboration, 53, 197; designs, 209; entanglement, 9, 28, 55, 197, 203; fungal hyphae, 43–44; linguistic, cultural, and rhetorical differences, 28, 111, 199; mycelial network, 138; polyphonic assemblages, 10, 48, 107, 131; reciprocity, 38; rediscovery, 127; relationships, 205–6; sites of inquiry, 11, 13; social media, 19, 38, 98, 113; string figuring, 51–52; temporal labor, 162; tentacular thinking, 52–53, 160; textual meaning, 77–78; unintentional design, 124; unpredictable encounters, 31, 114, 131; wayfinding, 112; writing labor, 7
"In Memory a Night Visit to Chengtian Temple," 195
indeterminate/indeterminacy: becoming-with, 79, 125; boundaries, 42, 44, 58, 69, 76; chronotopic figuring, 53; co-emergence, 129; entanglement, 27, 39–40, 46, 55, 78, 97, 107, 204; fungi, 44; identity practices, 30, 112; meaning, 75, 90; multilingual writing, 7, 28, 79, 97, 116; multimodality, 14; mushrooms, 34; mycelial networks, 38, 138; natural, cultural, and literacy others, 8, 10, 108; personal narrative, 70, 72, 75; reciprocal partnerships, 38–39; social media, 132, 139; strategic silence, 145, 160, 164; textual meaning, 77–78; unintentional design, 45, 46; unpredictable encounters, 13, 14, 30, 31, 47, 113, 120, 130, 137, 206; writer/researcher, 53, 77, 112

Indigenous cultures, 36, 47–48
induction experiences, 152
innovation: conventional tropes, 88; cultural differences, 34, 55, 75; multilingual writers, 81; parody, 88; unpredictable encounters, 12–13, 44, 46, 120, 123–24, 137
inquiry. *See* sites of inquiry
inscriptions, 128, 129
instructional language. *See* pedagogical practices
instructor-facilitated peer review, 21, 24, 99, 101f, 102, 103f, 104–6, 175, 212
intellectual labor: multilingual writing, 59, 199, 215; translation process, 81, 82, 83, 107, 109
Intensive English Program (IEP), 16
interconnectedness, 46–47, 78, 136–37
interdisciplinary polyphony, 48, 175
international students. *See* multilingual students; transnational students
intersection, reader-writer-text dynamic, 97–98, 102, 107–9, 124, 127
intertextual allusions, 195–96
interview research method, 25, 27, 167
intra-active/intra-action: boundary redrawing, 40, 42; memory, 90; open articulation, 38–39, 53, 55; shifting entanglement, 12, 54; string figuring, 51–52; temporality, 163; unpredictable encounters, 113–14
inventive stage of writing process, 17, 24, 125, 116–17, 144–45, 181–82
IRE (initiation, response, evaluation), 58

Japanese anime, 22, 61, 132, 143
Jobs, Steve, 171
Jordan, Jay, 59
journal writing, 193–94

Kang, Yu-Kyung, 172
Kell, Catherine, 164–65
knotting/knots: chronotopic figuring, 209; cultural, literacy, and familial histories, 148; entanglement, 55; natural, cultural, and literacy others, 11; open articulation, 207–8; semiotic fibers, 53; spacetime, 54; string figuring, 51–52; teacher conferences, 183, 185; tentacular thinking, 160; translation labor, 106; unpredictable encounters, 139–40
knowledge-making: boundaries, 40; cross-disciplinary writing, 166; emergent assemblages, 45, 52, 131

Lam, Eva, 130
language differences: asset-based pedagogy, 16–17, 198; audience expectation, 72, 115, 174; disruption, 11, 28, 42; entanglement, 171; first-year writing (FYW) class, 20–21, 62, 211; genres, 85; innovations, 4, 34, 44, 46, 75; knowledge, 169; literacy brokers, 217f; multilingual writing, 31, 208; negotiation, 4–5, 34, 55, 74, 75, 135, 191, 197; norms, 110; pedagogical instruction, 177; poetry assignments, 192; reflective writing, 24, 190–91; rhetorical differences, 102–4; shared vocabulary, 176; sites of inquiry, 17, 23, 52, 89, 107, 109–10, 113–14, 173–74, 188, 191–94; social media, 7, 137; translation labor, 80; unpredictable encounters, 12–13, 111; writing-related knowledge, 196
language practice, 6, 167, 190, 192
Law, John, 41
Lemke, Jay, 54
lexical issues, 169
life-in-becoming-with, 52, 79
linguistic resources, 73–74, 187–88
literacy brokers, 176, 217f
literacy landscape, 57, 61, 79
literacy practices: accessing, 167; activities, 57; artifacts, 193; assembling, 167; classical texts, 195–96; differences, 204–6; entanglement, 40, 43, 47, 55, 68; familial trajectories, 117, 155–61; home language, 134–35; identity, 20, 160, 192; indeterminacy, 30, 39–40, 46; making meaning, 147; memes, 22, 156; migratory processes, 5; otherness, 91, 108, 111, 137–39; public scrutiny, 159; self-censorship, 117, 160; spaces, 6, 8–9, 147; strategic silence, 123, 132, 146, 159; student writers, 3, 171–72, 216f; trajectories, 105, 208; tropes, 88, 121–22
lived experiences: classroom activities, 181, 193; emergent patterns, 45, 52; entanglement, 95, 97; gaps, 19–20; multilingual students, 70, 129, 172–73, 206–7; spacetime, 161–63; strategic silence, 30, 123
lived spatiality, 29, 60, 61, 62, 65, 79
logical reasoning, 94, 96
Lunsford, Karen, 195–96

material resources: becoming-with, 204; chronotopic figuring, 146; classroom environment, 58, 180, 181, 198, 212; ecocomposition, 8; entanglement, 40, 96, 107, 170–71; first-year writing (FYW) class, 168, 187, 198; inscriptions, 129; knotting, 207; literacy practices, 55; meaning making, 41, 68, 77, 92; memory, 128; multilingual writers, 34, 47, 91; natural, cultural, and literacy others, 200, 204; negotiation, 47, 74, 92; sites of inquiry, 199–200; spatiality, 8–9, 29, 57–58, 60, 62, 65; survival strategy, 161; tools, 83; tentacular thinking, 160
Matsuda, Paul, 28
matsutake mushrooms: biodiversity, 213; entanglement, 36; indeterminacy, 120; polyphonic rhythm, 49, 215; unpredictable encounters, 44–46
matter/mattering, 43, 60, 68, 69, 77, 163
meaning making: chronotopic figuring, 13, 34, 155; collaborative translation, 75, 92–93, 106; cultural differences, 34, 191; entanglement, 41, 196–97; identity practices, 147; inscriptions, 128, 129; material configurations, 68, 77, 92; multilingual writing, 30, 56, 196–97; negotiation, 47, 74, 189; semiotic practices, 50–51, 66, 68, 160; student agency, 129–30; translation labor, 80, 85
memes, 22, 156
Memoir assignments: audience expectations, 126; auditory details, 65–68, 70–72, 88–89; class identity, 149–50; drafting, 70, 126, 130; embodied experiences, 24, 89, 90; emergent assemblages, 52, 63, 131; inscriptions, 128, 129; literacy others, 91; multimodality, 38, 65–66, 69, 129, 148f; peer reviews, 24, 25, 75, 84, 91; strategic silence, 123, 151; unintended consequences, 45–46, 131–38; unpredictable encounters, 29, 67, 112–13, 116–17, 118f, 119–20, 123–24, 125, 132
memory: becoming, 140; entanglement, 12, 76, 117; inscriptions, 128, 129, 130, 131; meaning, 42, 49, 53, 67, 130; open articulation, 13, 54; rediscovery, 125–31; reflection, 117, 120, 125, 128, 195, 196; semiotic artifacts, 164; sensory, 66, 88; social media, 111, 127f; spatial-temporal boundaries, 78, 116, 129–30, 140, 141, 161, 165; tentacular thinking, 8, 53; translation labor, 89; unpredictable encounters, 65, 114, 118f, 119, 120, 126, 131; visceral feelings, 27, 64, 67, 90, 198; wandering, 54
metacognitive awareness, 83, 176
metalinguistic awareness, 80, 83, 176, 190, 198
metaphor/simile, 10, 22, 173
migration, transnational students, 3, 5
mobile writing process: artifacts, 205; co-emergence, 55; digital tools, 14, 57, 107, 112–13, 135, 139; entanglement, 23, 28, 41, 47, 179; home languages, 21, 211; meaning, 41,

84, 110; memory, 69; natural, cultural, and literacy others, 27, 92; polyphonic assemblage, 34, 138, 164; rhetorical styles, 88, 210; spatiality, 79; temporality, 163; tentacular thinking, 8; textual meaning, 4, 206; translation labor, 22, 85, 86, 108; unpredictable encounters, 112, 139

modeling, 181, 212

monolingual writing: academic units, 30, 167, 200; disciplinary terminology, 180; disruption, 11, 28, 42, 191; multilingual students, 73, 177–79, 183; negotiation, 5; pedagogical practices, 30, 81, 108

Mother Tongue, 64

multicultural texts, 193–94

multilingual students: academic literacy, 167, 210; agency, 129–30, 175; becoming, 29, 46–47, 52, 67, 79, 108–9, 124–25, 146, 183, 204–6; boundaries, 40, 44, 58, 68, 67, 76, 77; class identity, 20, 154, 163–64, 195, 199, 208; collaboration, 8, 33, 75, 97, 100, 109, 201; cultural differences, 6, 17–18, 31, 33, 64, 95, 97, 100, 111, 186, 197–98; deficit perspective, 99, 106, 110; embodied experiences, 4, 24, 96, 100, 109, 154, 171, 183, 212; extracurricular activities, 5, 119; familial influence, 117, 146–47, 206, 208; induction experiences, 152; interconnectedness, 46–47, 136–37; language differences, 62, 111, 167, 173, 174, 208; lived experiences, 30, 57, 70, 95, 97, 172–73, 197–98, 206–7; material configuration, 34, 47, 68, 91; meaning making, 30, 41, 56, 129–30, 196–97; monolingual classrooms, 179, 183; reflective sharing, 154; relationship-building, 29, 169–72; self-sponsored reviews, 21, 171, 210; shared first language, 172–73; social media, 7, 121–22, 124, 125, 209; strategic silence, 123, 154, 161–65, 208; teacher authority, 117, 173, 175, 182–83; temporal experiences, 34, 162–63; transformative encounters, 29, 38–39, 45, 46, 69, 74–75, 97, 131; translation labor, 108, 199, 211; tutoring, 168–70; unintended consequences, 45–46, 137–38; unpredictable encounters, 31, 67, 112–13, 116–17, 118f, 119–20, 123–24, 180, 206–7

multilingual writing: affective meaning, 4–6, 67, 99, 100, 117; asset-based curriculum, 16–17, 167–68, 197–98; audience expectation, 72, 94–99, 115, 126–27, 140, 161–62, 210; authentic voice, 211; authorial intention, 95, 98–99, 140; bridge writing class, 16–17, 22, 72, 115, 187; chronotopic figuring, 13, 34, 207–9; digital tools, 5, 112–13, 139–40, 217f; disruption, 4, 28, 42; entanglement, 167, 168, 185–86, 200–4; first-year writing (FYW) class, 20–21; genre conventions, 88; grammar, 18, 103–4; indeterminate meaning, 39–40, 46, 79; innovation, 44, 46, 81; linguistic choices, 31, 73–75, 108, 110, 130, 168; literacy brokers, 217f; literacy resources, 33, 57, 79, 111, 167, 171–72, 191–92, 204–8; logical reasoning, 94, 96; natural world, 33, 42, 61, 67; negotiation, 47, 74, 94–97, 189, 210; parallel structure, 71, 99–100; peer review, 21, 24, 75, 93f, 101f, 102, 103f, 104–6, 202–3; screenshots, 96, 122f, 127f, 128–29; semiotic repertoire, 6, 34, 50, 53, 66, 68, 78, 111, 117, 183, 201, 217f; sites of inquiry, 17, 23, 52, 97, 109, 113–14, 197–98; spatiality, 29, 34, 60–62, 65, 79, 130–31; textual meaning, 101, 106–7; word choice, 94–96, 102–4. *See also* writing process

multimodal activities: embodied performance, 38, 196; pedagogical language, 181, 212; screenshots, 65f, 66, 122f, 127f, 128–29; textual meaning, 4, 69; writing assignments, 17, 147, 148f, 193–94

multisensory orientation, 38, 60, 64, 65f, 66, 70, 212

multi-species relationships: entanglement, 35–39; material practices, 36; multilingual writing, 38; mushrooms, 33–39; pet companions, 59; sympoiesis, 36; trans-ontology, 37

Murakami, Haruki, 195

mushrooms: becoming-with, 36; boundary redrawing, 33; entanglement, 10, 37, 41–43, 175, 214, 215; indeterminacy, 44; meaning making, 34; permeability, 61; polyphony, 47–49, 124; reciprocal relationships, 35; unpredictable encounters, 45, 112

mycelial networks: chronotopic figuring, 53; entanglement, 37, 39; indeterminacy, 38, 138–39; reciprocal relationships, 35, 43–44

natural, cultural, and literacy others: becoming-with, 11–12, 79, 108; entanglement, 63; established relationships, 137, 200; literacy events, 27; multilingual writing, 7, 14, 206; open articulation, 42, 55; tentacular thinking, 52–53; unpredictable encounters, 33–34, 113–14, 204; visceral feelings, 206

negotiation: cross-language, 135; disciplinary differences, 191; dominant narrative, 30; emergent process, 45, 52, 188; entanglement, 94, 95, 97; language differences, 4–5,

34, 55, 74, 176–77, 191, 197; literary spaces, 6–9; material configuration, 47, 92; meaning, 189; multilingual sources, 102, 210–11; social differences, 191; time-space relationships, 192; teacher assessment, 197; translation labor, 81–82, 108; translingual practices, 94, 210; unpredictable encounters, 29, 120, 123–24, 137–38
networks/mobile networks: boundary redrawing, 69; becoming-with, 39; collaboration, 8; commute time, 55; digital spaces, 5, 18, 26; eco-composition, 8–9; entanglement, 38, 41, 205; fungi, 35, 36, 37; globalization, 15; interconnectedness, 138; peer support, 21; polyphony, 53; pop culture, 123; semiotic repertoires, 6; spatiality, 61; translation labor, 83, 92–93; transnational students, 74, 84, 91, 106, 201; unpredictable encounters, 43–47
Nordquist, Brice, 54–55

objects of inquiry. *See* sites of inquiry
observation research method, 24, 25, 167
one-on-one conferences, 181–82
ontological differences, disruption, 28, 107, 113–14, 209
open inquiry. *See* sites of inquiry
otherness, 108, 109, 209
outlining, 216*f*

Pahl, Kate, 164
parallel structure, 71, 86, 88, 99–100
paraphrasing skills, 211–12
parental surveillance, 156
pedagogical bans, 182–84
pedagogical practices: academia, 175; asset-based, 209–12; bridge writing class, 16–17; classroom activities, 178–80; collaboration, 8, 176–78; cultural differences, 178, 180–81, 184, 211–12; exclusionary language, 187; first-year writing (FYW) class, 17, 168; monolingual/monocultural, 17–18, 30; multimodal activities, 17, 38, 65*f*, 66, 69, 129, 181, 212; orientation, 177–78, 184–85; irregularities discussion, 18, 176; sites of inquiry, 17, 23, 52, 113–14, 211–12; teacher conferences, 182; topic novelty, 115, 184; translation process, 210–11; Western cultural contexts, 180; writing instructors, 21, 186
peer review: annotations, 24, 93*f*; digital tools, 103*f*, 104–5; edits, 93*f*, 94; feedback, 22, 202–3; first-year writing (FYW) class, 21, 217*f*; instructor-facilitated, 21, 175; Memoir assignments, 24, 70, 91, 116–17; multilingual writers, 202–3; multisensory orientation, 38, 60, 64, 65*f*, 66, 70, 212; revisions, 17, 75, 103*f*, 104–5, 177; side comments, 93*f*, 94; social media, 121–22, 124, 125, 133*f*, 134–36; strategic silence, 123, 161–63; time limitations, 104–5
peer-led modeling, 18
Perl, Sondra, 58–59
personal narrative, 70, 72, 74–75, 139, 151, 163–64, 208
personification, 22, 87, 88, 90, 173
physical labor, 60, 81, 82, 83, 107
Pigg, Stacy, 58–59
piggybacking, 178
plagiarism, 202
plantationocene, 209
poetry writing assignments, 192–97
political trajectories, 123, 144, 163–64, 208
polyphonic assemblage, 34, 138, 164, 168
polyphonic conversation, 31, 113
polyphony, 31, 47–49, 105–7, 123, 164, 175–76; temporal, 48–49, 147
positionality, 22–23, 97–98
post-humanist view: becoming-with, 11–12, 90–91, 109; boundary redrawing, 33, 39, 76–77; data collection and analysis, 26–27; entanglement, 10–11, 41–43, 55, 68, 78, 170, 199–200; fungi, 35, 36; meaning, 69; research ecology, 61; unpredictable encounters, 13, 45, 46
prescriptive grammar, 177
Prior, Paul A., 49, 50, 52, 140, 161, 195–96
professional engagement, 165, 187, 206
prompted think-aloud, 216*f*
public scrutiny: class identity, 134, 150–55; literacy practices, 159; rhetorical silence, 143; second-generation rich, 20, 145; self-censorship, 117, 132–34; social media, 121–22, 148–49; sociopolitical trajectories, 156–58; strategic silence, 123, 156–57

read aloud feedback, 169
reader interpretation: critical reading, 21, 64; friction, 96; intertextual allusions, 195–96; multilingual writing, 88, 124, 127; reflective practices, 24, 196; writing process, 54, 97
reader-writer-text dynamic: friction, 96, 98; intersection, 97–98, 102, 107, 109, 124, 127; literacy trajectories, 105; positionality, 23–24, 97–98
reciprocal partnerships/reciprocal relationships: friendships, 92; fungi, 10, 35,

170–71; multi-lingual writers, 205; open assemblages, 55; peer mentorship, 202–3; professional relationships, 153, 154; self-sponsored reviews, 171–72; semiotic fibers, 160; unpredictable encounters, 31; writing labor, 38–39, 51–52, 166, 170–7
recruiting writing center consultants, 172–73
referential norms in academic writing, 110
reflection: community context, 190–91; comparative, 188, 189; cultural contexts, 67, 190–91; drafting, 70, 126, 130, 196; embodied experiences, 154; home cultures, 188; pedagogical instruction, 154; poetry assignments, 192–93; reading, 64, 196; writing process, 54
relationship-building, 29, 171–72
remaking meaning. *See* meaning making
Remix writing assignment, 16, 70
representational logic, 68, 129
research methods. *See* data collection and analysis
research participants, 14–15, 19–23, 62–69, 114–16
reviewing process: digital tools, 206; instructor-facilitated, 175; self-sponsored reviews, 21, 84; translingual, 173; writing center consultation, 168–69; writing process, 54, 97, 144–45
revising sessions, 216*f*; clarification, 102; curriculum, 167; digital tools, 206; document format, 102; entanglement, 95–96; goals, 17, 167; Memoir assignments, 70, 84, 116–17; peer reviews, 21, 24, 103*f*, 104–5; self-sponsored reviews, 21, 84; Western-centric perspective, 99–100; writing center consultants, 169–70; writing process, 54, 91, 144–45
rhetorical differences: canonical texts, 88; Chinese, 173; classical texts, 87, 195–96; collaboration, 75, 109, 171; deficit perspective, 211; disruption, 11, 28, 42; language irregularities, 18, 101–4, 190; meaning making, 34, 191; mentors, 171; multilingual writers, 169, 197, 208; resources, 187–88, 197–98, 201; shared vocabulary, 176; sites of inquiry, 17, 23, 52, 109, 113–14, 173, 191–94; social media, 124, 137; translation labor, 80–84; unpredictable encounters, 29, 111–13, 120, 123–24
rhetorical strategies: audience expectation, 72–73, 115, 126–27, 174, 210–11; embodied performance, 196; embody emotions in scenery, 87; genre convention, 87, 88, 96; hyperbole, 22; innovation, 34, 46, 55; literary tropes, 6, 88; metaphor/simile, 10, 22, 173;

negotiation, 4–5, 34, 47, 55, 74, 191, 210–11; parallelism, 71, 88; personification, 22, 87, 88; reflective writing, 24, 190–91; risk-taking, 115–16; self-censorship, 117, 160; strategic silence, 30, 123, 142–45; survival strategy, 161; values through objects, 194–95
Roozen, Kevin, 128
Rule, Hannah, 58–59, 198, 203, 204

scaffolding, 18, 176, 211–12
screenshots, 96, 122*f*, 127*f*, 128–29
second-generation rich. *See* class identity
self-censorship: familial trajectories, 155; literacy practices, 117, 160; public scrutiny, 132–34; social media, 122–23, 136
self-sponsored peer reviews: drafting, 70, 83, 99, 101, 126; identity, 5–6; Memoir assignments, 70, 84, 91; multilingual writing, 21, 99, 106, 171, 210; sites of inquiry, 176; translation labor, 211
semantic choices: cultural meaning, 190; language irregularities, 18, 103–4; parallelism, 71, 86; social meaning, 190; translation process, 108
seminar-style classroom instruction, 179–80
semiotic repertoire/repertoire of semiotic and material resources: artifacts, 164, 217*f*; becoming-with, 76–79, 204–5; boundary redrawing, 11, 42, 44, 58, 69, 90; chronotopic figuring, 13, 34, 50–53, 160, 161–65, 207–9; colloquialisms, 73, 74; digital technologies, 23, 84, 130–31; educational trajectories, 23; emergent assemblages, 45, 46, 52, 91, 131; entanglement, 9, 40, 41, 47, 55–56, 61, 107, 160, 197, 201, 203, 217*f*; fungi, 37; indeterminacy, 46–47; knowledge, 10, 40, 183; literacy pedagogies, 23; memory, 117, 131, 164; multilingual writing, 3, 4, 6, 34, 197, 201, 217*f*; multimodality, 38, 65–66; natural, cultural, and literacy others, 42; open inquiry, 191–92; relationships, 12, 107, 108–9, 205; remediation, 66; representationalism, 68; shifting, 5; social media, 22, 124, 137; spatiality, 3, 57–58, 60, 69, 164; strategic silence, 149, 155, 159; tentacular thinking, 52–53; translation labor, 83, 108, 135; unpredictable encounters, 12, 29, 31, 47, 63, 67, 111–13, 120, 123–24; writing across differences, 19, 30. *See also* meaning making
semi-structured interviews, 25, 27, 216*f*
shared frames of reference, 172–76
Sheldrake, Merlin, 34–35, 39, 43, 44, 47, 53, 124, 139, 141, 145
Shipka, Jody, 6, 50, 66

side comments, drafting, 93f, 94
silence. *See* strategic silence
sites of inquiry: bridge writing class, 16–17; chronotopic figuring, 13, 34, 185; classroom activities, 181; disciplinary differences, 185–86, 191–92; language differences, 23, 107, 109–10, 173, 174, 185–86, 188, 191–94, 211–12; literacy brokers, 176; multilingual writing, 197–98; rhetorical differences, 109, 173, 191–94
self-sponsored conversations, 176; social differences, 191–92; translation labor, 86; unpredictable encounters, 113–14
Slam Dunk, 194
SnapChat, 113
social differences, 190, 192–93, 197–98
social media: activities, 209; audience expectation, 124–25, 148–49; class identity, 155; commenting peers, 121–22, 132; engagement, 18–19; familial influences, 113, 155–56, 159; government surveillance, 156; interconnectedness, 46–47; multilingual writers, 209; peer comments, 22, 133f, 134, 135, 136; research data, 27; self-censorship, 117, 136; spacetimes, 129, 137; strategic silence, 123, 148, 159; temporal experiences, 129–30, 162–63; unpredictable encounters, 29, 47, 112–13, 116–17, 118f, 119–20, 123–24, 128, 132, 137. *See also* WeChat
social relations, 28, 82
sociohistorical meaning, 9, 174
sociopolitical trajectories, 156–57
Sotomayer, Sonia (Justice), 193
spacetimes: class identity, 160; differences, 31; digital literacies, 6; identity practices, 147; lived experiences, 161–63; multilingual writing, 202; narratives, 147; social media, 124, 137; textual meaning, 206; unpredictable encounters, 29, 44, 47, 112–13, 120, 123–24, 140; writing process, 55, 129
spacetimemattering, 12, 163
spatial boundaries: classroom environment, 58, 181, 209–10; disruption, 11, 41–42; ecocomposition, 8–10, 61, 68–69; embodied forms, 29, 39, 44, 57, 62, 65; multilingual writing, 34, 130; poetry writing, 193; strategic silence, 123, 144
spatial-temporal contours, 58, 65, 98, 129–30
sports tropes, 184–85
Stewart, Mary Amanda, 192–93
strategic silence: chronotopic figuring, 13, 30, 161, 163–65; class identity, 145, 150–52, 156–57, 159, 161; embodied experiences, 155; enforced imposition, 162; entanglement perspective, 160–61; entanglement, 159; familial teaching, 146, 149–52; *gaman*, 142; government surveillance, 156–57; historical trajectories, 151–55, 159; identity practices, 117, 132; idiosyncratic decision-making, 161, 164; literacy practices, 132, 146, 159; Memoir assignments, 151; multilingual students, 144, 154, 163–65, 208; peer review, 161–63; public scrutiny, 156–57; rhetorical practices, 30, 142–45; social media, 123, 148, 159; temporal labor, 161–63
string figuring, 13, 23, 27, 51–52, 114, 131, 147, 185, 186
student agency, 129–30, 182–83
student experiences, 15–18, 117, 167, 178–80
Su, Shi, 189, 195
subject/object, 39–40, 46, 68, 69, 76, 77
symbiotic associations, 78, 100
sympoiesis, 36
syntactic complexity: language irregularities, 18, 103–4; parallelism, 71, 86; translation labor, 80; writing center consultants, 169
syntax structure: drafting, 99–100; metalinguistic awareness, 190

Takayoshi, Pamela, 6
Tan, Amy, 64, 193
teacher authority, 182, 183, 197
teacher conferences, 182, 183f
teacher interviews, 25, 27, 217f
teacher-conference review: drafting, 70, 99, 102–3; Memoir assignments, 91; multilingual writing, 99, 101, 175; multisensory orientation, 38, 60, 64, 65f, 66, 70, 212; revisions, 177
teaching of writing. *See* writing instruction
temporal experiences; literacy events, 65; multilingual writing, 34, 129–31, 162–63; social media, 124, 125, 162–63; strategic silences, 123, 161–63; translation labor, 29; writing process, 55, 141
temporal polyphony, 48, 49–50
tentacular thinking: chronotopic figuring, 209; hyphae/hyphal tip, 13, 38, 43; multilingual writing, 8, 108, 176; natural, cultural, and literacy others, 52–53; semiotic fibers, 160, 164; strategic silence, 165; unpredictable encounters, 113
Test of English as a Foreign Language (TOEFL), 16
textual meaning: authorial intention, 136; chronotopic figuring, 13, 34, 209; cross-

language, 4, 136; cultural differences, 108; deficit perspective, 211; discursive differences, 108; dominant tropes, 109–10; indeterminacies, 39–40, 46, 77–78; linguistic differences, 75, 108; literary trajectories, 105; multilingual writing, 101; multisensory orientation, 38, 60, 64, 65f, 66, 70, 212; spacetimes, 129, 206; translation process, 106–8

theory, pedagogical innovations, 46, 167

think-aloud, 216f

time limitations, feedback, 104–5

time-space relationships, 192

TOEFL (Test of English as a Foreign Language), 16

training, writing center consultants, 172–73

transcultural awareness, 192

transfer of meta-knowledge of writing, 197

transformative encounters; emergent assemblages, 45–46, 52, 131; entanglement, 38–39, 69, 97, 123–24; literacy others, 137, 138, 139; personal narrative, 29, 70, 72, 74–75; unpredictable encounters, 12–13, 44, 114

translanguaging, 81

translation labor: alternative options, 108; audience expectation, 72, 108, 115, 189, 210; auditory details, 70–72, 85–86, 88; back-translation, 89, 93, 94; boundaries, 81–82, 90; collaboration, 75, 100, 106, 188–89; connotations, 85, 86; cross-linguistic problem solving, 75, 80; cultural structures, 83; cyclicality, 81, 82; dialectical conventions, 80; digital tools, 82, 83, 84, 107, 108, 112–13, 134–35; drafting, 85–86, 105–6, 130; embodied experiences, 83, 90; emotional labor, 81, 82, 83, 107; frameshifting, 107; grammatical properties, 85; historical trajectories, 108; idioms, 71, 73, 74, 85, 89, 93, 94, 132, 134, 199; individual, 106; intellectual labor, 81, 82, 83, 107; linguistic structures, 75, 83, 108; materials tools, 83; Memoir assignments, 70, 131–34; metalinguistic awareness, 80; multilingual students, 108, 199, 211; multiple languages, 193; narrative, 188; negotiation, 81–82, 108, 210–11; physical labor, 81, 82, 83, 107; properties, 90; rhetorical practice, 12, 80–84; scaffolded instruction, 211–12; self-sponsored reviews, 21, 211; semiotic resources, 83, 108; sites of inquiry, 52, 86; spacetimes, 29; syntactic complexity, 80; syntax structure, 190; temporal episodes, 29; textual meaning, 85, 106–8; unpacking, 107; verb inflection, 86; vocabulary-building, 18, 22, 80, 177; writing process, 4–5, 29

Translation Narrative assignment, 188–92

transligual theory, 46, 94, 81, 167, 173, 174

transnational students: cultural differences, 185, 192–93; digital literacy, 5, 130–31; embodied experiences, 3–4; first-year writing (FYW) class, 17, 72, 115, 134, 187, 198; friendships, 91–92, 172; language practices, 167, 192, 201; literacy practices, 3, 6, 92, 192; multilingualism, 3, 4, 73–74; negotiation, 6, 192; poetry writing, 193–94; semiotic repertoires, 3, 4; textual meaning, 109; Translation Narrative assignment, 188–92; youth culture, 5, 22, 208

trans-ontology, 37

trust-building, 169–70

Tsing, Anna, 44, 48, 97, 164, 209

tutoring practices, 15–18, 21, 117, 169–72

undergraduate writing groups, 172–73

unintended consequences, 45–46, 131–38

unintentional design, 45, 46

unpacking, 107, 212

unpredictable encounters: affective meaning, 4, 6, 67, 99, 100, 117; audience expectation, 115, 126, 127, 137; authorial intention, 137; becoming-with, 11–12, 29, 46–47, 52, 67, 124, 125, 140; digital tools, 112–13, 139–40; feedback, 22, 178–79; historical trajectories, 120; innovation, 44, 46, 47, 137; Memoir assignments, 63, 117, 125, 132; multilingual living, 206–7; multilingual students, 12–13, 31, 180; natural worlds, 44–45, 61; negotiation, 137–38; shapeshifting, 139; sites of inquiry, 113–14; social media, 7, 116, 117, 118f, 119, 123–25, 128, 132; spacetime, 44; writing process, 79, 111–12

valuation systems, 109

values through objects, 194–95

verb conjugation, 102–4

verb inflection, 86

visceral reactions: artifacts, 193; assemblages, 47, 137; becoming-with, 76; cultural, natural and literacy others, 14, 34; intra-action, 90; memory, 27, 67, 99, 131; wandering, 53–54; world-in-articulation, 7

visual orientation. *See* multimodal activities; multisensory orientation

vocabulary-building, 18, 22, 80, 177

voice memo, 14, 26, 93, 98

wander/wandering: chronotopic figuring, 47; indeterminacy, 44; multilingual writing, 39, 50, 139, 207; polyphonic rhythm, 131; research methodology, 53; strategic silence, 160; tentacular thinking, 52, 53; unpredictable encounters, 124
Wang, Sicong, 145
Wang, Zhaozhe, 28, 172
Wargo, Jon M., 113
wayfinding, 112
WeChat, 18, 21, 22, 26, 65f, 95, 118f, 122f, 128, 132, 133f, 134–36, 139, 217f. *See also* social media
Weisser, Christian, 9, 78
Welcome to St. Paul, 73
Western genre expectations: academia norms, 179–80; auditory details, 70–72, 88; dominant tropes, 109–10; drafting, 99–100; individual authors, 9, 204; rhetorical differences, 87; writing process, 200
Witte, Stephen, 90
word choice, 94–96, 102, 103, 104
world-in-becoming, 10, 40, 76, 77, 93
writing artifacts, 128, 217f
writing assessments: collaborative translation practices, 109; cross-cultural, 185–86; historical trajectories, 147–48; multimodal imagery, 17, 38, 69, 70, 71f, 128–29, 147, 148f; student agency, 129–30, 182–83
writing center consultants, 63, 70, 91, 116–17, 168–70, 172–73, 211
writing classes. *See also* bridge writing class; first-year writing (FYW) class
writing instruction: collaborative translation, 75, 109; cross-language negotiation, 211; culture shock, 19–20, 186; disciplinary jargon, 177; discursive tools, 179; entanglement, 185–86, 200; interdisciplinary polyphony, 48, 49, 175; multilingual writing, 17, 175, 202; research-informed, 188; Western perspective, 200; writing instructors, 21, 179
writing process: academic, 62; annotation, 97, 128; assumptions, 207; brainstorming, 216f; collaboration, 8, 29–30, 75; conversation, 54; decision-making, 97–98; drafting, 54, 84, 70, 91, 126, 130, 144–45, 216f; ecocomposition, 8–10, 61, 68–69; ephemeral happenings, 112–13, 139–40; inscriptions, 128–29; institutional spaces, 168; intellectual labor, 59, 119, 215; interconnectedness, 46–47, 78; inventive stage, 17, 24, 116–17, 125, 144–45, 181–82; note-taking, 54; outlining, 216f; personification, 87; physical labor, 59; reading, 54, 64, 88, 95, 124, 127, 169; reciprocity, 38–39, 51–52, 166; revisions, 17, 54, 91, 93f, 94, 144–45, 216f; rhetorical differences, 80–84, 100, 168–69, 201, 208; risk-taking, 115–16; shapeshifting, 139; spacetimes, 6, 31, 44, 55, 129, 202; temporal polyphony, 48–50, 55, 65, 130–31, 141. *See also* multilingual writing
writing researcher, 39–40, 43, 46, 53, 77
writing reviews, 75, 109
writing transfer, 112
writing-related knowledge, 144, 196
Writing, Rhetoric, and Composition, Department of, 16
youth culture, 5, 22, 208

Zamel, Vivian, 212
zombie fungi, 39

About the Author

XIQIAO WANG is assistant professor in the University of Pittsburgh's Composition, Literacy, Pedagogy, and Rhetoric program. She received her PhD in language, literacy, and culture from Vanderbilt University.

Drawing on sociocultural theories of literacy, translingualism, and science studies, her research has examined the changing forms and functions of composition in the broader context of global migration.

Her research has appeared in a coauthored book titled *Inventing the World Grant University: Chinese International Students' Mobilities, Literacies, and Identities*, as well as professional journals such as *Research in the Teaching of English*, *College Composition and Communication*, *Journal of Second Language Writing*, and *Computers and Composition*, among others. Her research has been supported by grants such as the Spencer Foundation Small Research Grant (2025), College Composition and Communication Research Initiative (2014, 2025), and the Fulbright Specialist Program (2018).

www.ingramcontent.com/pod-product-compliance
Lightning Source LLC
Chambersburg PA
CBHW060554080526
44585CB00013B/559